Losing
Our Souls

Losing
Our Souls

THE AMERICAN EXPERIENCE
IN THE COLD WAR

Edward Pessen

IVAN R. DEE CHICAGO

1993

Library of Congress Cataloging-in-Publication Data:

Pessen, Edward, 1920–

Losing our souls : the American experience in the cold war / Edward Pessen.

p.   cm.

Includes bibliographical references and index.

ISBN 1-56663-037-1 (alk. paper)

1. United States—Foreign relations—1945–1989.   2. Cold War.   3. United States—Politics and government—1945–1989.   4. Subversive activities—United States—History—20th century.   5. Internal security—United States—History—20th century.   6. Political culture—United States—History—20th century.   I. Title.

E840.P375   1993

327.73—dc20   93-11241

To Frank Thornton, Eddie Timpone, Jesse "Tex" O'Quinn
Wherever They Are

CONTENTS

PUBLISHER'S NOTE

EDWARD PESSEN died December 23, 1992, after a distinguished career as a scholar and teacher of American history. He had been Distinguished Professor of History at Baruch College and the Graduate School and University Center of the City University of New York, and was at the time occupying the Edna Gene and Jordan Davidson Chair in the Humanities at Florida International University in Miami.

Less than two weeks before his death Mr. Pessen had sent to his publisher the manuscript of *Losing Our Souls*, its major revisions having been completed after a dialogue between author and editor. In the course of preparing the book for publication, the publisher saw a need for additional minor revisions and additions. With the consent of Adele Pessen, these were accomplished by Athan Theoharis, professor of history at Marquette University and an authority on aspects of American cold war history who had earned Mr. Pessen's respect. Mr. Theoharis's alterations and additions reinforce Mr. Pessen's major arguments in the book.

PREFACE

FROM THE closing days of World War II in the summer of 1945 until the end of 1991 when the Soviet Union finally crumbled, the United States pursued a hostile policy against its wartime ally and against the forces of international communist subversion that American leaders claimed the Soviets controlled and directed. Rarely has a great nation been so successful in achieving the goals of its foreign policy as was the United States in the cold war. Almost immediately after it was created in 1947, the National Security Council issued secret policy papers calling on the United States government to wage "economic, political, and psychological warfare" to bring about the "collapse of the Soviet Union," the overthrow of the Soviet Communist party, the dismantling of Soviet armed forces as well as the Soviets' political and economic order, and the liberation of its Eastern European empire. All of this has come to pass. Who can doubt that American policy was instrumental in destroying the Soviet state? And yet, as I shall try to show, our cold war policy, for all its success in dissolving the USSR, was so grievously flawed that the United States may never fully recover from its effects upon our values, our freedoms, our politics, our security, the conditions of our material life, the quality of our productive plant, and the very air we breathe.

The undeniable repulsiveness of many Soviet institutions and their actions, both at home and abroad, doubtless convinced many Americans of the rectitude of a policy directed against so repressive an adversary. A few years ago, as I was standing in the airport in Reno, the city where the Organization of American Historians had just held its annual meeting, an eminent historian came by and asked about my latest scholarly project. I told him I was working on a critical study of United States cold war policy. He appeared puzzled. "But wasn't Stalin evil? Wasn't the Nazi-Soviet pact a bad thing? Didn't the Soviets commit aggression against Finland?" he asked. The implication of his questions was that reprehensible Soviet conduct justified American policy. He had cited only pre–World War II Soviet misbehavior; he could have substantially enlarged his catalogue of Soviet misdeeds by adding numerous examples of Soviet misbehavior after the war. But what my colleague overlooked is that the impressive array of deplorable actions by Soviet leaders, from Lenin and Stalin through Gorbachev, did not necessarily justify the cold war policy of the United States. It is understandably comforting to a government when its chosen adversary is loveless. It becomes so much easier to enlist popular support for a hostile policy against such a state. But an unattractive adversary does not validate everything done in the name of combating the adversary. During the cold war the United States did deplorable things to people and governments having nothing to do with the Soviet Union while American policymakers insisted that our victims were agents or puppets of the Soviet design for world conquest.

There is by now a massive literature on the cold war, much of it excellent. Many books provide detailed accounts of events, their evidence drawn from patient investigations of archival materials, their claim to our attention resting on the fullness and in some cases the vividness of their narrative. I have read and profited from these writings. Mine, however, is not such a book. Instead I have sought to answer important questions about the post–World War II policy of the United States toward the Soviet Union. What precisely was that policy? (A nation's policy is not confined to what its leaders say it is.) Are there enduring principles of foreign policy that best serve the people of a democratic republic? And, if there are such principles, was our cold war policy guided by them? What reasons were presented by American leaders for waging the cold war, and how well do these reasons stand up to critical scrutiny? What were the chief means the United States relied on to implement its cold war policy, and what light do these means throw on our policy and its professed objectives? What have been the consequences to date of the cold war for the United States? And, finally, how are we sensibly to assess American cold war policy in light of the evidence? These are the questions this book discusses.

I have written this book because critical examinations of the nation's cold war policy are not in long supply. A society is better served when the deficiencies in its government's behavior are exposed than when they are ignored. As Hans Christian Andersen noted in *The Emperor's New Clothes*, rulers tend not to be favorably disposed toward critics, as their subjects well understand. Most people refrain from calling governmental imbecilities by their rightful name out of fear of incurring the wrath of their leaders. In his great Farewell Address, George Washington warned that "real patriots" who would in the future oppose a foreign policy they believed detrimental to the true interests of the nation would run the risk of being "suspected and odious"—for the policy was likely to be popular because of the government's power to shape public opinion. Clark Clifford's advice that President Harry Truman acted on—to stigmatize sharp criticism of the nation's new cold war policy as helpful to the Soviet enemy and therefore possibly subversive—no doubt induced some Americans to hold their tongues rather than ask the hard questions that might have been asked.

Criticism of policy always serves the public interest, even when the criticism is wrongheaded, by compelling a reexamination of issues that is vital to the well-being of any society.

I have been greatly influenced by an observation made by John Quincy Adams in 1847, shortly before his death. A stranger had written him requesting Adams's advice on how to go about writing a history of the war with Mexico that was then in progress. Adams, who had been a Harvard professor before becoming secretary of state, after that the sixth president of the United States, and finally an antislavery congressman from Massachusetts, had won a deserved reputation for learning and intellect as well as for integrity and patriotism. Adams told his correspondent that the United States was in the wrong with regard to all the important issues leading up to the war with Mexico. He then added, "The historian, you know, must have no country." This was striking advice, coming as it did from an ardent nationalist who had strongly supported the Monroe Doctrine. What Adams meant, of course, is that the historian serves his or her country by appraising its behavior with no less detachment and criticism than he would appraise the behavior of any other country. The scholar's task is not to please the state by approval of its every act but rather to serve the community by calling its attention to and condemning governmental misbehavior.

It has long been fashionable to describe critics of orthodoxy as naysayers, revisionists, and other terms suggesting that what makes such people critics is not the troubled state of affairs but the troubled state of their minds. Perhaps so. A critic is not necessarily reasonable because his detractors delight in denying that he is. I don't know whether or not I am a congential iconoclast, but I have written a book that the evidence of the past forty-seven years demanded be written.

Important to me have been the writings and statements of onetime American officials who, in Robert Jay Lifton's felicitous phrase, have attained "retirement wisdom." Sharp criticism of our cold war policy by Eleanor Roosevelt or by George F. Kennan, Jerome Wiesner, Robert S. McNamara, or

McGeorge Bundy, men who played crucial roles in formulating and executing that policy, must be respectfully attended. I have also been edified by the criticism of our policy made by former admirals, marine corps officers, Manhattan Project scientists, state department officials, CIA officers, senators and congressmen—all of them conversant with the details and nuances of policy and its implementation, all of them beyond the reach of the slanderous allegations directed at critics less eminent.

I wish also to acknowledge the invaluable suggestions, criticism, and encouragement given me by Henry Steele Commager, Carl N. Degler, James MacGregor Burns, Alfred F. Young, Ronald W. Pruessen, Göran Rystad, Robert Cuff, Walter LaFeber, Martin Jay Sherwin, Gregg Herken, Richard J. Barnet, Thomas J. McCormick, Stanley I. Kutler, Athan Theoharis, Richard Gid Powers, and, above all, Melvyn P. Leffler. Needless to say, any errors of fact and deficiencies of interpretation are entirely mine. My friends Edward Margolies, Stanley Buder, and Myrna Chase have patiently and helpfully listened and responded to my observations and questions during the many years I have worked on the theme. The stimulating questions and responses by faculty, administrators, and students at Florida International University to the public lectures on the cold war which I presented there in 1992, as the Edna Gene and Jordan Davidson Professor of the Humanities, were invaluable. Certainly they stimulated me to think further about important issues. In Ivan Dee I have found a publisher intellectual whose taste for written comment that is sensible, pithy, and well founded has compelled me to refine my thoughts and my prose in order to try to approach his exacting standards. My wife Adele has, as always, given me indispensable spiritual and material support during the years in which I have wrestled with this project.

The dedication is to my best World War II buddies of Company A of the First Battalion of the 318th Regiment of the

Eightieth Infantry Division of the Third Army, who joined me in vowing to spend one night each year in a foxhole to remind us of the miseries of war and to do what we could to make World War II our last war.

E. P.

Miami, Florida
December 1992

Losing Our Souls

CHAPTER I

※

American
Cold War
Policy

THE cold war was the most unusual war the United States ever fought. It was by far the longest of all American wars. In common with most of the wars the United States entered into, it was not declared by Congress. But unlike such wars as those we fought in the nineteenth century against Indian tribes and early in the twentieth century in the Philippines and in Mexico, it was not a shooting war. Cold war tensions may have led the United States to engage in hot wars in Korea and Indochina, but the two great antagonists of the cold war, the United States and the Soviet Union, at no time fired weapons in anger against each other.

The cold war had neither a precise beginning nor ending. Different experts assign it different starting times and termination dates. All we know for certain is that it appears to have begun some time between the closing days of World War II and the president's declaration of the Truman Doctrine on March 12, 1947, and to have ended during the closing months of Mikhail Gorbachev's ascendancy in the Soviet Union and the early years of the Bush administration in the United States. Not the least unusual feature of the cold war was the breadth of United States

objectives in pursuing it. For in contrast to previous wars which
we fought to achieve limited territorial changes, if any, our
goals in the cold war were global in scope.

In a conflict that had no fixed starting time, the United States
never presented a formal, comprehensive statement of its cold
war aims. American cold war policy evolved over time—albeit
a brief period of time. Its essential features are contained not
alone in presidential proclamations or in the public utterances of
other political leaders. Whoever would understand American
cold war policy must pay attention as well to secret policy
directives emanating from such government agencies as the
National Security Council (NSC), the Central Intelligence Agency (CIA), and the Joint Chiefs of Staff (JCS)—guidelines to
foreign policy actions that were classified when they were first
issued. We have learned of these important clues to the American government's cold war policy only because of relatively
recent disclosures, whether in the writings of retired U.S.
military and civilian officials, in the multivolume transcripts of
Senate committee and presidential commission investigations of
the CIA and other federal agencies' covert operations, or in the
reports of scholars and journalists enabled by the post-Watergate
Freedom of Information Act (FOIA) to extract at least part of
the secret records of government cold war actions.

Perhaps the best clue to the nation's cold war policy is the
government's performance in waging it. For while a government's policy statements may or may not be acted on, its actions
and their anticipated consequences throw a bright light on what
a government is up to and most clearly reveal its policy.

One can speak of *the* cold war policy of the United States
because for all of its inevitable shifts and turns of focus,
whether "containment," "liberation," "détente," "mutual assured destruction," or other modifications in tactics or strategy,
the policy at its core remained unchanging.[1] Through the administrations of Harry S Truman and Ronald W. Reagan, and all the

presidents in between, the great object of American detestation was the Soviet Union. As recently as 1983 President Reagan called the USSR the "evil empire." Earlier in the postwar years American leaders, by word and deed, treated the Soviets as the deadly enemy not only of the United States but of freedom-loving states everywhere in the world. As the only nation in the aftermath of World War II that enjoyed the wealth and power necessary to do the job, the United States took on what its leaders called the historic and unavoidable responsibility of doing whatever was necessary, however costly, onerous, and dangerous, to allay the Soviet threat to humankind.

Since the U.S. charged that the postwar Soviet Union was an imperialistic state dedicated to extending its power over the entire world, as after World War II it had swiftly established its control over Eastern and much of Central Europe, one vital element in American cold war policy was to block the further expansion of the Soviet empire. Containment of the USSR and its influence was a crucially important step—but only a first step, not an ultimate goal. For, as George F. Kennan in 1946–1947 reasoned, successful containment was likely to create deep strains within the Soviet Union that its Stalinist leadership would face only with great difficulty.[2] But since the goal of destabilizing and destroying the internal Soviet order was un-likely to be achieved by indirection alone, U.S. policy called for active American-assisted measures within the USSR's Eastern European satellite states and within the Soviet Union itself, to supplement containment pressure in weakening and ultimately bringing down the USSR. In sum, our policy called for the United States to do what was necessary to bring about the collapse of the Soviet Communist party and of the Soviet order over which the party presided, and the overthrow of pro-Soviet regimes in Eastern Europe.

American objectives also ranged well beyond the territorial confines of the Soviet empire. Treating the entire world as an

arena of mortal combat between the Free World and the forces
of totalitarianism, American policymakers sought to prevent the
emergence of communist or pro-Soviet regimes anywhere on
earth. Acting on the premise that those who were not for us
were against us, American leaders were also cold if not hostile
toward noncommunist but neutralist governments and movements. Our goal was a world composed of anti-Soviet, pro-
American states. Because right-wing despotisms could be counted
on not only to be anti-Soviet but to crush socialist and pro-
Soviet parties and movements within their midst, the United
States gave financial, military, and diverse other forms of
assistance to foreign groups and parties intent on establishing
such regimes. And when such despotisms were in place, Washington did all it could to maintain them in power. Even before
Jimmy Carter became president, American leaders spoke of
their concern for freedom and human rights in countries aligned
with the United States—even when these countries brutally
suppressed dissent. However sincere were the American leaders
who expressed such concern, U.S. policy was to prop up
anticommunist regimes, however despotic, as long as they
were clever enough to promise freedom and avoid embarrassing
the United States with measures so outrageous as to be certain
to evoke a storm of opposition in our country and abroad.[3]

The cold war policy of the United States was directed against
an ideology as well as against a particular state. For according
to American policymakers, what made the USSR even more
menacing than Hitler to the U.S. and other freedom-loving
nations were the doctrines to which Soviet leaders were so
fanatically devoted. If they strained to take over the world, it
was because the theories of Marxism-Leninism urged them on.
If Soviet leaders sought to destroy religion, undermine the
family and its values, and transform men and women from
spiritual beings into mindless automatons eager to serve an
all-powerful state, it was because they had become slavish

devotees to atheistic communism. American policy therefore was to oppose individuals and organizations as well as governments that were sympathetic to the doctrines of Marxism-Leninism.

American cold war policy sought to prevent the accession to power of those in thrall to these perverse doctrines, to undermine them in places where they enjoyed great influence, and to turn popular opinion against them by depicting their beliefs in lurid terms. Achieving this last objective took some doing, in view of Marxist communism's glorification of the working classes, social and economic justice, and peace, and its denunciation of exploitation, racism, imperialism, fascism, and war. Adding to the U.S. problem was the success of communism in evoking sympathy from millions of working people the world over, including Catholic France and Italy, as well as from such admired individuals as George Bernard Shaw, Sean O'Casey, Jean Paul Sartre, and Jawaharlal Nehru.

In appraising communist theories, American policymakers did not so much accentuate the negative; they confined themselves entirely to the negative. One effective way of doing so was publicly to interpret the undeniable brutalities of Stalinist Russia as the inevitable by-product of government by Marxist-Leninists, wherever such governments might take root. But American policy of stigmatizing and destroying the influence of communist theory did not rest entirely or even primarily on a presentation of superior ideas or on an attempt to change minds by intellectual means. Creating a political atmosphere in which sympathy or even tolerance for communism and Marxism was dangerous to the health and reputation of those who were accused of it, was an important objective of American policy. Such an atmosphere was likely to be more persuasive than brilliant argument in anathematizing communism.

While it was scarcely emphasized in American leaders' public rhetoric in the struggle to safeguard the Free World from Soviet assault, an important objective of American policy was the promotion of a world economy congenial to American manufacturers, bankers, businessmen, and investors. Achieving this goal required the rebuilding of viable capitalistic economies in the industrial nations of Western Europe, a goal which the Marshall Plan sought to achieve when it was initiated in 1948. Tactics for creating an economic climate suitable to American interests elsewhere in the world differed from one country to another, affected by diverse factors, political and cultural as well as economic. Whatever a foreign nation's level of technological and economic development, American policymakers sought what in some instances they called "social peace" and the absence as well of the militant trade unions and political movements likely to foment strikes or disorders.[4]

It is impossible to disentangle economic from other motives in the formation and execution of American cold war policy. Not surprisingly, most American businessmen had no objections to exorcising communism, radicalism, and militant trade unionism, whether at home or abroad. Their interest in foreign governments focused on how they responded to the wishes of American investors and bankers rather than on how much they lived up to the ideals of Thomas Jefferson. True, there were mavericks among these businessmen. It is germane, however, to note that detailed studies of the careers of our leading cold war officials reveal that to an inordinate degree they had been businessmen or lawyers who served large corporate firms and, more important, that their "world views" or ideologies were almost invariably sympathetic to the presumed interests of American big business.[5] Officials in the Pentagon and the armed forces, whatever their earlier careers, regularly exchanged military command for business leadership, without having to modify outlooks that appeared identical to those of corporate managers. The question, however, is not about the earlier careers and political persuasions of American leaders but about their actions during the cold war. These actions signify their determination to make the world safe and as profitable as possible for American businessmen.[6]

In pursuing its cold war policy the United States engaged in an unprecedented buildup of its armed forces and its arsenal of conventional and nuclear weapons. While this program is best described as one means to accomplish U.S. cold war objectives, the vast scope of the buildup, going far beyond any plausible defensive need, and the near certainty that it would induce the Soviets to invest vast sums in an attempt to maintain a military balance of power with the U.S., raise questions about its purpose. American political and military leaders often stated publicly that war with the Soviet Union was not only inevitable but imminent. In the early years of the cold war the U.S. maintained a great advantage over the Soviets in the quantity and quality of nuclear weapons. Combined with our refusal to ban nuclear weapons in warfare, was this an indication that one aim of our policy was war with the Soviet Union? And if, as secret military surveys disclosed in the early 1950s, the cost in money, destroyed planes, and lives and Western European territory lost in defeating the Soviets would be unacceptable, was it American policy—not simply a *means* of executing policy—to create an escalating arms race? For such a competition was certain to fortify cold war tensions, enhance American power, increase the influence of the military both at home and abroad, stimulate the economy, bring lavish profits to defense contractors and business opportunities to Pentagon retirees, create a large constituency for a continuing military buildup in the fully employed and well-paid labor force making the weapons, and, not incidentally, accelerate the deterioration of the Soviet Union's lagging domestic economy.

*

The cold war policy of the United States was bold, dynamic, and unprecedented. Never before had the nation adopted a hostile, in some ways a warlike, stance against a foreign state with which we were at peace, a state that had not attacked us and was known by our intelligence to have no inclination to attack us. Never before had we waged a warlike campaign against an ideology, philosophy, or doctrine. And never before had we in peacetime entered into a series of alliances and established military bases around the earth, ringing the territory of a foreign state.

The swiftest glance at recent events seems to establish that the United States successfully achieved the chief objectives of its cold war policy. The Soviet empire has crumbled. The Eastern European satellites have broken the shackles that bound them, achieving independence and installing—for the most part—representative democratic governments in place of their ousted Soviet puppet regimes. The former Soviet Union has withdrawn from Afghanistan, ceased intervening in Third World affairs, and cut off its financial and military aid to radical or Marxist regimes and movements. Marxism seems almost everywhere to be in retreat. And, most dramatic of all, the Communist party has not only been removed from power in what used to be the Soviet Union but it has in some places been outlawed. The Union of Soviet Socialist Republics has ceased to exist, replaced by what at this writing is called a commonwealth composed of those former Soviet republics that chose to join it. Amidst the debris, the United States stands alone as the sole remaining superpower, clearly the victor over its twin enemies—the Soviet Union and Marxism-Leninism.

And yet questions about American cold war policy remain. That the United States achieved its major objectives does not prove that the policy and its goals were therefore in the national interest. Questionable ends do not become worthy because they are attained. As I shall show, American policy and the means of implementing it have had negative as well as positive consequences. It can be argued that even if the bad effects outweigh the good, it does not necessarily mean the United States was wrong in waging the cold war. For it is conceivable that not adopting the anti-Soviet and anticommunist postwar policy might have hurt the United States more than the worst effects of pursuing that policy. I shall also examine that possibility.

Another way of gauging the wisdom of our cold war policy is to ask how closely it lived up to the enduring principles of foreign policy that should guide the behavior of a democratic republic. The Founding Fathers of the United States believed that there are such principles and that they would be as valid in the nation's maturity as they were in its infancy. The chapter that follows examines the extent to which our cold war policy repudiated these principles.

CHAPTER II

The Foreign Policy Principles of a Democratic Republic

THE Founding Fathers who established the American Republic believed there were timeless principles that should guide the nation's behavior in its relations with other nations. These principles are worth pondering, coming as they do from the minds of the men who led this country first in its struggle for independence from Great Britain and then in creating the federal Constitution under which we still live.

In addition to being patriots whose love of country was manifested not by brave words alone but by self-sacrifice and courageous acts that put their lives at risk, the nation's founders were uncommonly learned, conversant with the history of nations and international relations dating back to classical antiquity. And as leaders of the colonies and, after the American Revolution, of the national and state governments, they were men of rich practical experience in political affairs. Not the least of their claims to our attention was their wisdom. They were high-minded, but they understood the limits as well as the importance of morality in the government of human beings, the necessity in the real world of tempering abstract ideals with practical good sense. They knew too that the best of leaders would at times fall short of meeting their responsibilities to the people. In view of men's proneness to lapse from the requirements of morality and good sense, the Founders believed it necessary to proclaim principles for guiding the nation's future leaders in the conduct of foreign affairs, principles that would serve as a compass. If heeded, they would enable the nation to avoid destruction and to prosper.[1]

They were quite aware of their inability to anticipate the future shape of this and other nations. Yet they understood that great if unpredictable changes would occur during the centuries that followed, changes certain to transform the world they knew. They believed nevertheless that the foreign policy principles that would best serve the nation in their own time, when the United States was small and weak, would serve it as well in the future, when it was great and strong. For the fundamental needs and interests of the people, and the duty of responsible leaders to pursue policies designed to secure these needs and interests, were unchanging, unaffected by inevitable alterations in the world.

The clearest statement of these enduring principles of foreign policy is George Washington's Farewell Address.[2] It was actually a written message that Washington presented to a Philadelphia newspaper in September 1796, toward the end of his second term as president. The address covers two large themes. The first is the need for unity to deal with the domestic requirements of the nation. The second concerns the appropriate path the nation should follow in the international arena. It is the foreign policy ideas which interest us here.

The few people who know anything at all about the Farewell Address think it was little more than a warning against "entangling alliances." (That famous phrase was in fact spoken by Thomas Jefferson in his presidential inaugural in 1801.) Washington's farewell contained much more than advice about avoiding "foreign entanglements." It is advice that has been neglected and, in the rare instances when it has been consulted, has usually been misunderstood or distorted. For a long time the address has been read aloud to the U.S. Senate every year on Washington's birthday. On every other day of the year the Senate typically ignores or repudiates the first president's recommendations.[3]

Undoubtedly because he thought the nation's foreign policy goals so obvious, Washington alludes to them only implicitly in his address. They are the goals to which even Machiavellian political leaders would pay lip service—peace, security, and enhanced prosperity through trade and commerce with other nations. To a world grown jaded with politicians who talk peace and make war, to a people increasingly inclined to acquiesce in the Clausewitzian dictum that war is nothing more than one among a variety of means—acceptable means—of conducting foreign policy, there is something instructive in the abhorrence of the Founding Fathers for war. They regarded war as a barbaric practice, an irrational way of resolving differences between nations, the plaything of despots, the scourge of international relations. They subscribed to Christopher Marlowe's indictment in *Tamberlaine*: "Accurst be he that first invented war."

Washington's loathing of war was visceral as well as intellectual. He had of course experienced war firsthand. Unlike many commanders turned practical politician, after the Revolution Washington, far from forgetting the horror of war, devoted himself to banishing it from human affairs. When he urged that the United States "never unsheath the sword except in self-defense" and told his countrymen than he "devoutly pray[ed] that we remain at peace to the end of time," he gave every evidence of meaning it. A decade before he presented the address, Washington had stated that his "first wish" was that war should be forever "banished from the earth," and he later championed the cause of a universal language as a project that might "one day remove many of the causes of hostility from amongst mankind." A scholar who combed the historical record for every Washingtonian deed and utterance on the subject concluded that Washington's "antipathy to war... appears to have been genuine."[4]

Washington was high-minded but he understood the limits of idealism. World peace was a lovely goal but a goal that was beyond the power of American statesmen or those of any other nation to attain. It would be achievement enough for American leaders to keep their own nation at peace, thereby teaching the world that hateful war is not necessary to a nation's security and prosperity.

Washington knew that war is not easily avoided. It was because human beings were divided into separate nations, each pursuing its own interests, that nations had to adopt a foreign policy in the first place. In a world composed of nations that were typically governed by amoral leaders bent on aggrandizement, keeping the United States at peace would be no easy task. For history had shown that such rulers, far from abhorring war, seemed rather to dote on it. When waged successfully, war brought great wealth, new territories and resources, cheap labor, and captive markets to the victorious ruling classes. "Whence come wars," Socrates had asked, "but from the stomachs" of rulers? Outfitting and arming the military brought great profits to some, steady employment for many others. Nor were the blessings of war solely material. Victory in war brought glory and prestige to rulers and warriors. Powerful armies could deter and if necessary suppress dangerous disorders at home. War could easily divert popular attention from a government's failure to deal effectively with domestic problems. When artfully propagandized, war was a matchless device for inspiring people to devote themselves to, even die for, the state. And war had a seductive appeal to persons of a certain emotional makeup, to males who believed it the great authenticator of manhood.

But none of the charms of war could mask the maimings and deaths it inflicted, the devastation and suffering invariably resulting from it. Not having to answer to the people of their nations, despots, oligarchs, and the powerful elites that ruled most states were free to indulge their passion for war. Republics led by clever demagogues could incite popular support for wars of aggrandizement almost as easily as could absolute monarchs. Thus the duty of responsible leaders truly devoted to the welfare of their people was to avoid war if humanly possible. The great purpose of Washington's Farewell Address was, on the one hand, to remind future leaders of this increasingly democratic Republic that keeping the nation out of war must be their overriding goal and, on the other hand, to show them how to achieve that goal. If, as the faithful knew, there are many paths to heaven, responsible leaders of a republic must learn, if they do not already know, the several paths to peace.

We must "observe good faith and justice towards all nations. Cultivate peace and harmony with all." Washington explains that "religion and morality enjoin this conduct; and can it be," he asks, "that good policy does not equally enjoin it?" Justice as well as self-interest require us to "maintain inviolate the relations of peace and amity towards other nations." To Washington, as to other of the Founding Fathers, the dictates of idealism here were not in conflict with those of realism. Both compel the United States to maintain the friendly relations with foreign states that are most likely to "maintain inviolate" the peace among them. Happily, the world was so structured that government behavior one knew intuitively to be just was also behavior that enhanced the material and practical interests of the nation.

Choosing his words carefully, Washington calls on his successors to maintain friendly relations with *all* nations. It is not for us to pick and choose among nations. American leaders are not to dole out friendly treatment to the favored few whom they most admire. As individual human beings, the leaders of a republic will have personal preferences among men, nations, political systems, political philosophies. But as responsible leaders whose task is to represent the interest of their politically and philosophically diverse population in maintaining peace with all nations, their duty is clear.

If we must behave toward all nations in an equally friendly way, it is not because their leaders deserve it but because our interests require it and morality approves it. Washington recognized that some nations were more attractive than others. Changing unlovely foreign regimes for the better was not the task of any nation, the United States included, but a task rather for the people living under that regime. It would be no more appropriate for the American government to adopt a hostile policy toward a state which harbored distasteful internal institutions than for a self-righteous foreign state to mistreat us because both in Washington's time and later we treated non-white Americans unjustly. No state was good enough to set things right in another. As students of history, the Founders knew that ancient Athens was doubtless freer and in many ways far more attractive than Sparta. And yet, as Thucydides had explained, Athens was no less imperious in its behavior toward weak neighboring states than was Sparta, no less culpable in bringing on the tragic Peloponnesian War.[5] States governed one way rather than another were neither more nor less dangerous because of the fact. American policy toward them should be based not on how they had treated third parties but on how they behaved toward us.

It was axiomatic that great powers were amoral. They had become great powers by conquering or dominating weaker nations. Friendly treatment of them was not a reward for their previous misdeeds but simply a sensible means of encouraging them to reciprocate our own amicable behavior. It was bad enough that nations too often went to war for what their governments considered their interests. It would be intolerable for a nation, itself imperfect, to justify making war on another nation which had done it no harm because of that nation's mistreatment of others. An all-too-rare good sense had led nations to condemn war justified on such grounds—grounds that, once accepted, would ensure perpetual war.

Washington recognized that in urging his successors to show forbearance toward warlike nations and treat them in a friendly fashion he was holding the United States to a demanding standard of international conduct likely to be met by no other nation. The greater the pity for the benighted people of great powers, whose lives were rarely free of the hardships and sacrifices required in preparation for war, the misery and suffering attendant on engaging in war, the few rewards accruing to ordinary people from the spoils of war! To live in a nation disinclined to wage wars for conquest and equally opposed to making war for "reasons of state" was good for the bodies as well as the souls of the people so fortunate.[6]

The most remarkable example of Washington's belief that moral behavior toward other countries was profitable to the United States was his advice that it would be "worthy of a free, enlightened, and at no distant period, a great nation, to give mankind the magnanimous and too novel example of a people always guided by an exalted justice and benevolence." For, he continued, "who can doubt that in the course of time . . . the fruits of such a plan would richly repay any temporary advantages which might be lost by a steady adherence to it?"

Given what we know about people and their governments, it may seem unrealistic to ask them always to abide by the golden rule in their treatment of other nations. The problem is not with the request, for it may well be right that ethically admirable behavior is in the long run self-interested behavior. The problem rather is with cantankerous, frequently irrational human beings, tragically capable of actions that, like those of the scorpion in

Aesop's fable, they cannot resist taking even when they know them to be self-destructive. Washington was acting on the premise later given voice by the poet—"What's a heaven for?" Future American leaders would not likely always be wise enough to heed Washington's advice, nor would the people be keen enough always to discern government misbehavior and courageous enough to condemn it when it occurred. But that such a sound and wise policy was difficult to execute was no reason not to edify the people about its characteristics or to refrain from trying to achieve it.

Among Washington's points is that our delight, say, at wealth that might pour into the country as a result of conquest, reminiscent of how Romans danced in the streets when their legions confiscated the Macedonian treasury, would turn out to be transitory when accounts were finally settled. As moralists, Washington and other of the Founders agreed with George Mason's observation at the Constitutional Convention in Philadelphia that Providence would inflict great calamities on nations that committed great atrocities.[7] Thinking of slavery, Jefferson later wrote that he "trembled that God is just." As realists the Founders concluded that the human costs of military conquest, the financial costs of maintaining the forces necessary to perpetuate the subjugation of others, the political hatred of those conquered, and the bitter dissent provoked by conquest among high-minded people in our own nation outweighed the ephemeral and unequally distributed profits of war.

The implication of the enjoinder that we treat all nations in a friendly manner was that our future leaders not pick and choose among foreign states, as though our amicable treatment of them were a reward for good behavior. Washington makes the point explicitly when he advises his successors that "nothing is more essential than that permanent inveterate antipathies against particular nations and passionate attachments for others should be excluded" from our conduct. Anticipating the famous maxim of

Lord Palmerston a half-century later, Washington reminds future
American statesmen that individuals have friends, nations have
interests.[8] Since political leaders are human, they will inevitably
prefer some nations to others. But the new republic's responsible leaders must play no favorites. By all means treat admirable
states well, certainly no worse but no better than we treat less
attractive states. Washington continues: "The nation, which
indulges towards another an habitual hatred or an habitual
fondness, is in some degree a slave: it is a slave to its animosity
or to its affection, either of which is sufficient to lead it astray
from its duty and its interest. Antipathy in one nation against
another disposes each more readily to offer insult and injury, to
lay hold of slight causes of umbrage. . . . The nation, prompted
by ill will and resentment, sometimes impels to war the government, contrary to the best calculations of policy. . . Excessive
partiality for one foreign nation and excessive dislike of another, cause those whom they actuate to see danger only on
one side. . . ." Statesmen who would bend their nation's foreign
policy to their personal political or ideological preferences
would be guilty of arrogance and dereliction of duty, not to mention poor judgment. If peace or the avoidance of unnecessary
war is truly America's passion, as it should be, it follows that
we should indeed avoid "inveterate antipathies against particular
nations."

Neither Washington nor any of the other Founding Fathers
believed in peace at any price. But it was their aversion to war
for light cause or for the cause of nations other than our own
that prompted their suspicion of entangling alliances. That was
why the Farewell Address stated that "the great rule of conduct
for us, in regard to foreign nations is . . . to have with them as
little *political* connection as possible." For it would be "unwise
in us to implicate ourselves in the vicissitudes of [Europe's and,
by implication, other continents'] politics," or in the "combina-
tions and collusions of her [or their] friendships or enmities.

Our detached and distant [geographical] situation invites and enables us to pursue a different course. . . . Why forgo the advantage of so peculiar a situation? . . . Why, by interweaving our destiny with that of any part of Europe, entangle our peace and prosperity in the toils of European ambition, rivalships, interest, humor, or caprice?" Although "we may safely trust to temporary alliances for extraordinary emergencies," absent such emergencies " 'tis our true policy to steer clear of permanent alliances with any portion of the foreign world."

These strictures against "interweaving our destiny" and entangling our prosperity in the toils of foreign rivalries, intrigues, and hostilities over which we have no control have been branded "isolationism" by critics of the Farewell Address. The charge is a serious one in an American society that has come to regard isolationism as a dereliction if not a betrayal of duty. After all, doesn't the United States have a duty to be involved in the affairs of the world? But nothing in Washington's final message commands the United States or its citizens to avoid friendship, close contacts, and substantial commercial and financial relationships with other nations. Such relationships with other societies do not require us to unite with them, form permanent military alliances with them, or send our troops to fight alongside them in wars of their making. Maintaining close ties with other nations, while refraining from formal political and military connections with them in the absence of emergencies requiring such connections, is not isolationism except in the usage of those to whom involvement means nothing less than war or preparation for war.

The Founding Fathers had great faith in international commerce as a means both of cementing good relations with America's trading partners and enhancing its own prosperity. In Washington's phrase, "liberal intercourse with all nations" was recommended not only by religion and morality but by "policy, humanity, interest." And "even our commercial policy should hold an equal and impartial hand: neither seeking nor granting exclusive favors. . . ." In the short run, compelling weaker states to make products accessible to us under terms of our choosing might enlarge American profit margins and, when the products had military uses, promote our security. But such a policy would offend morality and humanity. And in the long run its seeming material benefits would be outweighed by its unacceptable political and economic costs. For it was as true for nations as it was for individuals: what did it profit them to gain the world but lose their souls?

Washington was devoted to peace; his final message was essentially a recipe for achieving it. He nonetheless understood that maintaining peace would not depend on the United States alone. Friendly, impartial treatment of all nations was good for the soul, for the pocketbook, and at worst would deprive perverse foreign rulers bent on war of the pretext for waging it against us. But there were such rulers and governments likely to interpret U.S. weakness as an invitation to commit aggression against us. One necessary means of ensuring our security and enhancing our prospects for peace was to build military forces capable of deterring attack. Fortunately, our geographical situation was favorable, with two great oceanic barriers to invasion from east and west and militarily weak and unthreatening states north and south, making it unnecessary for us to create the "swollen military establishment" that Washington feared could threaten republican government. Since it was in the interest of the United States to forswear subjugation or domination of other states, it would be sufficient to our needs "to keep ourselves, by suitable [military] establishments, on a reasonably defensive posture." In the "extraordinary emergency" created by the threat of imminent attack on the United States by an aggressor too powerful to be resisted successfully by American forces alone, we might "safely trust to temporary alliances."

These, then, were the measures by which our future governments could achieve the three great goals of foreign policy: peace, security, and prosperity.

Washington had no illusions that his successors would honor these principles. He "dare[d] not hope" his sentiments would "make the strong and lasting impression [he] could wish" and thus prevent the nation he loved from "running the [dismal] course which has hitherto marked the destiny of nations." But these were doubts not about the wisdom of the course he had charted; rather they were doubts about the capacity of later generations to depart from the forlorn patterns of international behavior followed by amoral states and hew instead to the path conducive to enduring peace and happiness. Washington's concern about the behavior of his successors in the highest office turned out to be justified.

The United States began to repudiate Washington's recommendations long before the Civil War. Some critics have argued that whatever value the address may have had in its own time, its principles were made obsolete by the changes that overtook the United States, and the world, in the nineteenth and twentieth centuries. Observing that admirers of the address fail to note "the peculiar context of the times in which Washington issued his solemn warning," a modern historian reminds us that times have changed radically. Since in our own time "jet planes, long-range bombers, submarines, atom and hydrogen bombs can penetrate the most formidable barrier," and since too "the outposts of the nation have moved to farflung places whose very names were unknown to Americans in Washington's day," this scholar thinks it "highly probable that [Washington] would have been the first to disavow the interpretations which have been placed upon his doctrine of 'entangling alliances.'"[9] Not very likely. Washington's clearly expressed words to the contrary suggest that he would have stuck to his guns, continuing to believe that his prescriptions were permanently applicable. One suspects that a Washington returned to life would ask, rather,

why and how we came to have farflung outposts. The real
question, however, is not what a resurrected Washington would
think but whether the technological and other changes of the
past two centuries have indeed undermined the validity of his
ideas.

By the late nineteenth century the United States had become,
as Washington hoped we would, a country with a "population,
riches, and resources [which] when combined with its peculiarly
happy and remote situation from the other quarters of the
globe," made it possible for us "to bid defiance, in a just
cause, to any earthly power whatsoever." Washington believed
his principles would apply despite the transformation of American life and the world around us because peace, security, and
prosperity through commerce would continue to be the nation's
foreign policy goals. Just and friendly behavior toward all states
would best ensure attaining these goals, whatever the state of
our technology, the size of our treasury, the numbers in our
population. Expanding our wealth and resources through successful wars waged by a preeminent military machine would be
as unjust, as certain to leave bitterness in their wake in our
maturity as they had been in our youth. War had, if anything,
become less permissible because far more horrible than Washington's generation in its worst nightmare ever dreamed it could
be. The means of destruction had become more powerful, the
walls between military personnel and noncombatants had crumbled, the carnage had grown far more devastating.

During the early twentieth century, well before the advent of
the Soviet state, the United States many times flouted Washington's advice that we cultivate peaceful relations with all nations,
particularly in Central and Latin America, China, and the
Philippine Islands. We did so not because our size, wealth and
power permitted such action. We did so because our leaders
elected to use our strength, as did imperial powers, to compel
weaker states and peoples to give us what our leaders wanted,

whether resources, cheap labor, naval bases and fueling stations, or most-favored-nation commercial and financial advantages. These deviations from the principles of the Farewell Address were dictated not by historical necessity but by imperial ambitions, arrogance, and the racial chauvinism that permeated the foreign policy of Washington's successors in high office.

Like other states pursuing amoral policies abroad, the United States and its leaders invoked lofty justifications for this imperial performance, justifications that, if they were unlikely to satisfy skeptics, might at least mollify a nationalistic public. Abetted by racist, jingoistic, and acquiescent publicists and scholars, American statesmen proclaimed their honorable intentions, motivated by sentiments of Christian uplift and an awareness of the obligations attendant on our racial and cultural superiority, and that our actions were congruent with the dictates of biological and social science.[10] From the vantage point of the late twentieth century these earlier justifications for what Theodore Roosevelt called our Large Policy are intellectually deficient as well as hypocritical. In fairness to the surprisingly popular antiimperialist movement at the turn of the century, a great number of Americans were not buying either the policy or the rationalizations presented in its defense. For better or for worse, however, the expansionists prevailed, first in Congress, then in the minds of the people, but for reasons having little to do with the technological changes that overtook the nation after the Civil War. Washington's principles were repudiated less because the facts of life compelled them to be than because his successors loved power and aggrandizement more than peace, morality, and justice—precisely as Washington had feared they would.

The clearest feature of the cold war policy of the United States is how thoroughly it abandoned every one of George Washington's recommendations for achieving peace, security, and prosperity through commerce on equal terms with all nations. Long before the cold war American leaders had moved sharply away from the kind of foreign policy envisioned by the Founding Fathers. But the policy adopted by the American government in the aftermath of World War II represented the sharpest break ever with the principles of the Farewell Address.

During the cold war years U.S. leaders hardly "cultivated peace and harmony" with all other nations. American behavior toward them was not "always guided by an exalted justice and benevolence." In opposition to Washington's advice U.S. leaders instead promoted "inveterate antipathies"—long enduring, if not permanent—"against particular nations." The nation was indeed "impel[led] to war" in Korea and Vietnam that, in the opinion of many, was "contrary to the best calculations of policy." "Excessive dislike" for "one foreign nation" caused us to see "danger only on one side." The counsel that "in regard to foreign nations [we should] have with them as little political connection as possible" was repudiated. Nor was Washington's advice heeded against interweaving "our destiny" and entangling "our peace and prosperity in the toil of [foreign] nations' ambition, rivalship, interest, humor, [and] caprice." U.S. policymakers did not "steer clear of permanent alliances with any portion of the foreign world" and instead went far beyond Washington's insistence on a "reasonably defensive posture." In our "commercial policy" we did not hold out an "equal and impartial hand." We did not "maintain inviolate the relations of peace and amity" toward those we called our adversaries.

Nor was American cold war policy less at odds with the clear implications of the Farewell Address. We did not assiduously seek to avoid war. American leaders indeed acted as though their responsibilities extended to embracing the interests of nations other than our own. They sought to achieve victory abroad for the kind of political, social, and economic order they approved. Presidents treated some nations as permanent friends and intervened in the internal affairs of nations around the globe. In pursuing foreign policy based on their "private affections" for some states and systems, our leaders failed to act impartially toward all nations. They violated the implicit Washingtonian principle that both the internal institutions of a foreign state and its external behavior toward third parties should be a matter of indifference to us. And, in violation of what Felix Gilbert called Washington's warning "against the danger of letting ideological predilections or prejudices enter considerations of foreign policy,"[11] U.S. policymakers largely based the nation's foreign policy precisely on such "predilections and prejudices."

Where the foreign policy urged on the nation by its Founders was predicated on the overwhelming importance of peace, the cold war policy put in place by our postwar leaders was predicated on the overwhelming importance of things other than peace. American statesmen of course talked peace. If public rhetoric is the clue to the hearts of politicians, peace was our leaders' passion in the forty-five years after World War II. But if deeds matter, not peace but the sword was on their minds.

That statesmen are inclined to put their motives in the best possible light does not mean that the explanations they offer for their behavior are insincere. Even when their justifications seem farfetched, they demand close attention. For whether right or wrong, sincere or insincere, the arguments propagated by a nation's leaders are revealing about their priorities and political strategies. At the least they disclose what the government wants the public to believe are the nation's objectives. When publicized widely and effectively, ideas have great influence on the public mind, whatever their intellectual shortcomings. Where policy justifications are blatantly unpersuasive or out of touch with the facts, they leave the distinct impression that those presenting them intended to mask the real wellsprings of their policy. Government objectives hidden from the people more than likely cannot stand close scrutiny. All of which is to say that no serious appraisal of U.S. cold war policy can ignore the justifications offered by American leaders for adopting that policy.

The foreign policy principles presented in George Washington's Farewell Address are an impressive blend of high moral purpose and practical good sense. Repudiating these principles, the architects of American cold war policy in effect argued that the unprecedented dangers confronting the United States at the end of World War II left them no alternative but to brush aside Washington's recommendations and administer the nation's foreign policy along principles more responsive to harsh new realities.

CHAPTER III

🎋

American Justifications for Waging the Cold War

In the immediate aftermath of World War II, the great majority of Americans told pollsters they continued to have the positive feelings toward the Soviet Union that had been awakened during the war by the sacrifices and military feats of our "heroic ally."[1] American political and military leaders, as well as those of Britain and France, had lauded the Soviet people for their courage and endurance, the Red Army for its dominant role in crushing Hitler's Wehrmacht, and Joseph Stalin for his cooperation with the Western democracies, despite what Roosevelt and Churchill called his understandable disappointment at the long-delayed opening of a second front in Europe.[2] Doubtless it was inevitable that the love feast of wartime would fade with the coming of peace. Few alliances outlast the defeat of the enemy. The removal of the common danger loosens the cement that binds states joined together out of self-interest.[3] What was unprecedented was both the speed of the breakup of the Grand Alliance that had won World War II and the celerity with which the leaders of the United States and the Soviet Union turned on each other.

Within months of the defeat of the Axis powers, American

leaders were describing the USSR as a dangerous threat to the United States. Soon the U.S. government convinced its hesitant friends in Western Europe that the three separate Western zones of occupation in Germany should be unified, the shattered West German economy rebuilt, and Germany's armed forces resurrected.[4] To effect this shift and ensure the popular support necessary for success, President Truman and his key advisers needed a massive propaganda campaign to transform the public's approval of the USSR into fear and loathing. American leaders mounted that effort, presenting diverse justifications for the government's sharp and sudden reversal of its wartime policy. In essence they charged that the postwar misbehavior of the Soviet Union created an unprecedented threat to the safety and security of the United States and the world, leaving us no alternative but to take military and other measures necessary for dealing with this mortal danger, whatever the cost, whatever sacrifices these measures entailed.

How well do the Truman administration's explanations for the cold war stand up to critical scrutiny? Other writers have of course addressed this question.[5] But the conclusions reached by these critical investigators do not appear to have had much influence either on the public at large or on the media that dispensed information about the cold war. Most of the nation's newspaper and magazine publishers, editors, syndicated columnists, and television commentators depicted the origins and events of the cold war very much as the president wished them to be depicted.[6] The viewpoint presented might very well have been valid; there is, after all, no law that official pronouncements must always be false. What is disturbing is the uncritical way in which the molders of American public opinion typically disseminated the government's viewpoint about why the nation went to war against Soviet-directed "international communist subversion." For, as the complex historical record confirms, the accuracy of the American case was by no means self-evident. It seems incontrovertible that the media chose to portray the cold war as they did not because they were persuaded by a serious investigation of the issues but rather because they chose to play the American government's game.

In any case, while particular features of American cold war policy, such as the Vietnam War or the Bay of Pigs invasion of Cuba, were widely questioned and condemned, the underlying policy that led to these engagements was spared harsh criticism in most of the media. The few sharp challenges to that policy were largely ignored, and the public was taught to suspect that subversion might be lurking behind critiques certain to be helpful to the "enemy."[7] Americans who unquestioningly supported the government's cold war actions and justifications as patriotic would have been surprised to discover that to George Washington, "real patriots" were citizens who had the integrity and courage openly to condemn popular policy which they considered bad policy, even at the risk of becoming "suspected and odious" for their temerity.

No single utterance or document contains all the charges against the Soviet Union and the international communist subversion that U.S. officials claimed the USSR directed. Between 1945 and 1947 President Truman and civilian and military officials in his administration, as well as other influential individuals in and out of government, presented this indictment in piecemeal fashion. In public addresses, press conferences, interviews, congressional hearings, executive department documents, and statements read to the press or made to broadcasters, administration leaders charged that not only the postwar behavior of the USSR but its doctrines and very way of life posed a deadly threat to the safety and security of the United States and the world.

The Truman administration's chief accusations against the Soviet Union were these:

The USSR had rearmed after World War II despite the destruction of Nazi Germany and Japan. Soviet possession of "armed forces far in excess of those necessary to defend its territory" was telltale proof of a plan for military aggression.[8]

By 1985 Secretary of Defense Caspar W. Weinberger charged that Soviet noncompliance with agreements on atomic weapons limitations constituted a "threat to vital American interests." Earlier, in a 1946 report commissioned by President Truman, White House aides Clark Clifford and George Elsey concluded that Soviet dishonoring of wartime agreements confirmed that Soviet leaders sought world domination. As early as April 23, 1945, President Truman had warned Soviet Foreign Minister V. M. Molotov, in what Admiral William D. Leahy called "plain American language," that relations between the U.S. and the USSR could no longer be "on the basis of a one-way street." When Molotov objected that "I have never been talked to like that," Truman responded, "Carry out your agreements and you won't get talked to like that." Two years later the president accused the Soviets of not honoring the agreements reached at Yalta in February 1945, Potsdam in July 1945, or any other Allied wartime agreement concerning their postwar responsibilities and actions.[9]

The Allies' wartime agreements had dealt with issues involving the governance of postwar Europe, Asia, and other portions of the globe. The Soviet violations most emphasized by American leaders concerned Poland and Eastern Europe. President Truman accused the Soviets of repudiating the agreements on the nature and means of installing the postwar Polish government, making high-handed demands regarding Poland's borders, not permitting free elections, repudiating the "Declaration on Liberated Europe," and using threats and force to take over not only Poland but Czechoslovakia, Hungary, Rumania, Bulgaria, and Albania, and dominating Yugoslavia, turning these nations into satellites of the USSR. Soviet treatment of Eastern Europe was in itself brutal. What made it unacceptably threatening, said American leaders, was the fact that Stalin regarded Soviet subjugation of Eastern Europe as only a first step, a prelude to Soviet moves against Central and Western Europe.[10]

The United States denounced Soviet behavior in postwar Germany as violations of the Yalta and Potsdam accords. Truman administration officials accused the USSR of demanding exorbitant reparations payments from the Germans, improperly removing machinery and equipment from Germany, brutally mistreating the German civilian population, and stalling on a peace treaty. In 1948 President Truman responded with an airlift to break what he called the illegal Soviet blockade of Berlin, a blockade intended to back up the Soviet claim that the Western allies had forfeited their rights to the western portion of Berlin by their actions in unifying their occupation zones in West Germany.[11]

At Yalta the wartime allies had agreed to form an international organization to work to prevent a recurrence of the aggressions and wars that had disfigured the world during the first half of the twentieth century. Although the United States had itself introduced the proposal that gave each of the Big Five (the U.S., USSR, Britain, France, and China) a veto in the Security Council of the UN, American leaders and the media regularly condemned the Soviets for thwarting the will of the majority by their excessive use of the veto.[12]

American leaders discerned a dangerous threat in a number of other Soviet actions that, though not in violation of wartime agreements, were no less disquieting for what they claimed to be violations of international law and acceptable norms of conduct among nations. The civil war that raged in Greece after 1945 and threatened to upset restoration of the monarchy supported by the United States and Great Britain came to be portrayed by the Truman administration as an attempt by Soviet-controlled communists to turn Greece into a Soviet puppet state. Indeed, Secretary of State George C. Marshall in 1947 darkly warned that a victory for the Greek guerrillas "might open three continents to Soviet penetration." Such warnings set the stage for the president's "Truman Doctrine" speech on March 12, 1947, to a joint session of Congress, characterizing the conflict in Greece as part of a mortal global struggle "between alternative ways of life."[13]

In 1947 President Truman and George F. Kennan, then a State Department adviser, further accused the Soviets of committing "indirect aggression" by their intervention in the internal affairs of France and Italy. Both men privately concluded that an electoral victory by the Communist parties in those two crucially important countries was so unthinkable that the United States might have to resort to force and risk starting World War III should covert financial assistance to Italian and French anticommunists fail to avert such a calamity. For Italian and French Communists were puppets of the Soviet state.[14]

The Truman administration also condemned Soviet postwar actions in the Middle East, accusing the Soviets of working with procommunist forces in northern Iran to dismember that country, using coercion to try to extract unwarranted oil concessions from the Iranian government, violating their agreement to pull Soviet troops out of the country by March 2, 1946, and planning to invade Iran. President Truman warned that Soviet failure to honor the deadline for withdrawal of military forces from Iran could lead to a general war.[15] In August 1946 the president interpreted the Soviet request to Turkey that the two states provide for joint defense of the Dardanelles as an aggressive demand signifying Soviet plans for expansion. He swiftly sent U.S. warships to the region. His response was not surprising, as earlier in the year he had written to James Byrnes that "there isn't a doubt in my mind that Russia intends an invasion of Turkey and the seizure of the Black Sea Straits."[16]

The administration also charged that Soviet rejection of the Baruch Plan for international control and the ultimate elimination of atomic weapons, a plan which the U.S. brought to the United Nations in June 1946 (at a time when it alone possessed atomic bombs and the know-how and means to make them), indicated the USSR's willingness to ignite a dangerous arms race in its drive for world domination.[17]

Yet, while American leaders were making these charges and branding the USSR a dangerous outlaw state, they were aware that a fair number of Soviet postwar actions were in fact consistent with the wartime summit agreements, moderate, even cooperative. In a February 1946 speech to the Soviet public, Stalin described the United States and Britain as "freedom-loving countries" which even before the German invasion of the USSR in 1941 had been fighting a war of "anti-fascist liberating character" against the Axis powers, and whose wartime alliance with the Soviet Union had been instrumental in achieving victory. Even after Winston Churchill's "Iron Curtain" speech in Fulton, Missouri, on March 5, 1946, Stalin told a Western correspondent that the English-speaking nations are "strong for [the] maintenance of peace." Shortly after the Nazi surrender the Soviet ruler told American emissary Harry Hopkins that as a world power the United States would of course "have to accept worldwide interests." Hopkins reported that when Soviet Foreign Minister Molotov rejected the American proposal that there be no veto in the UN Security Council on discussion (as on action), Stalin in Hopkins's presence told his foreign minister, "Molotov, that's nonsense!" and forthwith accepted the proposal. Professor Vojtech Mastny, a bitter critic of the Stalin regime, reports that Stalin disapproved of the Czech communists' action in demanding a disproportionate number of ministries in the postwar Czech government. Mastny further reports that Stalin had curbed the spring 1945 Yugoslav advance into Corinthia, "enabling the British to take control of the province"; that the USSR, far from seeking to maintain a military presence in Hungary and Central Europe, instead "sought the broadest possible range of collaboration" and "passed over opportunities to install the local Communists in power." In 1946 the Soviet Union approved free elections in Hungary and Czechoslovakia as well as in Austria, with whom they later signed a peace treaty.

That same year Ambassador Walter Bedell Smith reported from Moscow on the USSR's efforts at mediation in Iran and in the Chinese civil war, and their settlement of border disputes with Afghanistan. In a January 1947 report the U.S. Central Intelligence Group cited eight examples of moderate and conciliatory Soviet behavior in Central and Eastern Europe and in the UN.[18] But nothing the Russians might do deflected American leaders from their campaign to demonize the Soviet Union. Dating from Truman's presidency, American political leaders chose to construe seemingly irreproachable Soviet behavior as mere tactics designed to lull the West into complacency.

In the years immediately following the Japanese surrender, for example, some U.S. officials urged that Washington respond positively to unexceptionable Soviet actions and to Stalin's urgent request that the two sides meet to resolve their important differences through negotiation and compromise. But such voices went unheard. Instead President Truman elected to follow the advice of those who argued that the Soviet Union had never abandoned its goal of world conquest, that its intentions were always malevolent. In the phrase of a planning document approved by the Joint Chiefs of Staff, the "basic objective" of the USSR was "unlimited expansion of Soviet Communism, accompanied by . . . the territorial expansion of Russian imperialism." The State Department claimed that the Soviets had established control over Eastern Europe as a "prelude to further expansion." In 1946 Chief of Naval Operations Admiral Chester Nimitz warned that the Soviets were preparing to blockade, bomb, and invade England and to launch submarine attacks on American coastal cities, while Ambassador Smith urged Washington not to be taken in by the improved Soviet behavior in Asia he had reported in June 1946. "The Russians," he warned, had not abandoned their "predatory aims." Similarly, the Central Intelligence Group cautioned against misreading the eight examples of Soviet moderate and conciliatory behavior it had discerned in 1947: these "new tactics of compromise and conciliation [had] been adopted merely as a matter of expediency." The Kremlin had "not abandoned any of its long-run objectives." In the eyes of American policymakers, the Soviet Union could do no right.[19]

American leaders knew these malevolent intentions because they were confident in their knowledge of the beliefs that animated every Soviet action. It was idle to negotiate with Soviet leaders because they adhered to Marxist-Leninist doctrines. From the administration of Harry Truman through the first administration of Ronald Reagan, U.S. leaders ceaselessly attacked this "fanatical Soviet faith antithetical to our own." How, asked Secretary of State John Foster Dulles in testimony before the Senate Foreign Relations Committee, could "there be any permanent conciliation" between the U.S. and the USSR when Soviet communism "believes that human beings are somewhat superior animals?" The Marxism-Leninism depicted in American cold war propaganda glorified an all-powerful state ruled by a self-appointed elite dedicated to stamping out religion, the family, humane values, freedom, and democracy while inciting its spiritually enslaved followers to destroy the institutions and governments of noncommunist countries. Communists relied on means both treacherous and brutal in their attempt to communize the world and subject it to the control of the amoral dictators who ruled the Soviet Union.

The USSR, American officials charged, was more dangerous than Nazi Germany because Soviet doctrines masked their sinister objectives with high-sounding promises of social justice, equality, and world peace—promises that were capable of attracting the gullible of the earth. If, as NSC policy papers in the late 1940s warned, the Soviets' very internal order was an unacceptable threat to our freedom and security, it was because their system had been created in a Marxist-Leninist image and was ruled by men bent on imposing on the world a social, economic, political, and intellectual order similarly abhorrent.[20]

As turmoil and civil war racked the postwar world, U.S. officials concluded that Soviet leaders aimed to exploit disorders in China, Africa, Asia, and the Middle East to further their own sinister purpose of world conquest.

This catalogue constitutes the bill of indictment drafted by American leaders against the post–World War II Soviet Union. Informed people by now know that some of these accusations were somewhat exaggerated. When President Truman "scared hell" out of the American people in his Truman Doctrine message, as Senator Arthur Vandenberg had urged him to do, supporters of this anticommunist policy understood that the president's denunciation of "indirect aggression" by "totalitarian regimes" was not intended to be a factual summary in a scholarly disquisition.[21] What was distinctive about American presidents' criticisms of the postwar Soviet Union however, was not that some of the charges were exaggerated but that virtually every one of them was distorted, undocumented, false, or known by those making the charges to be exaggerated. Indeed, a number of the high American officials who condemned the Soviet Union's allegedly threatening postwar behavior privately conceded that it was not threatening at all.

In some cases policymakers who had earlier found nothing culpable in Soviet actions swiftly reevaluated them once the U.S. decided to wage cold war. Now they discerned a sinister character. It is of course the prerogative of diplomats, no less than of other people, to change their minds. It is disconcerting, however, when they do so to whip up public loathing of a state they have decided to demonize.

The Truman administration's charges against the Soviet Union exaggerated the danger. State Department documents reveal that at the end of World War II, United States armed forces were greater than those of the USSR. In May 1945 the Red Army numbered roughly 11,365,000 men. Commencing to demobilize the following month, by 1948 Soviet armed forces had shrunk to 2,874,000 troops. Many of these soldiers were occupation troops, as the Joint Chiefs knew, and their level of expertise was comparatively primitive. Western land forces outnumbered those of the Soviet Union; Soviet air and naval forces were markedly inferior both in quantity and quality; while the United States alone possessed atomic bombs. The American charge that the Soviet Union maintained armed forces "far in excess of those necessary for defensive purposes" was nonsense, and we knew it was nonsense. At a time when U.S. military leaders knew that Soviet forces lacked the numbers, capacity, and technological sophistication to attack Western Europe, as well as the productive plant necessary to sustain such an attack, President Truman and high administration officials harangued the American people about the monstrous Soviet military threat.[22]

Had American policymakers really convinced themselves that the Soviet military had to be curbed and their armed forces and weaponry reduced, one would think that they would have promoted disarmament. Not a bit of it. Speaking for the State, War, Navy, and intelligence departments, presidential counsel Clark Clifford in September 1946 advised President Truman that in view of our military superiority, the United States "should

entertain no proposal for disarmament or limitation of armament
as long as the possibility of Soviet expansion exists." For,
according to Clifford and other influential American officials,
the Soviet Union would retreat only in the face of superior
military power. To restrain the Soviet Union, "the United States
must be ready to wage atomic and biological war."[23] Well
received by the president, Clifford's counsel throws a revealing
light on the U.S. plan for international control of atomic bombs
put forward three months earlier in the UN, in June 1946 by
Bernard Baruch.

Convincing the American public that the Baruch Plan was an
unselfish American proposal for ridding the world of atomic
weapons—which at the time the United States alone possessed—
was probably the Truman administration's most brilliant propaganda coup of the cold war. As Gregg Herken, the leading
authority on the proposal, has observed, the Baruch Plan was
not designed to achieve agreement on international control and
ultimate elimination of atomic weapons. Rather, it "did not
differ in substance from an ultimatum the United States might
have given Russia to forswear nuclear weapons or be destroyed." The plan called for an international authority to
supervise the control and destruction of atomic materials; if the
authority found the Soviet Union guilty of noncompliance with
its directives, it could vote to inflict "condign punishment" on
the USSR. Chief of Naval Operations Chester Nimitz scored the
"incongruity that [under the Baruch Plan] the atomic bomb is
necessary to enforce an agreement to outlaw it." And there was
to be no veto to protect the Russians against a majority decision
to punish them. To assure Soviet compliance with the authority's directives, its members could, as an American official
observed, "open up" and "transform" Soviet society. Dean
Acheson and David Lilienthal, whom President Truman had
earlier empowered to formulate a program for international
control of atomic weapons, at the time called the drastic

changes in their plan suggested under the Baruch proposal "a manifest provocation to the Russians if not an implicit invitation to failure." No wonder influential Americans concerned about the horrors of an atomic arms race—such as Cord Meyer of the American UN delegation, Chester Barnard, president of the New Jersey Bell Telephone Company, George F. Kennan, and Walter Lippmann—urged the United States to withdraw the plan. Even a Baruch staff member conceded that the plan was "obviously unacceptable to the Soviets" and put forward "with the full realization that they would reject it." But President Truman would not back down, presenting the plan to the USSR on a take-it-or-leave-it basis and rejecting slight modifications that even Baruch thought harmless.[24] Soviet rejection of the Baruch Plan, far from constituting yet another example of Soviet intransigence, thus appears to be precisely the response likely to have been made by any state in similar circumstances. Worse, this response had been expected. For, as Herken has noted, "The Russians obviously could not accept the American plan for its one-sidedness."

Presented publicly as a high-minded proposal to rid the world of a terrible weapon, the Baruch Plan had been put forward for precisely opposite reasons. Indeed, H. E. Evatt, the pro-American Australian chairman of the UN Atomic Energy Commission at the time, rejected criticism of the Baruch Plan on the grounds that "we might want to use the weapons" against the USSR.[25] The U.S. Joint Chiefs wanted it both ways, saying, "The bomb should continue to be at the heart of America's arsenal, and a system of controls should be established that would prevent the Russians from developing the weapon." That Baruch shared this impossible dream is clear from what he told John Foster Dulles at the time: "The only thing that stands in the way of the overrunning of Europe today is the atomic bomb. . . . Once we outlaw that, there is nothing to stop the Russian advance."

In opposing the Baruch Plan the Soviet Union opposed not so much a plan to rid the world of atomic weapons but one designed to give the world that impression while ridding the USSR of the capacity to join the United States in possessing such weapons.[26] Soviet opposition to atomic weapons and an atomic arms race was manifested in the Gromyko Plan, presented to the UN on June 14, 1946. The Soviets were no doubt sincere in calling for the abolition of weapons they did not have! And then, responding in October 1946 to the Soviets' proposed compromise between the two plans, one that J. Robert Oppenheimer thought worthwhile for not requiring the destruction, only the dismantling, of existing American atomic bombs, Baruch "turned a deaf ear to indications that the Russians might be seeking a way out of the impasse."[27]

American leaders were accurate in accusing the Soviet Union of violating the Grand Alliance's wartime agreements for postwar Europe, Asia, and other parts of the world. The USSR did not fully comply with the Yalta and Potsdam accords. Yet these charges were disingenuous at best. None of the signatories, including the United States, fully honored the wartime pacts. John Foster Dulles told the U.S. Senate in 1947 that the U.S. "should not [feel] bound in any way to the commitments of Potsdam."[28] The leading scholarly authorities on the Yalta and Potsdam conferences have favorably compared Soviet compliance with the accords with our own. Diane Clemens correctly observes that the Soviets not only made most of the concessions at the Crimean conference (as Secretary of State Edward R. Stettinius, Jr., noted) but "generally complied with the Yalta decisions sponsored by and beneficial to the West." Melvyn P. Leffler, in his recent review of the two nations' records in honoring the Yalta, Potsdam, and armistice accords, concludes that "the Kremlin's pattern of compliance with wartime agreements in the immediate aftermath of World War II appears no better or worse than the American record." If "American disillusionment was great [it was] because American leaders misled the American people about the real meaning of wartime agreements." These and other students of the agreements point out that what American postwar leaders called Soviet violations of Yalta were in fact Soviet violations—or, more accurately, challenges—of unilateral American attempts to revise and reinterpret Yalta accords that, once the shooting stopped, we no longer wished to honor. By "seeking to backtrack on concessions granted [to the USSR] at Yalta," American leaders "stimulated legitimate questions from the Soviet leaders about their own compliance record." And that record was imperfect because American officials "concluded that [the Soviets] had little to gain from adherence to wartime agreements." "Allegations of Soviet noncompliance" were instead used as "a smokescreen to legitimate the lifting of restraints on American actions" designed to deprive the Soviets of the gains and assurances we had conferred on them during the war. American leaders were determined to repudiate wartime compromises with the USSR not because of Soviet noncompliance or malfeasance but because the U.S. had changed its strategy toward the Soviet Union.[29]

The two major Polish issues at Yalta concerned the borders of Poland and the composition and means of creating the postwar Polish government. The border issue was resolved without great difficulty, as the U.S. and the British agreed to cede a slice of Poland's eastern territory (to the Curzon Line) to the Soviet Union. The Poles were to be compensated by having their other border extended westward into what had formerly been German territory (to the Oder-Neisse Rivers). The government issue, in contrast, was thornier.

As they drove through Poland to expel the German armies,

the Soviets had installed a procommunist government in the city of Lublin as the provisional national government of Poland. At Yalta Stalin had called for Western recognition of this regime. Churchill countered with a proposal to establish a "fully representative" new Polish government, composed primarily of representatives of the anti-Soviet Polish government-in-exile in London and democratic leaders within Poland. Insisting that to the USSR, Poland was a "life and death" issue, and that under no circumstances could he permit an anti-Soviet government to be elected in Poland, Stalin won agreement from Roosevelt and Churchill for a compromise solution to this problem. The Lublin government was to be "reorganized on a broader democratic basis with the inclusion of democratic leaders from Poland itself and from Poles abroad." As Leffler points out, "there was no mention [in the Yalta agreement] of the government becoming 'fully representative' " or of supervised elections for the reorganized provisional government of Poland. In a letter two weeks before his death, FDR reminded Churchill that "the wording of the [final] agreement gave more emphasis on the Lublin Poles than on the other two groups from which the new government [was] to be drawn." FDR recognized that to disregard Lublin's claim to preeminence (the position that was taken almost immediately after his death by his successor, Harry Truman) would rightly "expose ourselves to the charges that we are attempting to go back on the Crimea decision." In sum, Roosevelt agreed with Stalin's subsequent reminder to Truman that the Crimean conference had agreed on the Lublin government as "the core, that is, the main part of a new reconstructed Polish government of national unity."[30]

When the Yalta agreements were reached in February 1945, the conference and its achievements were quite popular in the West. The Soviet Union had repulsed the Nazi armies, and its military contribution was needed to defeat Germany. American military and political leaders hoped to induce the Soviets to join the war against Japan, and regarded the USSR's agreement to do just that as justification for concessions to assure our "heroic ally" security against future invasions across Eastern Europe. But popular or not, the compromises agreed to at Yalta led the USSR to believe that its security interests in Poland and Eastern Europe had been recognized and accepted by the West. Furthermore, as the strongly anti-Soviet scholar Adam Ulam noted, "Stalin and his associates must have felt they had stated their postwar ambitions and aims to their Western associates during the course of the war and that their allies' reaction had been . . . of the kind to encourage them to pursue their aims." Charles DeGaulle believed that the "rapid 'Sovietization' of Eastern Europe had been agreed to at Yalta."[31] White House Chief of Staff Admiral William D. Leahy told first Roosevelt and then Truman that, for all the conference's references to free elections and self-determination in liberated Europe, the language was so vague and so open to interpretation that the USSR "could stretch it all the way from Yalta to Washington without technically breaking it." Since, according to John L. Gaddis, FDR "by his actions had led the American people to expect free elections in Eastern Europe, while at the same time leading the Russians to expect a free hand," the USSR could scarcely be found culpable for doing what it believed it had Western approval to do.[32]

Long before the Bolshevik Revolution, tsarist Russia had "considered the paramount influence of Russia in [the countries bordering Russia] as a . . . *sine qua non* of Russian security," whatever the forms of government or the domestic arrangements of these countries. Isaac Deutscher makes the interesting point that had the Soviet Union been truly interested in winning the affection of the people of Eastern Europe for the USSR and Soviet-style communism, it would not have exacted the "heavy reparations . . . from Hungary, Bulgaria, Rumania, Finland, and East Germany [that] would make the name of Communism as

well as that of Russia odious to the people of those countries."
For all the Soviet boilerplate about their fraternal love of the
working classes of Eastern Europe and the Balkans, their brutal
behavior underscores the pragmatism of their actions, not to
promote the ideology of communism but to ensure their security
against attack from Germany and their desire for retribution.[33] At
the Moscow foreign ministers' conference in December 1945,
Stalin "reminded Secretary of State [James] Byrnes that Ruman-
ian troops had marched to the Volga, Hungarian armies had
reached the Don, and Nazi naval vessels had moved unhindered
through Bulgarian waters." At Potsdam Stalin had said bluntly
that "a freely elected government in any of these countries
would be anti-Soviet, and that we cannot allow." Stalin's
position was clear, and the West did not challenge it.[34] President
Truman's report to the American people three weeks after
Potsdam that Bulgaria and Rumania "are not to be spheres of
influence of any one power" "flatly contradict[ed] everything
he knew and had recognized to be true."[35]

In succeeding years, however, American leaders publicly denounced Soviet behavior in Poland and Eastern Europe as
unacceptably threatening, a prelude to a Soviet drive on Central
and Western Europe. Former State Department official Louis
Halle has written that the Truman administration's postwar
foreign policy would only have "made sense" on the premise
that "Moscow was determined by fraud or violence, to establish
its . . . domination over the entire world."[36] But the administration had uncovered no credible evidence that Moscow sought
such domination. To the contrary, a number of influential
American leaders, some of them architects of our cold war
policy, themselves disbelieved this charge. They agreed with
Hans J. Morgenthau's conclusion that domination of Eastern

Europe was a tsarist Russian, not a Soviet, idea, and that it was grounded in pragmatic considerations of defense and security, not in alleged Marxist-Leninist dreams of world conquest.

Secretary of War Henry Stimson in April 1945 told a conference of American leaders that the Soviet Union's demands in Eastern Europe were motivated not by goals of world conquest but by concerns for Russian security, concerns with which he sympathized. These countries had never known democracy. John Foster Dulles had earlier compared the Soviet position toward Poland with American treatment of Texas and Panama— pragmatic behavior in each case. Agreeing that security, not ideology, dictated Soviet policy in Eastern Europe were Admiral Leahy, General Lucius Clay, State Department adviser Robert Murphy, Charles E. Bohlen, and an aide to Bernard Baruch. And, at the same time Senator Arthur Vandenberg was publicly warning of Soviet plans for imminent war and conquest, the Joint Chiefs concurred with the findings of a secret 1946 navy intelligence report that, far from scheming world domination, the USSR's policy was defensive in nature and sought only "to establish a Soviet Monroe Doctrine for the area under her shadow, primarily and urgently for security."[37]

Nor were American charges of Soviet malfeasance in postwar Germany any more accurate. For, as some American officials themselves conceded, Soviet behavior scarcely constituted a threat to the United States and the West. Rather, it was characterized by forbearance in view of the devastation recently inflicted on her by Germany's armed forces.

At Yalta the Soviets had requested and won President Roosevelt's approval of reparations payments from Germany to the value of ten billion dollars—a sum that did not match the cost of the destruction the Russians had suffered. FDR and Stalin had

nonetheless acquiesced in Churchill's insistence that the reparations committee which the conference established to set final
reparations terms not work from that or any other precise figure.
In any event, Roosevelt and Churchill had accepted the principle of high German reparations. After Germany's surrender in
May 1945, however, the Truman administration retreated from
FDR's commitments at Yalta. By the time of Potsdam, five
months later, the U.S. rejected the twenty-billion-dollar figure
(half of which was to go to the Soviet Union), disavowed the
earlier agreement for four-power control of the industries of the
Ruhr, and denied the Soviet request to take reparations in kind
from Western occupation zones as well as from their own zone.
Soviet Foreign Minister Molotov was further advised that German payment for loans from the West would have to take
precedence over reparations to Russia. The foreign minister
observed that the Russian people would find it hard to understand why the claims of "Wall street bankers" had a higher
priority than their need for partial repayment from their German
malefactors. Like it or not, he and Stalin accepted it. In
Clemens's phrase, the West had "made reparations [to the
USSR] at first difficult and then, later, impossible." In a clear
violation of the Yalta agreement, the United States in May 1946
"unilaterally suspended the delivery of reparations from the
American-occupied zone in Germany." We did so even though
Lucius Clay, the U.S. general who headed the American occupation zone and who gave the order, had found no fault with the
Soviet performance in postwar Germany. In response to General
Eisenhower's queries about Soviet obstructionism, Clay in July
1946 said, "It is difficult to find major instances of Soviet
failure to carry out agreements reached in the quadripartite
government of Germany."[38]

When agreeing to the four-power occupation zone for postwar
Germany, the Soviets had accepted a zone in eastern Germany
that covered about 40 percent of the country, contained 36

percent of the population, and only 33 percent of Germany's industrial capacity. Philip E. Mosely, who was a member of the American delegation to the Big Three's European Advisory Commission, later wrote that, in view of its suffering and its outsized contributions to the war effort and victory, "the Soviet Union might have claimed a larger share of Germany for itself." The Russians did resort to extralegal commandeering of German property and equipment. But, as an American diplomat observed, the French took "everything, including the kitchen stove" out of their territory, and "our own soldiers [were] 'liberating' [everything in sight]. But the criticisms were leveled only at the Soviets."[39] Stories of Soviet soldiers' postwar atrocities in Germany, published in *Life* and other magazines, were regarded with amusement in my own infantry outfit. After the Nazi surrender some of my buddies initiated their nightly routine of guarding German prisoners of war by shooting rounds of machine-gun bullets into the compound—aiming, it is true, below the knees. And we unceremoniously took the prisoners' cameras and other personal valuables. Our feeling was that the Nazis were a bad lot.   *personal*

By 1947 the United States had not only lost interest in negotiating a four-power settlement of Germany but had come to oppose it. As Secretary of State George C. Marshall put it, our new aim was to "see that [Germany] is better integrated into [a] Western Europe" that would accept a West German state and a West German army. This was a far cry indeed from former Treasury Secretary Henry Morgenthau's wartime plan for turning Germany into a pastoral state and our commitment to denazification, demilitarization, and deindustrialization. As State Department official Charles E. Bohlen observed, American leaders' postwar rethinking could not be attributed to anything the Soviets had done or not done in Germany. Even Truman's secretary of state, James F. Byrnes, was convinced that the Soviets desired only what they had asked for at

Yalta—ten billion dollars in reparations and four-power control to insure the continuing demilitarization of the country. Brushing aside Soviet objections, Truman won British and French support at the London Conference in early 1948 for the establishment of a West German state. Stalin objected to this development, but he did not publicly challenge it. He told U.S. Ambassador Walter Bedell Smith that he "did not want to embarrass the Western governments by forcing them to backtrack publicly on the London agreements."[40]

Shortly after Truman turned down Stalin's desperate proposal of May 1948 for the powers to work out a negotiated settlement of outstanding issues involving postwar Germany, the USSR instituted what turned out to be its futile blockade of West Berlin, cutting off land access to the city from the Western occupation zones in Germany. Interestingly, Secretary of the Army Kenneth Royall found some logic in the Soviet position that the forthcoming abandonment of four-power control of Germany, instituted by the West, removed the basis for the quadripartite control of Berlin. Although the great city was located in the Soviet zone, each of the four powers had been given a district in it from which to administer their occupation zones in Germany. But the affair was not to be settled by logic. Blessed with atomic bombs and far greater power than the Soviets possessed, the United States chose to direct an airlift rather than follow General Clay's recommendation for in effect initiating World War III by using force to restore Western land access to Berlin. The airlift broke the blockade.[41]

Despite these events, Soviet postwar behavior in Germany was, as American officials conceded, no threat to the United States. In recreating a strengthened, pro-Western German state, and later incorporating West Germany within the NATO alliance, we charged that sinister Soviet actions and intentions compelled us to do it. American diplomats on the spot, like critical scholars at home, could discern nothing more malevolent in Soviet actions than a desire for reparations and a militarily impotent Germany that the West had earlier approved.

In view of Stalin's nonintervention in the civil war that raged in postwar Greece, American accusations of the Soviet threat in that country had to be phrased carefully. Secretary of State Marshall, Secretary of War Robert Patterson, Under Secretary of State Dean Acheson, and other high-ranking officials, culminating with the president in his Truman Doctrine speech of March 12, 1947, accordingly warned that a "communist" victory in Greece would result in countries in Europe, the Middle East, and even in Africa and Asia falling like dominoes. The Soviet Union, while avoiding direct involvement in the internal struggle, would supposedly exploit "communist" success in Greece to use its new territorial base as a launching pad for the further expansion of imperialistic communism. These dire warnings were designed to "scare the hell" out of the American people, thereby enlisting their support for the financial sacrifices required if the United States was to succeed in maintaining what our own diplomat conceded was a brutal and corrupt Greek regime.

In fact, as a Chase Manhattan Bank representative in the area pointed out in 1947, the people of Greece, "having lost faith in the government on account of its excesses and lack of action in improving the [bleak and deteriorating] economic situation, [were] beginning to look to the guerillas as their sole hope of deliverance. Corruption, . . . suppression of most civil liberties, economic and financial chaos and black markets [were] the order of the day in Greece."[42] The leading student of the events leading up to the civil war reports that "the Greek crisis was basically a domestic affair of long standing, compounded by Balkan tensions and rivalries. The Soviet Union not only did not

cause or aggravate the Greek situation but apparently disapproved of the . . . rebellion and instructed the Greek Communist
Party to refrain from resorting to violent tactics." Seeking U.S.
support, the Greek government instead promoted "the view that
Greece was fighting the very forces that threatened all Western
and democratic nations everywhere."[43]

Winston Churchill has reported that in 1946 Stalin had said
not a word of criticism to him when British-supported government forces killed large numbers of Greek communists. The
Soviet ruler was apparently determined to honor his 1944 understanding with Churchill that in return for British acceptance of
Soviet predominance in Eastern Europe, the USSR would not
challenge British and, subsequently, American predominance in
Greece and Western Europe. Two years later Stalin condemned
Yugoslavia for aiding the Greek guerrillas. To ardent cold
warriors who insisted that the Soviet Union could do no right,
Stalin's forbearance was of course construed as simply a tactic.
Although the Soviet Union was neither altruistic nor transformed by a sudden reverence for the principle of nonintervention; it was motivated, as always, by self-interest. In this case
that meant brushing aside communist internationalists' calls for
"fraternal revolutionary solidarity," in order to continue to
enjoy Western support for what the Soviets most valued—assurance that the governments of Eastern Europe would be in
friendly hands.[44]

President Truman and George Kennan, then a State Department
adviser, charged the Soviet Union with "indirect aggression" in
France and Italy that, if it resulted in Communist electoral
victories, would have to be countered by American armed
intervention to roll back the Reds.[45] Since Truman's words were
uttered privately, it is not clear whether he would have actually

started World War III over the matter. This proved unnecessary in any event. Relying on the newly created Central Intelligence Agency, the Truman administration successfully funneled monies to ensure a Christian Democratic party victory in the 1948 Italian elections and to forge a counterpart anticommunist trade union movement in France. Fearful of Soviet influence, the administration did not hesitate to intervene in the internal affairs of Italy and France—and did so covertly through the CIA.

The feared communist "takeover" in France and Italy would have resulted from a victory by the Communist party and its political allies in democratic elections. The USSR during the war had agreed to the dissolution of the Comintern in order, as Stalin told a Reuters correspondent, to expose the "Nazi lie" and "calumny that Communist parties in various countries were acting not in the interest of their people but on orders from outside."[46] The fact remains that the American charge of indirect Soviet aggression in the two countries was based not on evidence that the Soviets had gone back on their pledge but on the presumption shared by cold warriors that communists and their political allies everywhere were Soviet puppets, if not agents. Interestingly, their puppetry became unacceptable only when it threatened to succeed, and to do so by legal means. American leaders seemed convinced that the millions of French and Italian Catholics who belonged to or supported the Communist party did not properly understand the perils of their membership or their attraction to radical politics. For the communists' popularity in France and Italy had been based on a unique set of historical circumstances: a widespread knowledge of the heroic role played by communists in the antifascist movement, communist leadership in the trade unions, the identification of admired artists and intellectuals with the party, memories of communists' role in fighting the Franco regime in Spain, and the not yet dormant popular enthusiasm for the Soviet army's role in turning back and destroying the Nazis.

Paradoxically, the charge of intervention in the internal politics of postwar Western Europe can appropriately be laid at the door of the United States. For it was Washington that regularly demanded the elimination of Communist ministers from the governing coalitions of France and Italy and made clear to them that our responses to their requests for aid would be strongly influenced by their performance in exorcising communists from government. Massive American funding of the Italian Christian Democratic party in 1948 was the first full-fledged covert operation undertaken by the newly created Central Intelligence Agency, as its agents pressed money into the hands of voters and used movie stars and mobsters to save Italy from the Red Menace.[47]

Additional questions arise about this particular American charge of aggression. If Truman and Kennan thought the Soviet Union guilty of committing aggression in Italy and France, whether directly or indirectly, why were their accusations so muffled, why made so secretly? If the intervention itself was culpable, why hold it criminal only if it succeeded? Just as President Eisenhower in 1956 opposed a national election in Vietnam because the wrong man would win, and Henry Kissinger in 1973 said we could not let Chile go "communist" because of the irresponsibility of its own people, so too President Truman in 1948 refused to accept the election of the "wrong" party in France or Italy. Washington evidently found comfort in attributing its unwillingness to accept uncongenial outcomes of democratic elections not to its own illiberalism but rather to an alleged Soviet perfidy. This left freedom-loving democrats no alternative but to ignore the popular will—the dangerously and unacceptably misguided popular will.

*

In the Middle East the USSR's postwar actions were also publicly interpreted by the Truman administration as part of the Soviet drive toward world conquest. In fact, as the United States government had reason to know, Soviet aims in the region were similar to Russian aims under the tsars. Soviet actions testified not to an ideologically driven pursuit of world power but a nationalistically driven search for security and for advantages in nearby countries—a search that, during the war just ended, had been sympathetically treated by the Western allies as understandable and unthreatening.

Soviet and British troops had occupied pro-German Iran from 1941 through the end of the war. A central element in the Iranian crisis that roiled the UN in 1946 was the USSR's tardiness in honoring its promise to withdraw its troops by March 2, 1946. Other sources of contention were the emergence of a pro-Soviet separatist movement in Iran's northern provinces and Soviet troop movements that were rumored to be the forerunner of a Russian invasion. Although the State Department prepared a map of the region purporting to show the Soviets' planned invasion route and their intended military objectives, it offered no proof to substantiate this allegation. The United States pounced on Soviet delay in removing all its forces from Iran as a frightening sign of wicked intentions. American leaders conveniently overlooked a number of U.S. failures to withdraw American forces from foreign countries in what the Joint Chiefs in 1946 described as "strict accordance with the time limitation provision of the existing agreement with the foreign government concerned." But our violations were justified by what the Joint Chiefs called "military considerations which [made] inadvisable the withdrawal of U.S. forces."[48]

On that fateful deadline date for troop withdrawal in Iran, the Soviets were in fact negotiating with the Iranian government the details of their complete withdrawal that was shortly to follow. But President Truman ignored Soviet requests that the issue be resolved by private diplomacy. Washington ignored as well the suggestion made by UN Secretary General Trygve Lie that "a debate in the Security Council...would probably intensify rather than ease the dispute." He was proved right, of course, the Truman administration having decided to provoke a crisis rather than promote a resolution of the issue. Nonetheless the crisis was resolved, and quickly, as a result of a secret settlement concluded by the Soviets and the Iranian premier. Before the year was out, American firms had won important oil concessions, highlighting one partial basis for the administration's aversion to Soviet influence in the area. Britain had long enjoyed oil concessions in what had been Persia, and it maintained them after the war. Clemens notes that "the Iranian controversy vividly illustrated the double standard which Washington applied to international affairs. Soviet demands for a concession [in oil] were 'interference,' Western demands were not. The Russians were baffled. They left their negotiating team in Iran and tried in vain to follow the rules established by the West. They did not yet realize that the Allies' rules were for the [Western] allies' exclusive benefit."[49]

In his Truman Doctrine speech the president called on Congress to come to the rescue of Turkey as well as Greece with money, arms, equipment, and "civilian and military personnel" to safeguard the peace of the world and the welfare of the United States. Truman had earlier written Secretary of State James Byrnes that there was no doubt in his mind that "Russia intends an invasion of Turkey and the seizure of the Black Sea straits to the Mediterranean."[50] Whatever may have been on the president's mind on January 5, 1946, when he wrote to Byrnes, he understood that Russian postwar policy toward Turkey signified no such initiative. Shortly before his Truman Doctrine speech the president chose to interpret the Soviet request to Turkey for joint Turkish-Soviet defense of the Dardanelles as an unacceptable demand which the United States must oppose; he sent part of the U.S. fleet to the region to signify our readiness to go to war to block Soviet expansion. As the leading scholar on the matter observes, "Even hard-line U.S. officials . . . acknowledged that the Soviets had not made formal demands, had acted with restraint, and invited further discussion."[51]

Russian interest in securing a base in the straits and access to warm water had long antedated the Bolshevik Revolution. The USSR claimed that the territory had belonged to Russia between 1878 and 1917. Its desire for the base had won a sympathetic hearing from Churchill at the Teheran Conference in 1943. During his October 1944 meeting with Stalin in Moscow, Churchill again expressed his approval of Soviet "access to warm-water ports." At Yalta FDR concurred that the 1936 Montreux Convention, giving Turkey sole control over use of the Dardanelles, should be revised. The Big Three formally approved the revision at Potsdam. Once again, a Soviet stand that during the war had been favored by the West, after the war was not only opposed but denounced by American leaders as aggression.[52]

Even before Japan surrendered, President Truman condemned Soviet behavior in eastern Asia, charging that it violated the Yalta and Potsdam agreements. Soviet commanders did in some instances give captured Japanese arms to Chinese communists, and the USSR delayed the departure of Soviet troops from Manchuria beyond the agreed-to February 1946 deadline. Yet the United States violated the deadline for American troop withdrawals in half a dozen countries and did so over the objections of some of their governments. And the Truman administration did not simply violate wartime accords concerning Soviet rights and responsibilities in postwar Asia; it pretended that the accords did not exist.[53]

As Leffler has pointed out, at Yalta FDR and Stalin had negotiated a secret Far Eastern protocol. In return for Soviet promises to enter the war against Japan shortly after Germany's capitulation, recognize Chiang Kai-shek's Nationalist government, offer no support to the Chinese Communists in the civil war, and accept Chinese sovereignty over Manchuria, President Roosevelt recognized the status quo in Outer Mongolia and Soviet annexation of the Kuriles and southern Sakhalin; ceded to the Soviets a naval base at Port Arthur; and recognized the "preeminent interests" of the USSR in the port of Dairen and in the Manchurian railroads. After Roosevelt's death "Truman and his closest advisers acted as if the United States had never entered into any secret agreement on the Far East."

Having decided on a policy of everywhere confronting the Soviet Union and blocking the extension of its influence and the strengthening of its security, the Truman administration was understandably unhappy with President Roosevelt's earlier recognition of Soviet objectives in the Far East. This recognition had of course been accorded out of an interest in Chiang Kai-shek's success in quelling the Red Chinese, in inducing Soviet acquiescence in American, not joint U.S. and USSR, control of postwar Japan, and above all in having the Soviets join the war against Japan. On being apprised at Potsdam of the successful explosion of the atomic bomb in the New Mexico desert, Truman now regretted the earlier concessions that had been made to the USSR at a time when military and diplomatic officials had thought Soviet participation in the war against Japan to be indispensable. Now we no longer needed them. Thus, "at the first cabinet meeting after he returned from Potsdam and after the [atomic] bombing of Hiroshima and Nagasaki, Truman [actually] denied the existence of any agreement relating to Manchuria." In a variety of ways, American officials sought to water down or get around the Yalta language that required "the heads of the three great powers [to ensure] . . .

that the claims of the Soviet Union shall be unquestionably fulfilled after Japan has been defeated."[54]

The fact is, then, that the Soviets honored the wartime agreements on Asia and did so because it was obviously in their interest. As American officials in China were aware, the USSR so fully lived up to its pledge to recognize and collaborate with the Nationalist government and not to assist its communist enemies that Chiang requested that Stalin delay Soviet troop withdrawals from China.[55]

Soviet demands concerning the organization of the United Nations, and Soviet actions in the UN after it began to function, were no less displeasing to the Truman administration than were their other postwar actions. If, however, the United States delegation at Yalta truly "considered the UN to be the crucial issue of the conference," Soviet behavior should have been at least slightly consoling to Americans who wished the new organization to play a constructive role in the postwar world. True, the Soviets at first demanded inordinate representation in the body. But they did back off. Even Churchill supported their later proposal that the Soviet republics of Ukraine and Belorussia as well as the USSR be accorded membership. He had "great sympathy for the request. . . . A nation so great as Russia with 180 million people would perhaps have cause to look at the British Commonwealth [with six members in the UN] with a questioning eye, if they had but one vote when their population far exceeds our own." Whatever the actual Soviet motives in opposing membership in the UN for Argentina, the character of that state and its policies during World War II were disconcerting not to communists alone. Soviet attempts to restrict the powers of a General Assembly composed largely of Latin American states disposed to vote with the U.S. on controversial issues was nationalist rather than internationalist behavior, but nevertheless understandable, and certainly not threatening.

American leaders scored propaganda points at home by denouncing the "excessive" vetoes of the USSR and impugning the motives underlying their incessant *nyets*, yet the U.S. would not have joined the UN without the right to a veto in the Security Council. At worst the Soviet performance at the UN reflected stubbornness combined with flexibility, nationalism, and security-mindedness rather than a missionary impulse to communize the world.[56]

A central element in the American indictment held that every Soviet action, however seemingly innocent it might appear on the surface, was actually sinister. Fanatically devoted, as we said they were, to the doctrines of Marxism-Leninism, Soviet leaders and their agents abroad worked ceaselessly to undermine and overthrow noncommunist governments. They relied on guile as well as force and coercion to bring about a world devoid of freedom, democracy, religion, and individual enterprise. This was the perception of Soviet communist theory taught to young patriots who joined the CIA, and it was widely disseminated among the American public.[57] It was a distorted perception, but to ardent cold warriors it was of course a useful perception. For it could not be refuted, certainly not definitively. Who could prove that world conquest was *not* on the minds of Soviet leaders? Skeptics might not accept undocumented assertions as to what the men in the Kremlin were thinking, but in the developing cold war atmosphere spreading over the United States, skeptics were in short supply.[58] How many would court the "odium" and suspicion that George Washington had presciently predicted would be the lot of those who challenged popular government policy? Since, as Justice Felix Frankfurter once said, historical truth has its claims to our attention, evaluating this American argument about Soviet intentions is essential.

Two questions arise. Is Marxism-Leninism what American leaders said it was? That is, did the doctrine demand that Soviet leaders work incessantly to impose a communist order dominated by the Soviet Union over the United States and the rest of the world? And was every important action by the rulers of the USSR taken in accord with the dictates of Marxism-Leninism? That is, were Stalin and his lieutenants essentially inflexible doctrinaires concerned primarily if not solely with fulfilling the demands of communist doctrine? The most disconcerting feature of the answers to these questions is the absence of evidence that America's postwar leaders were even interested in answering them.

These charges against the Soviet Union were not the product of a close reading of the writings of Marx and Lenin. Nor were they a result of an informed assessment of Stalin's sincerity in mouthing communist principles. The impression is unavoidable that these charges were made not because the leaders of the United States found them true but because, if believed, they would justify America's refusal to negotiate with the Soviet Union and Washington's policy of unremitting hostility toward the USSR. A serious reading of Marx, Engels, Lenin, and the other contributors to what the USSR called the principles of Marxism-Leninism points up the complexity of that canon. And Stalin's lip service to Marxist-Leninist principles notwithstanding, this man and those he dominated acted out of diverse motives, most of them having little to do with revolutionary principles. The lust for power, the paranoia, the nationalism no different from that which animated the Romanov tsars, loveless though these qualities might be, were far removed from revolutionary zealotry or fanaticism.

In formulating policy, the leaders of the postwar United States did not have the luxury that scholars have, of sifting through masses of evidence, taking however much time they think they need, to arrive at balanced judgments. But that political leaders must at times act swiftly does not mean they must act irresponsibly. It was irresponsible to formulate a fateful, enormously costly, and enormously dangerous policy on the basis of the unthinking anticommunism that informed U.S. policymakers' estimates of Soviet intentions, captured in the language of the now-famous National Security Council memorandum No. 68: "The [Soviet] design calls for the complete subversion or forcible destruction of the machinery of government and structure of society in the countries of the non-Soviet world and their replacement by an apparatus and structure subservient to and controlled from the Kremlin."

Whatever its grip on the minds and motives of postwar Soviet leaders, Marxism-Leninism is not quite the repulsive philosophy described to the American people by American leaders. It could command the devotion as well as admiration of tens of millions of people in Western Europe and in other noncommunist countries because of its humane and egalitarian social and cultural vision. In calling Soviet communism more dangerous than Nazism, America's cold war leaders were in effect saying that communism's condemnation of racism, war, inequality, and classic imperialism gave it a seductive appeal that Hitlerism could not match. Neither the doctrines of Marxism-Leninism nor the plans of the Soviet regime called for military conquest of Europe, in sharp contrast to the blueprint Hitler had published in *Mein Kampf*. Stalin's brutal suppression of political dissenters, for all its repulsiveness, fell a good deal short of Nazi extermination of entire ethnic and religious groups, not for what they had allegedly done but for what Nazi theorists called their biological or innate inferiority. Stalin's discriminations against Jews and Judaism did undercut Soviet protestations of respect for all ethnic and religious groups. But to suggest, as some cold warriors did, that there was little to choose between anti-Semitism in the USSR, where many Jews were employed in prestigious jobs, and anti-Semitism in Nazi Germany, where they were tortured and destroyed, glosses over this difference.[59]

While Marxism predicted that "socialist revolutions" would one day occur everywhere, and indeed called on the faithful to work toward that end, it scorned the notion that armed coups or the military invasion of noncommunist countries by socialist states were the means of bringing about the Great Day. Socialism would occur when the "internal contradictions" of capitalism in advanced "bourgeois" societies created both the conditions and the requisite class consciousness in the "laboring masses" that were ostensibly necessary for it to take hold. Lenin's supplement to Marxist theory sought to win acceptance of the successful Bolshevik takeover of power in technologically backward Russia as a classic socialist revolution, through a clever modification of the Marxist canon: Russia had been part of a world system of exploitative capitalism. By this reasoning the Bolsheviks and their allies among the Russian working classes and armed forces had struck against a weak link in the worldwide chain of capitalism. Discovering that not even Central Europe, let alone the world, was sufficiently inspired by the Bolshevik uprising to emulate it, Lenin and his successor Stalin put aside visions of world revolution, suppressed those who insisted on it, and focused their energies instead on building "socialism in one country"—their phrase for consolidating the power of the Communist party of the USSR, ruthlessly industrializing Russia, and destroying internal opposition to their plans and their control. All this was accomplished in the proclaimed interests of the "toiling masses," for was not the Communist party the "vanguard of the working class"? This arrogance did not, however, make those who proclaimed it a mortal threat to the United States.[60]

Scripture is so ample that the devil can cite it. One can wrench from Marxist-Leninist theology phrases suggestive of Soviet designs on the security of the noncommunist world. Yet

Western scholars of communist theory know that the official cold war version of it was a distortion. The aim of American leaders was to present a distorted assessment of Marxist-Leninist theory that would help frighten the American public into supporting cold war policy and accepting the enormous costs and dangers of that policy.

On November 23, 1941, Stalin wrote Churchill to say he agreed with him that the "difference in political systems in the USSR, on the one hand, and that of Great Britain and the U.S.A., on the other, should not and cannot be an obstacle to a favorable solution of the fundamental issues of ensuring our mutual security and rightful interests." Twelve years later, well after the cold war had begun, President Eisenhower observed that "any nation's right to form a government and an economic system of its own choosing is inalienable. . . . Any nation's attempt to dictate to other nations their form of government is indefensible."[61] Yet it was American cold war leaders who flouted the principle. Secret National Security Council documents and periodic public statements by U.S. officials charged that the very Soviet system constituted an unacceptable threat to our country. In the phrase of presidential candidate John F. Kennedy, in 1960, our "enemy is the Communist system itself—implacable, unceasing in its drive for world domination."

Somehow the United States had managed to live with that system since its birth in 1917. It was indeed death on domestic dissidents—as were other states and systems whose unattractiveness had been no bar to good relations between them and the United States. When the Soviet system was probably at its worst and most despotic, during the purges of the late 1930s, President Roosevelt understood that the great threat to world peace centered not in Moscow but in Berlin. And from 1941 until late 1945 the Soviet system and the men who ruled it cooperated in fighting the war and planning the peace. Was there a startling change in the Soviet system in late 1945 and 1946 that suddenly transformed it into a monstrous threat? Washington offered no evidence of it. But if the very domestic order of the Soviet Union was an important cause of the cold war, we would have to keep fighting it until that order disappeared. Given the effectiveness of what George Kennan later described as our demonization of the Soviet Union, why wouldn't the American people believe this charge against the state they had been repeatedly told was the source of all evil in the world?[62]

The most fascinating feature of American justifications for waging the cold war against the Soviet Union is not simply that they are tendentious but that our leaders knew or had reason to know that they were. The Soviet behavior that so riled Washington occurred in the immediate aftermath of World War II, the twenty or so months during which the containment policy was essentially hammered out, bombs and bases put in place, and worldwide covert operations instituted to execute that confrontational policy. Later Soviet actions in Hungary, Czechoslovakia, Cuba, Vietnam, and Afghanistan were undertaken after the cold war was under way. This is not to exculpate these later actions but only to recognize that however blameworthy they might be, they were not the cause of the cold war. No incredible leap of historical imagination is required to wonder whether, absent the cold war, some of the most tragic events of the forty years after World War II, in Korea, Vietnam, Nicaragua, Afghanistan, Indonesia, and Cambodia, might not have occurred.

If official justifications for the cold war were weak, the propaganda effort of America's cold war leaders nonetheless succeeded, despite its exaggerated, distorted character. To charge that Soviet intentions were invariably malignant, no matter how blameless their actions, was brilliant, since it was a charge that could not be definitively refuted. And increasingly to portray the cold war as an irreconcilable conflict between two ways of life, and to win public acceptance not only of that portrayal but of the implicit judgment that these profound differences caused the cold war—this was a public relations masterstroke. For who could deny that one way of life was free, open, democratic, and congenial to the blossoming of the human spirit, while the other was the antithesis of these ideals?

By almost every significant measure, the postwar United States was a far more attractive society than the Soviet Union. Once the cold war was depicted as a conflict between two diametrically opposed orders, there was little question which state deserved to win. Not only Americans but fair-minded and sensible people everywhere would agree. And who could doubt that blame for the conflict would be assigned to the less attractive of the contestants?

In Hans J. Morgenthau's passionate indictment, the U.S. government's policy was "the disheartening tale of a noble people ignobly led. The [Truman] Administration [was] both the author and protagonist of that tale, and to the Administration must be read this indictment and this prophecy: *You have deceived once; you must deceive again. . . . You have falsified the real issue between the United States and the Soviet Union into a holy crusade to stamp out Bolshevism everywhere on earth, for this seemed a good way of arousing the public. . . .* "[63]

American leaders did sincerely believe the explanations they gave for pursuing the cold war; nonetheless they stand condemned for adopting a dangerous and costly policy unnecessarily, on the basis of a flawed reading of Soviet actions and intentions.

It may be argued that in some instances leaders alone know all the facts and are wiser than the people they lead, that they must tell the people what Plato called wholesome lies for the people's own good. Not only is such a standard undemocratic, there is no evidence attesting the superior wisdom of the men who gave us Vietnam, the runaway arms race, and wholesale violations of privacy rights; who saw legal restrictions as problems to be surmounted and who, in the words of a secret government analysis of 1954, could offer this prescription for public policy: "It is now clear that we are facing an implacable enemy whose avowed objective is world domination by whatever means and at whatever cost. . . . If the United States is to survive, long-standing American concepts of 'fair play' must be reconsidered. . . . It may become necessary that the American people be made acquainted with, understand and support this fundamentally repugnant philosophy."

American leaders doubtless feared that disclosing their true reasons for pursuing the cold war would have damaged public support for a "fundamentally repugnant" policy or led to its rejection by the people. As later events were to show, once the assumptions of the cold war were critically accepted, public opposition to one or another aspect of the government's policy, or to its means of implementing that policy, could be discredited or circumvented by resort to secretly authorized and implemented programs. In the early 1980s, for example, the Reagan administration brushed aside respected polls and many local elections that demonstrated overwhelming popular support of a freeze on the manufacture of nuclear weapons.[64] But in launching a cold war policy that broke so sharply with American diplomatic precedent, and whose success depended on the support of Congress and the voting public, the architects of the new policy withheld reasons that were unlikely to win that indispensable public support.

What those reasons were is a matter of great interest and importance. They will be discussed after we examine the important means by which American leaders implemented cold war policy.

CHAPTER IV

✤

Treating the
Soviet Union
as the Enemy

Sʜᴏʀᴛʟʏ after the end of World War II American leaders began to speak of the Soviet Union as the enemy of the United States. The Truman administration and its successors supplemented words with actions of the sort that a nation takes only against an enemy. This American behavior is worth remarking because it broke with the enduring diplomatic tradition under which the United States knew enemies only when it went to war, and with a legal tradition which confined enemy status to nations and their nationals engaged in formal military conflict with the United States. The questions therefore arise: Can a foreign state with which we are not at war be the enemy of the United States? When a state has taken no action threatening invasion of the United States or an attack on American citizens and territories, can it be made the enemy of the United States on the basis of American leaders' distaste for that state and their appraisal of that state's suspected intentions?

These questions are worth pondering because during the cold war American leaders made an enemy of the Soviet Union, a nation with which we were not at war and which had not threatened to attack or invade our country. Our leaders did so on the basis of their extreme distaste for that state, its leaders, the ideas said to shape the behavior of these leaders, and supposed plans of the rulers of that state.

Words spoken by government leaders are themselves actions, highly significant actions. When Theodore Roosevelt called the presidency a bully pulpit, he meant that a president's words are likely to have a great impact on the thinking and mood of the country, directing the people to understand issues the way the president wants them to be understood. When presidents and other high officials describe a foreign state as the enemy, the public tends to react accordingly, for the intent of the words is to promote popular antipathy toward that nation.

The hostile words spoken by presidents and high-level federal officials affect the moods and policies of other governments as well, particularly those whom we have singled out as the enemy. Their leaders are almost certain to respond in kind. When our hostile phrases are joined by hostile measures, by war preparations and public threats to unloose our vast destructive power, the "enemy" will take measures of its own. They may indeed be menacing to us and create a situation that threatens war. Thus alleged enemies are transformed into enemies as we traditionally understand them.

One can assemble a lengthy catalogue of assertions by U.S. leaders labeling the postwar Soviet Union as our enemy. On February 22, 1946, George F. Kennan, the American chargé d'affaires at Moscow, sent an eight-thousand-word cable to the State Department for circulation among the nation's policy-makers. Regarded by many historians as the opening shot in the cold war, Kennan's "long telegram" described the USSR as a paranoiac state dominated by fanatical leaders who were deter-mined to wage a "deadly struggle" for the total destruction of their adversaries. They were our enemies because, according to Kennan, they thought it "necessary that the internal harmony of our society be disrupted, our traditional way of life be destroyed

...if Soviet power [was] to be secure." Kennan urged the United States to "adopt a wartime frame of mind" in dealing with this deadly foe. (Kennan was later to undergo a change of mind, but too late to deflect the Truman administration from pursuing the path of cold war he had implored it to follow.)[1]

George Kennan was hardly the first American diplomat to call Soviet Russia the enemy. In opposing diplomatic recognition of the USSR in 1919, Secretary of State Bainbridge Colby referred to the Soviet Union as an "enemy state." Nonetheless, before the onset of the cold war such hostile language was not companion to hostile action. In May 1945, as the war in Europe was ending, Acting Secretary of State Joseph Grew described the Soviet Union as our "certain future enemy." After the war General Leslie R. Groves, who headed the Manhattan Project, said that as early as the fall of 1942 he was convinced that Soviet Russia, not Nazi Germany, was our chief foe. "There was never from about two weeks from the time I took charge of this project [to oversee the creation of an atomic bomb] any illusion on my part but that Russia was our enemy," he continued, adding the fascinating comment, "and the project was conducted on that basis."[2]

When Leo Szilard, Albert Einstein, and other scientists in the U.S. and Britain finally succeeded in convincing the Roosevelt administration to launch the Manhattan Project, our original purpose had been to beat the Nazis to what informed scientists knew would be a dread weapon.[3] With the bomb in hand, after the end of World War II U.S. officials launched a massive effort to strengthen our atomic arsenal and did so even before the Soviet Union had committed any of the post–World War II acts that transformed it from friend to foe in the eyes of the U.S. government. After the war, denunciations of the Soviet "enemy" became much more common and more strident within both the executive and legislative branches.

Not five months after the shooting stopped in Europe, the

Joint Chiefs accepted as a basis for future planning an intelligence report calling for the atomic bombing of twenty major cities of the Soviet Union if that country developed "either a means of defense against our attack or the capacity for an eventual attack on the United States." This Joint Chiefs justification for launching a war of aggression against the Soviet Union was not simply a military contingency plan. At the time the Soviets had no atomic weapons of their own and would not have them for forty-four months. Bomb them if they create a defense against atomic attack, or if they learn how to make their own atomic bombs! The actual meaning of the Joint Chiefs report was that the United States should initiate war on the Soviet Union if it achieved a capacity *suggesting that at some future time it might be able to attack our country.* Surely only an enemy could be dealt with that way.

President Truman's later decision of June 1950 to send American forces into combat in the Korean War intensified American hostility toward the Soviet "enemy." Secretary of State Dean Acheson at this time told the Joint Chiefs that "the great trouble is that we are fighting the second team, whereas the real enemy is the Soviet Union." Confirming the consensus in Washington, Senator Lyndon B. Johnson asked publicly, why fight only the slave, North Korea, and let the master, the Soviet Union, be spared? "It is foolish," he continued, "to talk of avoiding war. We are already in a war—a major war. The war in Korea is a war of Soviet Russia." Johnson's syntax was confusing but his thought was clear. The notion that the Soviet Union was the real enemy of the United States in Korea was expressed so often that it became commonplace. When in 1951 Judge Irving R. Kaufman sentenced Julius and Ethel Rosenberg to death—as he had promised he would even before the trial began—after a jury found them guilty of conspiring during the closing months of World War II to pass atomic secrets to our then Soviet ally, Kaufman condemned them for having spied for the Soviet enemy and further for having invited communist aggression in Korea.[4] This is not the occasion for a detailed examination of the Korean War or of the Soviet role in it. Good evidence is still to be found in classified U.S. files and in the Soviet archives. But the most admired American scholarly authority on the Korean War thinks that what happened in Korea in 1950 was the continuation of a civil war, in which "our side," the government of Syngman Rhee, had several times before June 25 sent troops north of the 38th parallel, as on that fateful date North Korean troops poured into the south. Both sides had of course been armed and trained by their mentors, North Korea by the USSR, South Korea by the United States.[5] The U.S. had no evidence that Soviet troops participated in the border crossing of June 25 or in the fighting that followed. American officials' assertions that the USSR was the real enemy in the Korean War nonetheless confirmed the assumptions under-pinning U.S. policy: that any insurrection or radical political movement was aided, abetted, and directed by the Kremlin.

In April 1950 the National Security Council, created in 1947 to advise the president on foreign policy matters, presented President Truman with NSC-68, a document which became the secret blueprint for American policy toward the Soviet Union. After the Korean War broke out, NSC records show that the president on September 3, 1950, "approved the conclusions of NSC-68 . . . as a statement of policy to be followed during the next four or five years, and their implementation by all appro-priate Departments and Agencies of the United States govern-ment."[6] Kept secret for a quarter of a century, this "American blueprint for waging the cold war" not only spoke of the Soviet enemy but urged on the nation policies and actions that were swiftly set in motion, *treating* the Soviet Union as the enemy. To Paul Nitze and the other authors of the document, "The Cold War [was] in fact a real war in which the survival of the free world [was] at stake." Since in a real war the nation's adversary is indeed the enemy, calling the cold war a real war reveals that Nitze and his colleagues in the State and Defense departments had come to identify the Soviet Union as the enemy of the United States. The lurid motives they attributed to the USSR and its leaders may not have established that they were in fact the enemy, but President Truman did not need to be convinced of this, being himself quite ready to denounce the Soviet Union's deeds, thoughts, intentions, ways, and its very existence.

NSC-68 described the USSR as a "slave society. . . animated by a new fanatic faith, antithetical to our own," seeking to "impose its absolute authority" over the world. The "fundamental design of the Kremlin" was to achieve the "total submission" of all those under their control. Ready to accomplish their ends "swiftly and with stealth," the repulsive world of their design was one in which "the personality of the individual is so broken and perverted that he participates affirmatively in his own degradation." Whatever else might be said about this prose, it did not prove that the USSR was the enemy, however loathsome its nature, atrocious its actions, malevolent its motives. Thomas G. Paterson, a respected scholar of the cold war, may well be right that "NSC-68, most scholars agree, was a flawed, even amateurish document," which, among other things, "assumed a Communist monolith that did not exist, drew alarming conclusions based upon vague and inaccurate information about Soviet intentions," and "glossed over the presence of many non-democratic countries in the 'free world.' . . ."[7] NSC-68 might not have demonstrated that the cold war was a real war. Nonetheless, its draconian secret recommendations were approved by the president.

In moving ahead with the manufacture of awesomely destructive hydrogen bombs, a massive buildup of conventional weapons and forces, a large tax increase to meet the costs of this buildup, mobilization of American society behind the government's calls for "sacrifice" and "unity," a system of worldwide anti-Soviet military alliances, and unspecified covert operations within the USSR and the Soviet empire, and in rejecting further negotiations with the Soviet Union, the United States treated the USSR as though it were a wartime enemy—as NSC-68 urged. Washington's actions and the inevitable Soviet reactions to them were certain to increase world tension and help convince the American people that we were engaged in a real war against the Soviet enemy.

President Truman may have called the American intervention in Korea a police action, but it was of course war. Hot war against a communist army that was actually shooting and killing American soldiers further inflamed American public opinion against the Soviet "enemy" that had apparently instigated the aggression. In his journal entry for January 27, 1952, President Truman wrote that the time had come to present Moscow with an ultimatum warning that in case of "further interference" by the Soviet Union with our military actions against her Chinese satellite (the Chinese Communists having directly intervened in the Korean conflict in November 1950), the United States would go to "all out war" against both the Soviet Union and China, destroying Moscow, St. Petersburg [then Leningrad], and Stalingrad, as well as "Peking, Shanghai, and every manufacturing plant in China and the Soviet Union."[8] Fortunately this threatened attack did not take place, the "all out war" did not begin, the earth was spared the nuclear exchange that would have triggered World War III. But the president's soliloquy left no doubt of his readiness to suit the action to the word and his conception of all political and revolutionary crises as having been orchestrated and directed by the Soviet enemy.

NSC-68 was a new departure in United States policy toward the Soviet Union only in formally setting in motion a comprehensive series of hostile actions—actions approved by President Truman only after the Korean War broke out. The document's assumptions on the need to develop a strategy and the requisite means to wage cold, and if necessary, hot war against the USSR were already accepted by American leaders before we went to war in Korea. On the level of theory and belief, NSC-68 was simply a culmination of anti-Soviet ideas and policies which had guided the American government since shortly after the end of World War II. The creation in 1947 of the NSC and the Central Intelligence Agency, and the reorganization of the War and Navy departments into the Department of Defense were all measures designed to enable the U.S. to wage war, cold and hot, more effectively against the Soviet bloc. A year after its birth the NSC had prepared plans calling for American victory in the war against the communist enemy. In Gregg Herken's phrase, peace to the NSC "was to be only a prosecution of the Cold War by nonmilitary means." Whether by diplomatic pressure, atomic threats, or by destabilizing actions inside Soviet territory (in 1947 the CIA had been authorized to launch a psychological warfare strategy in Eastern Europe and the Soviet Union), the United States was to compel the USSR to change its "present concepts," disgorge Eastern Europe, and dismantle both its military system and its political and social order. These were war objectives.

Not that hostile U.S. operations inside the USSR waited on the establishment of the NSC. As soon as the war in Europe ended, young Henry Kissinger's detachment had been put "under orders" to utilize ex-Nazis in "a series of [secret] operations in Ukraine and elsewhere inside Russia."[9] In 1948 the NSC recommended that the president do what was necessary to bring about the "collapse" of Soviet communism; the means of choice required dismantling the Soviet military establishment and ending the power of the Communist party within the Soviet Union. Unconditional surrender was not to be demanded only so that the Russian people would more easily be able to move from support of their government to support of ours. And one year later the NSC's follow-up report to the president set forth the measures of "economic, political, and psychological warfare" that would "foment and support unrest and rebellion" in the Soviet empire.[10]

American threats to make war on the Soviet enemy were not confined to secret NSC policy proposals. Articles and public statements by air force generals Curtis LeMay, Carl Spaatz, and George Kenney openly proclaimed U.S. plans to drop atomic bombs on the Soviet Union in the forthcoming war between the two countries.[11] The revelation in September 1949 of the Soviets' successful test of an atomic bomb evoked panic in some American officials. Senator Brian McMahon, chairman of the Joint Congressional Committee on Atomic Energy, told David Lilienthal that the United States now must "blow them [the Soviets] off the face of the earth, quick, before they do the same to us—and we haven't much time."[12]

Through all the shifts and turns in American policy between the Truman and Bush administrations, and notwithstanding détente and intermittent thaws in the relations between the U.S. and the USSR, the image of the Soviet Union as the enemy persisted in the minds of American leaders.[13] Washington perfected its plans for nuclear destruction of the USSR and rejected calls for renouncing nuclear weapons or the "first use" of nuclear weapons. A little-noticed series of public statements by President Ronald Reagan and his secretary of state in 1982 indicated that covert American operations designed to destabilize the Soviet Union not only continued but were being broadcast to the world—if in somewhat euphemistic language. President Reagan, a great sports fan, described the NSC plan he approved as a "full-court press" within the Soviet Union, calling for the U.S. to "undertake a campaign aimed at internal reform in the Soviet Union and shrinkage of the Soviet empire." At a conference in Washington in October 1982 designed to find ways to "spread democracy to communist countries," Secretary of State George P. Shultz reiterated that "we will not ignore the individuals and groups in Communist countries who seek peaceful change."[14] This mild language did not camouflage a frank intention to intervene in Soviet affairs to bring about the changes that American leaders sought.

In sum, from the inception of the cold war to its end, presidents and their key advisers in many ways treated the Soviet Union as an enemy. American leaders publicly branded it the enemy and proclaimed an intention to overthrow its system, carve up its territory, and destroy its cities, reducing them to rubble in the "imminent war." To insure victory in that war, military alliances were formed with nations all over the world, the Soviet Union was ringed with bases for bombing operations, and planes armed with nuclear weapons were kept constantly in the air, ready at a moment's notice to launch a strike against the USSR. In the era of intercontinental ballistic missiles, American hydrogen bombs from silos on our land and submarines and ships at sea were aimed at thousands of Soviet targets. For almost half a century secret agents were deployed in the Soviet Union, not only to ferret out military intelligence but to destabilize and destroy their system. And through the FBI (as well as committees of Congress) those Americans suspected of excessively uncritical admiration of the Soviet "enemy" were treated as a traitorous fifth column. Such treatment was not confined to Communist party members but extended as well to liberal political leaders (Eleanor Roosevelt, Adlai Stevenson, Martin Luther King, Jr.), prominent writers (Norman Mailer, Dwight Macdonald), and even reporters (Harrison Salisbury, Peter Lisagor). As General Groves said, even when the Soviets were our supposed ally during World War II, he knew they were our enemy. The minority who agreed with him in the fall of 1942 soon swelled to a majority after the fall of 1945.

Now, that this conviction became widely accepted does not mean it was true. The question remains, was the Soviet Union truly the enemy of the United States? Under federal law and the

Constitution of the United States, as interpreted by the federal judiciary, an enemy of the United States is a foreign nation with which we are at war. On this count the Soviet Union did not qualify.

In the late-nineteenth-century federal case bearing most directly on the issue. *United States v. Greathouse*, Justice Stephen J. Field ruled that "the term 'enemies,' as used in [the Constitution] according to its settled meaning at the time the Constitution was adopted, applies only to the subjects of a foreign power in a state of open hostility with us."[15] In other cases the courts have affirmed that "an enemy is he with whom a nation is at war" and that "by the law of nations, an enemy is defined to be 'one with whom a nation is at war.' "[16] The section on "definitions" in the Trading with the Enemy Act of 1917, as amended, states that "the word 'enemy' as used herein, shall be deemed to mean any [subject, group of subjects, or] the government of any nation with which the United States is at war."[17] The eminent twentieth-century authority on the Constitution, Charles Warren, has concluded that the crime of giving aid and comfort to the enemies of the United States is an "act committed in connection with a war waged against the United States by a foreign power."[18] But these constitutional proscriptions were abandoned even by the Supreme Court during the cold war years. Upholding the conviction of the leadership of the American Communist party under the Smith Act in *Dennis v. United States,* the Court in effect found the party to be an agent of an international conspiracy to overthrow the U.S. government. Even then, the basis for the Court's ruling centered on the intended actions of American Communists within the United States.

Under international law, as well as under the United States Constitution and American judicial precedent, the Soviet Union was not the enemy of the United States because at no point after the close of World War II was it at war with the United States. No wonder the authors of NSC-68 and other ardent cold warriors declared that "the Cold War is a real war." Accept that claim and our cold war adversaries become the legal enemy of the United States. For war is a matter of the military forces of one nation firing weapons at the land or forces of another.

Ironically, for all the rancor and warlike measures generated by the cold war, the United States and the Soviet Union did not direct their military forces to fire on each other. Formal diplomatic contacts between the two nations were maintained. Both nations engaged in commerce with each other. Cultural and academic exchanges flourished and in time expanded. (In 1985 I was sent by the United States to be the Fulbright lecturer in American history in universities in Moscow, Leningrad, and Tbilisi.) American tourists visited the USSR; the country was not off limits. By the 1960s the two nations entered into armaments limitation and nuclear test limitation treaties and put in place a hotline to assure the swift contact necessary to prevent the outbreak of war between them.

Good sense and what George Washington and the Founding Fathers regarded as the true national interest confirm the wisdom of the legal principle that the only enemies of the United States are those nations and people at war with us. Once our political leaders are permitted to name as enemies nations they detest, but nations which have not made war on the United States, then law can be (and was) brushed aside; and, given the need for secrecy, foreign policy becomes the exclusive province of presidents and bureaucrats, a hostage to their personal ideological predilections. Secretary of State Dean Rusk might tell the Senate Foreign Relations Committee in 1961 that we were engaged in "a war to the death" with Soviet-directed international communism, but his statement proved that neither the USSR nor "international communism" was truly our enemy. It only showed that the cold war emboldened members of the executive branch to make policy without having their assumptions tested in fact or basing their decisions on lawful authority.[19]

CHAPTER V

✤

Nuclear Bombs for Freedom

ON being advised that a U.S. atomic bomb had destroyed Hiroshima, President Truman, who ordered the attack, said, "This is the greatest thing in history."[1] Most of the world did not agree about the nuclear bombs that wiped out Hiroshima and Nagasaki and the ever more destructive thermonuclear weapons that replaced them. In contrast to the United States, which from the dawn of the atomic era to the present has treated The Bomb as an appropriate weapon that we may use against our Soviet adversary, most of the nations and all of the great religions have gone on record opposing the use of nuclear weapons under any circumstances.[2]

The reasons for the world's antipathy are clear. Nuclear weapons above all destroy cities and massive numbers of innocent civilians. The thirteen-kiloton bomb used on Hiroshima ultimately killed and maimed several hundred thousand people. One multimegaton bomb of the sort now available could destroy tens of millions of people and wipe out cities the size of London, Moscow, and New York City. According to competent medical authorities, the impact on the United States of an all-out nuclear attack by us, *"even if unanswered by the Russians,"* would be catastrophic. "Cancerous leukemia would soar. A second generation of Americans would find it *difficult if not impossible to survive."* Civil defense would be exposed as farcical, since the heat in fallout shelters within five miles of a nuclear attack would reach 1,472 degrees. The shelters would become "crematoria in which people are simultaneously dry-roasted and asphyxiated."[3] On the basis of data drawn from the "defense plans" of the Federal Emergency Management Administration, Dr. Herbert Abrams, professor of radiology at Harvard Medical School, not long ago concluded that "within minutes of a 65 megaton [bomb] attack on the United States," 83 million people would be dead and 134 million more would die before the month was up.[4]

After Hiroshima and Nagasaki people did not have to be nuclear scientists to understand that the new weapon was horrifying. When he participated in the Manhattan Project, Edward Teller, later dubbed the "father of the H-bomb" and enthusiastic advocate of every escalation in the destructiveness of the American nuclear arsenal, regarded the atomic bomb he had helped create as "this dreadful thing," so awful that nothing could "save [the] souls" of those who made it.[5] Apparently unaffected by such guilt feelings, President Truman publicly claimed not to have lost sleep over his decision to use our only two atomic bombs against Japan, and after the Japanese surrender he ordered the production of atomic bombs to continue. He made The Bomb the "centerpiece" of postwar United States military strategy, evidently agreeing with those of his advisers who regarded it as the "winning weapon" both in the cold war and in the hot war with the Soviet Union they said was imminent.[6]

The nuclear weapons policies of the United States under the presidential administrations of Harry Truman and his successors were little deterred by negative public opinion, whether in the United States or the outside world. What Archbishop John B. Roach, Joseph Cardinal Bernardin, and other American Catholic bishops called our nuclear weapons "action policy"[7] was essentially unchanging through the cold war: make more bombs; make them increasingly powerful and accurate; deploy them at first in the air and subsequently on land, in the sea, and in space, zeroed in on the Soviet Union; make detailed plans for using them against the Soviet Union and other communist or hostile nations, whether in response to their attacks with conventional weapons or in preemptive strikes against them; oppose a ban on these weapons; reject calls that the United States join the USSR in promising never to initiate the use of nuclear weapons; induce public acceptance of nuclear bombs as no more unacceptable than any other weapons; and convince public opinion that American nuclear weapons policies had been adopted only out of grim necessity. The Soviets' successful test of an atomic bomb in the fall of 1949 doubtless fortified President Truman in his decision to order the making of the "super" or hydrogen bomb. But he had made The Bomb the centerpiece of U.S. military strategy even before the Soviets exploded their weapon.

Since public opinion was a vital element in what presidents called the cold war struggle for the hearts and minds of men, and since too American officials were quite aware of widespread revulsion for The Bomb, what the Catholic bishops called the American "declaratory policy" on The Bomb was necessarily ambiguous. For no matter how great their actual ardor for the new weapon, American leaders understandably felt it politic to try to camouflage it. Publicly they communicated a certain sadness that the monstrous Soviet threat had left the United States no alternative but to embrace this "dreadful thing." Since American leaders were indeed human and therefore prey to the inconsistencies that afflict our species, they did not always succeed in muffling their passion for the marvelous weapon that Winston Churchill said God had given the U.S.[8] And sometimes they grew impatient with perverse public opinion. The straightforward boldness in what the United States did with atomic and hydrogen bombs during the cold war, when combined with the contradictory and complex things American leaders said about their actions and motives, present an interesting challenge to the historian.

During the cold war American nuclear bombs were constantly aimed at the Soviet Union. Almost from the time the atomic bomb program of the United States got under way in the fall of 1942, influential American leaders regarded our Soviet ally as, at the least, a potential diplomatic target of our bombs. The scientists who finally induced President Roosevelt to launch the Manhattan Project appear to have thought only of beating the Nazis in the race to create the first A-bomb, thereby preventing Hitler from terrorizing the world. Joseph Rotblat, an English physicist who worked in the Manhattan Project, has written that in doing so he "never envisaged that we should use [the bomb], not even against the Germans. We needed the bomb for the sole purpose of making sure it would not be used by them."[9] Some government officials, as well as scientists, agreed with him. But President Truman did not. As earlier noted, General Leslie R. Groves, who headed the Manhattan Project, said after the war that he never doubted Russia was the enemy.[10]

Gar Alperovitz touched off a scholarly controversy a generation ago when he interpreted the U.S. refusal to accede to the scientists' request for a three-day delay in testing the first atomic bomb (on account of a technical problem they had encountered) as indication that President Truman was determined to exploit the results of that test during the Potsdam Conference.[11] Whatever may have been the president's reasons for opposing a delay in the test, observers at Potsdam reported that Truman was buoyed by the news that the July 16 test at Alamagordo had been successful. Churchill observed that the president was a "changed man" who now "told the Russians where they got . . . off" at the meeting of July 21. With the mighty weapon in hand, the president no longer needed the Soviet intervention in the war against Japan that President Roosevelt and U.S. military leaders had earlier sought and which Stalin had agreed to at Yalta. As Daniel Yergin has noted, "Truman and Secretary of State James F. Byrnes were now eager to end the [Potsdam] Conference so that the bomb might be used quickly and thus stave off, or at least slow, the Russian advance into East Asia." On the day following the July 21 meeting Truman "wrote out in longhand the order to use the bomb" against Japan.[12]

This is not the occasion for a detailed examination of President Truman's decision to order the atomic bombing of Japan and the changing explanations he gave for that decision. Germane to this discussion is that the evidence, some of it only recently unearthed, raises unsettling questions about the president's performance. In public statements he made after the war, Truman kept escalating the number of lives his decision had saved, the figure soaring from less than a quarter-million to more than one million in the space of a few years. Truman had also disregarded advice from Generals MacArthur, Eisenhower, Curtis LeMay, George C. Marshall, the Joint Chiefs, and Admiral William Leahy that it was unnecessary to "hit [Japan] with that awful thing." In Leahy's words, "The use of this barbarous weapon at Hiroshima and Nagasaki was of no material assistance in our war against Japan" since "the Japanese were already defeated and ready to surrender." Before he gave the order to atom bomb Japan, Truman had said privately, first in his diary and then in a letter to his wife, that "Fini Japan when [the Soviet entry into the war in the Far East] comes about."[13] After noting that American military authorities believed that even in a worst-case scenario involving a forthcoming invasion of a Japan that would hold out until late 1945,

"American deaths almost surely would not have been more than 20,000 and probably less than 15,000," Rufus Miles, a long-time American official, recently concluded that "our atomic bombing of Japan must have been based largely on other considerations than the saving of large numbers of American lives." Miles believes that falsehoods about both the need to use atomic bombs and the number of lives they saved "more than any other factor seemed to give legitimacy to the American use of nuclear weapons."[14] If, as General Groves is reported to have said, "the real purpose in making the bomb was to subdue the Soviets," one of the real purposes in using the bomb appears to have been to send a message to the Soviets.[15]

The demonstration of our capacity to atomize distant cities meant that "there was no reason for any concessions to Russia at the end of the war," advised Vannevar Bush, chief adviser on atomic matters to Secretary of War Henry Stimson. Stimson himself regarded the bomb as our "master card" in the game for "big stakes in diplomacy." Secretary of State Byrnes told President Truman that "the bomb might put us in a position to dictate our own terms" at the end of the war. It "would make Russia more manageable in Europe," he told a Manhattan Project scientist.[16]

The United States had not built, tested, and used its first atomic bombs chiefly to shorten the war against Japan and save hundreds of thousands of American lives; nor were the anti-Soviet possibilities of the new weapon an afterthought, a sudden inspiration that leaped into the minds of American policymakers only as they discovered that our wartime Soviet ally was becoming our postwar adversary. The top military leaders of the United States had argued that the bomb was not necessary to defeat or reduce the time needed to defeat Japan. Well before he ordered the atomic bombing of Japanese cities, President Truman knew of Japan's readiness to surrender under peace terms similar to those he found acceptable after the destruction of

Hiroshima and Nagasaki. Our military had reported that in the unlikely event of Japanese refusal to surrender until their mainland had been invaded, American casualties would probably have been less than one-tenth of the quarter-million figure that the president first offered as the number of lives our bombing had saved. Before he decided to use the bomb, Truman had told his wife that the war was really over. And the heads of the War and State departments applauded the new weapon for its supposed power to coerce the Soviet Union into accepting the postwar world envisaged by American leaders. Just as he brushed aside last-minute pleas by Manhattan Project scientists that the bombs not be used against civilian populations, General Eisenhower's description of The Bomb as a "horrible weapon" that would "only turn world opinion against the United States" did not deflect Truman from authorizing the bombing of Hiroshima and Nagasaki.[17]

President Truman's contradictory explanations for his decision to use the bombs against Japan offer further evidence of his determination. His public comment that he lost no sleep over his decision might indicate that he had no compunctions about using a weapon that he believed did not differ in kind from any other. Or it might betoken his attempt to mold public opinion by assuring the American people that their government, in having no qualms about using The Bomb, left them no good reason to sympathize with the concerns being expressed by scientists and others over the use of so dreadful a weapon. Truman's later claims that, by shortening the war, our bombing had saved hundreds of thousands of American and Japanese lives, confirm that the president understood that the new weapon was far from ordinary, requiring him to justify its use on humane grounds. His decision to continue producing atomic bombs, despite Japan's surrender almost immediately after the bombing of Nagasaki, reveals that even before August 6 the president's plans for American atomic bombs were not confined to what they would do to Japan. Truman's rationale soon shifted following the onset of the cold war. By 1949 he was saying that he had decided to make nuclear weapons the centerpiece of American strategy. The evidence indicates that even before the term "cold war" had come into use, the president had decided to rely on atomic bombs as a vital diplomatic and military tool in the struggle against the Soviet Union.[18]

In embracing nuclear weapons as they did, the Truman administration and its successors through the presidency of George Bush ignored centuries-old attempts, culminating in the Geneva Convention, to assure that noncombatant civilians were not to be targeted by nations at war. United States officials later argued that the neutron bomb and other "smart" nuclear weapons, as well as the counterforce doctrine they had temporarily adopted, were focused on military targets, and that this testified to a concern to limit damage to innocent civilians in the event of a nuclear war between the two superpowers. But in view of what United States officials knew would almost certainly be a massive Soviet nuclear response even to an American attack with "clean weapons," and the equally massive American attack on Soviet targets that would follow, talk of limiting nuclear destruction to military targets and personnel was essentially only propaganda. Nuclear bombs were not smart enough, even when aimed at military targets, to refrain from destroying civilian populations.[19] The more than fifty hydrogen bombs we were prepared to unloose on "military targets" in Moscow would spare no civilians.

The youthful Edward Teller of the Manhattan Project explained that he entered into a Faustian bargain with the angel of death. He decided to participate in creating "this dreadful thing" that would cost all who helped make it to lose their souls, "because the [scientific] problems" involved in making the bomb "interested [him] and [he] should have felt it a great restraint not to go ahead."[20] What enticed President Truman and his successors in the White House to clasp The Bomb to their breasts was not irresistible scientific curiosity but the irresistible political and military advantages they thought it would confer on the United States, advantages that extended beyond American competition with the Soviet Union.

What the Catholic bishops called American nuclear weapons "action policy" was all of a piece throughout the cold war. The United States continued after the surrender of Japan to keep manufacturing atomic bombs on close to a wartime basis. Shortly after the shooting stopped, the U.S. military began to prepare detailed plans for nuclear attacks on the Soviet Union, whether in preemptive strikes or in response to the outbreak of war between the two nations. Although the United States in 1946 brought to the UN the Baruch Plan for the international control and eventual elimination of atomic weapons, senior American officials, including Bernard Baruch, privately made clear that the United States had no intention of forsaking the atomic bomb. The Joint Chiefs clearly stated the real purpose at the time: "The bomb should continue to be at the heart of America's arsenal, and a system of controls should be established that would prevent the Russians from developing the weapon." U.S. officials rejected out of hand the Soviet plan presented to the UN on June 14, 1946, calling for a ban on atomic weapons, just as they continued thereafter to oppose all "Ban the Bomb" proposals, whether emanating from the USSR or any other source. Concluding after a careful study that earlier American plans for nuclear attacks on the Soviet Union would be too costly in planes and American lives lost, as well as in the loss of a Central and Western Europe overrun by Soviet troops responding to our bombing raids, the U.S. military had only postponed the date for a nuclear strike. Washington later abandoned "Dropshot," the Joint Chiefs' plan for launching a Western nuclear assault on the Soviet Union on January 1, 1957, when follow-up studies indicated that Soviet countermeasures would probably result in the loss of Western Europe, the destruction of Britain, and heavy damage to American cities. For by that time the Soviets had developed their own arsenal of hydrogen bombs. Regrettably, thought General Groves, the United States had not acted on the 1946 recommendation by the Joint Intelligence Committee that the United States initiate a nuclear attack on any "aggressor nation about to acquire the bomb." American military planners believed that the new concept of striking the first blow was not an act of aggression when executed against an "aggressor nation" such as the USSR.[21]

The Soviet explosion of an atomic bomb precipitated an accelerated and expanded U.S. nuclear weapons buildup, including the planned use against the Soviet Union and Soviet surrogates. President Truman ordered the building of hydrogen bombs so powerful that their destructive force was measured in megatons (millions of tons of explosive power, or one thousand times as great as the kilotons used for measuring the power of atomic bombs). Testing of ever more powerful hydrogen bombs was accelerated at the same time the disastrous effects of these tests on the atmosphere, the earth, the oceans, and on animal and human health were covered up. When public outrage at the poisonous consequences of atmospheric testing compelled the two superpowers to confine their tests to realms other than the earth's surface and the atmosphere, the United States at first refused to enter into a comprehensive test ban, but later agreed to work toward achieving it at some indeterminate future time.

The clear objective of American nuclear weapons policy was superiority rather than the parity in nuclear power approved by NATO. To achieve that superiority required testing of more powerful and precise nuclear weapons. American leaders publicly assured the world that they sympathized with the goals of movements to ban the bomb, deploring only the ineffectuality of the means used by adherents to attain their noble objective. At the same time American officials were secretly telling the Senate that a ban on nuclear weapons must be opposed as contrary to the interests of the United States.[22] Even as they publicly expressed revulsion for these "dread weapons" and justified them only out of bitter necessity, American leaders privately expressed quite different feelings about the very weapon they deplored. Thus, urging President Truman to go ahead with the manufacture of the hydrogen bomb, the Joint Chiefs emphasized that it was "folly to argue whether one weapon is more immoral than another," since "in the larger sense, it is war itself which is immoral." And at a secret meeting of the National Security Council on March 27, 1953, at a time when the Korean War was still being waged, President Eisenhower, Secretary of State John Foster Dulles, and others agreed that "somehow or other the taboo which surrounds the use of atomic weapons would have to be destroyed." Given "the state of world opinion" prevailing at the time, Dulles observed, "we could not use an A-bomb [but] we should make every effort now to dissipate this feeling." As the secretary of state later told a closed-door meeting of NATO in Paris on April 23, 1954, "the United States believed atomic weapons must be regarded as 'conventional' as non-nuclear weapons."[23] Varied evidence nonetheless indicates that American leaders failed to change public opinion from abhorrence to acceptance of The Bomb.

Some American officials evidently thought that giving our bombs such names as "Little Boy" and "Fat Man" might somehow humanize them. The psychologist Carol Cohn, who spent a year with "defense intellectuals" who "plan mass incineration of million of human beings for a living," doing so as though they were solving problems in theoretical mathematics, reports that they found solace in speaking of The Bomb in a "language [that was] abstract and sanitized . . . which never gives you access to the [actual] images of war." But cute names for bombs, and Pentagon references to clean weapons and surgical strikes, failed to transform public opinion from horror to amusement.[24] Continued public antipathy, however, had no effect on U.S. officials' determination to make more weapons, to make them more destructive than ever, to consider using them during the Korean and Vietnam wars, and to perfect plans for destroying "military and industrial targets" in the Soviet Union with many thousands of bombs.[25]

Observers as disparate as George F. Kennan, the Nobel laureate Hans Bethe, and Jerome B. Wiesner, adviser on nuclear weapons to Presidents Kennedy and Johnson, have pointed out that "we Americans," not the Soviets, "at almost every step of the road, have taken the lead in the development [and escalation of nuclear] weaponry." From the time of the first atomic and hydrogen bombs through MIRVing (or putting multiple nuclear warheads on ballistic missiles) to the Strategic Defense Initiative or Star Wars, the "central dogma" propelling the United States to be "the leading force in the [nuclear] arms race," according to Wiesner, was the notion that "whatever is technically possible must be done."[26] Whatever may have motivated them, American military, scientific, and political leaders pushed ahead without deviation in expanding and strengthening the U.S. nuclear weapons program.

With a Soviet nuclear weapons buildup that matched our own, United States officials cannot be faulted for rejecting unilateral nuclear disarmament. Soviet leaders, however, were evidently convinced that their weaponry could not match the accuracy of ours, that our technological and scientific superiority would doom them to perpetually lagging behind the United States, and that the costliness of a near runaway arms race would ultimately have disastrous effects on their economy. Thus the Soviets endorsed a freeze on the manufacture of nuclear weapons and delivery systems, a permanent test ban, and the elimination of "all [nuclear] stockpiles on earth," and even made a unilateral pledge never to initiate the use of nuclear weapons in warfare. United States officials rejected all these Soviet proposals that required agreement by the two sides. Presidents refused as well to emulate the Soviets' pledge of no first use, despite the plea of our four "wise men"—George Kennan, Robert McNamara, McGeorge Bundy, and Gerard Smith—that we do so. But as President Reagan told a group of reporters in 1982, since we would not abandon our policy of threatening to unloose hydrogen bombs on the USSR when we saw fit, no "useful purpose [would be] served in making such a declaration."[27]

American leaders did not merely reject a freeze on the manufacture and testing of nuclear weapons and a ban on their use. They also impugned the motives of those in the United States and elsewhere who advanced these proposals, stigmatizing them as unwitting dupes if not conscious agents of the Soviet Union. Nuclear "hawks" in and out of the U.S. government also denounced Jonathan Schell's book *The Fate of the Earth*, the TV film *The Day After*, scientific talk of a "nuclear winter" that would threaten to extinguish life on earth after a full-scale nuclear war, and other scenarios that focused on the allegedly horrifying effects of a nuclear exchange. William F. Buckley, onetime CIA employee and ardent anticommunist, charged that the activities of antinuclear Catholic priests encouraged "idolatrous veneration of human life."[28]

The massive American nuclear weapons buildup inevitably prodded the Soviet Union to create a vast nuclear arsenal of its own. By the 1980s the Soviets possessed more than twenty thousand nuclear warheads, many of them not impressively accurate but so monstrous in size and destructiveness as to be capable of exterminating most life and property in the United States many times over. Yet, for all their awesome power, Soviet nuclear weapons were inferior to the American arsenal. Even Caspar Weinberger, the secretary of defense in the Reagan administration who regularly cried "Wolf!" about the Soviet

Union's nuclear power, conceded that he would not exchange our bombs for theirs.[29] In contrast to the Soviet emphasis on ICBMs located in easily targetable land silos, the American "triad" of nuclear-armed missiles roughly divided among land-based ICBMs, planes constantly in the air or poised to strike from aircraft carriers, and SLBMs or missiles to be launched from our superior submarines, comprised a balanced and essentially invulnerable arsenal. The United States retained sufficient firepower to destroy the USSR even if the Soviets launched a massive and successful nuclear attack on American forces.

By the late 1960s both sides concluded that it was in their interest to enter into treaties limiting nuclear weapons tests and the size of their arsenals. In the ABM treaty of 1972 they agreed not to create large-scale defense capabilities against incoming ICBMs. Were such defenses permitted, the reasoning went, they would trigger an even greater and more unsettling race in offensive nuclear weapons, for whichever nation succeeded first in creating a viable defense might be tempted to launch a preemptive strike. Technological advances had made possible surveillance systems which enabled each side to check on the tests and other nuclear activities of its adversary.

Mutual agreement to impose limited restraints on the deployment of certain classes of hydrogen bombs by no means signaled the end of the nuclear arms race. Particularly during the Reagan administration, United States officials regularly charged that the Soviet Union violated joint nuclear weapons treaties. Although a number of these allegations were refuted by officials in NATO, the CIA, and other American government agencies, the charges provided a valuable backdrop for a continuous U.S. escalation in the power and precision of its nuclear weapons.[30] Something new in this buildup was the manufacture and deployment of "first-strike" weapons such as the M-X missile and the Pershing IIs which the Reagan administration installed in Germany. The M-X was a weapon whose power and precision would enable it to destroy Soviet ICBMs before they could be launched. The Pershings were not simply accurate but, according to a "senior Reagan administration official," they could "reach Moscow from West German sites and with [their] accuracy and 4 to 6 minute flight time, could knock out secondary command and control sites and render the Soviet Union unable to fire its land-based force of ICBMs."[31]

Experts considered first-strike weapons destabilizing because they threatened to destroy the adversary's nuclear weapons and its nuclear command posts—thus they might precipitate a launch-on-warning mode, with all the uncertainties involved in decision-making by inhuman—and imperfect—computers. Theoretically, mere knowledge of the fact that the other side had devoted money and effort to create weapons with the capacity to destroy your own attack force before it was launched, might lead you to get your weapons into the air, moving against their intended targets before the first-strike force destroyed them. Fears expressed by some critics of first-strike weapons—that they were likely to trigger a Soviet preemptive strike against the U.S. —fortunately were never realized. For all the Soviet emphasis of their relatively vulnerable ICBMs, American leaders knew they had a sufficient number of hydrogen bombs in and under water and in the air to commit unacceptable damage on the United States. In strict logic there may have been no point to making and deploying first-strike bombs unless they were to be used; but life, as Justice Oliver Wendell Holmes once said in a different context, is not logic. There can be little doubt that our precise new weapons increased Soviet anxieties about American intentions, making an already delicate situation even more fragile. William Van Cleave, of President Reagan's advisory committee on arms control, believed that deploying our "powerful and highly accurate MX [could] only be a first-strike weapon" to use in a "surprise launching [that increased] the likelihood of war" by tempting "the other side to launch first."[32]

On March 23, 1983, President Reagan proclaimed his Strategic Defense Initiative (SDI) or Star Wars program, designed, he said, to "free the world from the threat of nuclear war." By destroying incoming ballistic missiles, SDI would supposedly render nuclear weapons "impotent and obsolete." Most of the nation's scientists, engineers, and computer experts did not agree, more than two thousand of them in the academic community finding SDI not only "technologically unfeasible," but "ill conceived and dangerous"—it was a "step toward the type of weapons and strategy likely to trigger a nuclear holocaust." Although the president initially spoke of sharing the new technology with the Soviet Union, saying, "I will be happy when the Soviets can shoot down our missiles just as we can shoot down theirs," by 1985 the Pentagon thought such sharing "unlikely." Thereafter the president ceased making what retired admirals Gene R. La Rocque and Eugene Carroll dismissed as "this wholly incredible promise." It was incredible in asking the Soviet Union "to sit by for many years while the U.S. developed its space defenses, knowing too that our [Defense Department] was seeking military advantage in space and spending vast sums on offensive missiles capable of evading, deceiving, jamming or outmaneuvering Soviet defenses."[33]

Star Wars was not what it seemed. For the Strategic Defense Initiative was also a strategic *offense* initiative. Robert C. Aldridge, a former designer of the Trident missile, observed that "although the American people [were] led to believe that SDI is defensive, that is far from the case." The beam weapons of SDI had to be powered by nuclear explosions. The R & D Associates defense consulting firm hired by the Pentagon to "explore the use of lasers in a space-based missile defense system powerful enough to cope with the ballistic missile threat can also destroy the enemy's major cities by fire." As the military analyst Fred Reed has observed, "Star wars, if it works, will be an offensive weapon of absolute power."[34]

At the same time they were proposing to use space for purposes of defense, Reagan administration officials were planning to "wage war effectively from outer space" by achieving "space superiority." Thus in "the fighting" that an air force master plan predicted would be "actually taking place in space," the United States would prevail. In a speech to the American Society of Mechanical Engineers in December 1985, John Gardiner, SDI's director for systems, revealed that SDI would alter the nuclear weapons balance to the advantage of the United States, even should the USSR deploy a defensive program in space. For since "the forces of the two sides are asymmetric," with a far greater proportion of ballistic missiles in the Soviet nuclear arsenal than in our own, "as you turn up the gain on the defense against ballistic missiles . . . the situation moves . . . sharply in our favor with ballistic missile defenses."[35] Star Wars would enhance American prospects for prevailing in the nuclear war in space and, in the language of General Charles A. Gabriel, air force chief of staff, assure "more rapid conflict termination or increased survivability" for the United States in the ground and air war against the Soviet Union.[36]

After Mikhail Gorbachev's ascension to power in 1985, the changes he introduced in both the domestic and foreign policies of the Soviet Union dramatically improved relations between the USSR and the United States. Subsequent nuclear weapons treaties radically reduced the number of weapons in Europe and the overkill capacity of the two sides' weapons arsenals. But although President Reagan—for what American cold warriors regarded as one scary moment—seemed ready to agree with Gorbachev's proposal to get rid of *all* nuclear weapons, the moment passed. The United States and the Soviet Union continued to maintain their largely redundant nuclear weapons forces, and Star Wars research and planning continued, barely deflected by the end not only of the cold war but of the Soviet Union. The extinction of the Great Soviet Threat, whose existence had supposedly compelled the United States to launch the nuclear arms race, by the summer of 1992 had had slight effect on U.S. nuclear weapons plans. Planes may no longer have been constantly in the air, ready at a moment's notice to launch their hydrogen bombs on the former Soviet Union. But the warheads on missiles in silos in the American heartland and in submarines continued to be aimed at targets in the renamed Commonwealth of Independent States. Vague references by some congressmen to the possibility of a drastic reduction in the U.S. nuclear weapons arsenal in coming years appear to have had little effect on President George Bush's plans to retain a massive nuclear weapons force capable of destroying any and all nations several times over, and on our policy of reserving the option of initiating the use of hydrogen bombs in any future American military action. The Bush administration continued to reject "no first use."

United States nuclear weapons action policy was remarkably consistent before, during, and in the immediate aftermath of the cold war. During World War II atomic bombs were developed and used militarily against Japan, diplomatically against the Soviet Union. After the war vastly more powerful hydrogen bombs were developed while a variety of ways were devised to direct them to Soviet and hostile targets, and to deploy them around the earth. While agreeing to some restraints on testing and on the numbers of several classes of these weapons, U.S. officials refused to accept a total cessation of testing. They also opposed a ban on their use and calls for their destruction by both sides, and rejected the plea that the United States join the Soviets in renouncing first use.

At the same time American leaders proposed and started work on a plan to enable the U.S.—and the USSR—to destroy

incoming ballistic missiles, a variety of new weapons and de-
vices were created to ensure U.S. nuclear superiority in space
as well as in the air and on the earth below. American leaders
talked parity while in fact striving for and achieving superiority.
And these same leaders opposed and impugned the motives of
individuals and groups within and outside the United States that
demanded a freeze on the manufacture and testing of thermonuclear bombs, the destruction of nuclear arsenals, and the renun-
ciation of nuclear weapons in warfare.

Washington's *declared* nuclear weapons policy was designed to
justify and beautify the nation's nuclear weapons action policy.
The relatively few defections from the U.S. cause by nations of
the Free World during the cold war indicate that this declaratory
policy worked. American leaders' nuclear weapons policy and
our justifications for it did not evoke defections, certainly not on
the part of friendly governments. But that arguments prevail
may be due not to their validity but to the power of those who
present them, and the fear their power inspires. When tested for
logical consistency and good sense, our declared policy does not
come off well.

American leaders' awareness of widespread antipathy to The
Bomb, and the importance to them of modifying this hostility,
compelled them to speak of our understanding of, even our
sharing in, this popular revulsion. But at times they forgot
themselves and spoke the language of lust if not love of this
"dread weapon." They called it the "winning weapon," and
within months of the close of World War II air force generals
publicly proclaimed their intention to rain atomic bombs on the
Soviet Union. Diatribes against books, films, and scientific
arguments that emphasized the appalling consequences of nuclear war betrayed an enthusiasm for The Bomb and a readiness

to use it in war on the part of those who criticized these vivid scenarios of nuclear horrors. Joint Chiefs memos deplored the "folly" of arguments about the morality of nuclear weapons. High government officials periodically asserted that, in Henry Kissinger's words, we had to get our money's worth out of these costly toys by using or threatening to use them. President Eisenhower observed that the American public, having paid so much to make, test, and deploy these weapons, would question government hesitancy to use them. Upon becoming president, Eisenhower abandoned the concerns he had earlier expressed about Hiroshima and, like our other cold war leaders, came to accept the ordinariness of The Bomb.[37]

The most important official justifications for U.S. nuclear weapons policy were pragmatic. Describing The Bomb as a deplorable necessity conveyed to the world what American leaders evidently hoped was a comforting suggestion—that the United States had embraced The Bomb out of an unavoidable need to counter the menace of Soviet totalitarianism. Unfortunately, these justifications do not stand up to critical scrutiny.

A persistent explanation for U.S. nuclear weapons policy in the aftermath of World War II was that The Bomb was the great equalizer. It redressed the imbalance between the massive conventional forces of the Soviet empire and the modest forces of the United States and its allies. For, as Bernard Baruch and General Groves told the world in 1946, we needed atomic bombs "as a counterbalance to the enormous military establishment maintained by Russia." A generation later President Reagan sounded the same note when he said at one of his rare press conferences that "our strategic nuclear weapons . . . are the only balance . . . that we have to the massive buildup of conventional arms that the Soviet Union has on the Western front or the NATO front." The USSR and its Warsaw Pact allies did indeed have a massive military machine. But so did the United States and its NATO allies. As American leaders knew, Western forces were better trained, better armed, and more reliable. Western antitank weapons neutralized the great Soviet tank forces; American ships, in or under water, outperformed their Soviet counterparts; American planes and pilots were superior.[38]

Commencing with President Truman's shifting justifications for his decision to atom bomb Japanese cities, his successors were never at a loss for explanations of American nuclear weapons policies. Their high-sounding explanations stressed the U.S. need to achieve a military power that approximated the great military power of the USSR. The argument for lives saved was questionable. Similarly unpersuasive were official references to an imaginary Western deficit in conventional military power as justification for a massive nuclear weapons buildup.

The chief argument presented by American leaders in justifying their nuclear weapons policy was deterrence. According to the Truman administration, the United States had decided to continue building nuclear weapons after the end of the war principally to deter Soviet military aggression in Western Europe and elsewhere. Only U.S. possession of The Bomb and proclaimed readiness to use it protected the "almost defenseless" Free World from invasion by hordes of Soviet and later Warsaw Pact troops. As General Eisenhower told Bernard Baruch in 1946, "the existence of the atomic bomb in our hands" was the deterrent to the planned Soviet sweep across Western Europe and to "aggression [elsewhere] in the world." President Reagan later claimed that "deterrence is essential to preserve peace and protect our way of life."[39]

American leaders made ever widening claims for the deterrent effects of nuclear weapons. In addition to forestalling the sweep of Soviet and Warsaw Pact forces across Europe, the American nuclear arsenal would deter a Soviet takeover of the Middle East, a Soviet nuclear attack on the Free World, the outbreak of World War III. This deterrence argument commanded support even from those rare persons who were otherwise skeptical about the nation's cold war policy in general, its nuclear policies in particular. Theodore Draper, a critic of nuclear weapons in their "war-fighting" capacity, accepted their "war-deterring" capacity. After the showing of the anti-Bomb film *The Day After* on national television, Carl Sagan told the viewing audience that while The Bomb was monstrous and much of our policy objectionable, deterrence might yet constitute the best hope for peace. The nation's Catholic bishops rejected deterrence "as an end in itself" or as an "adequate strategy as a long-term basis for peace" in their 1983 pastoral letter criticizing American nuclear weapons policy. Yet the bishops did find deterrence an acceptable, if dangerous, "transitional strategy" or temporary "step on the way toward a progressive disarmament," if "only in conjunction with [the sincere pursuit of] arms control." And a 1986 *New York Times* editorial praised nuclear weapons for having offered a "great benefit against small risk of overwhelming disaster," since "because of the nuclear shadow (or deterrent), American and Russian troops [had] never met in combat."[40]

There is no question but that each superpower's knowledge of the other's capacity to inflict unacceptable punishment, if not total destruction, acted as a deterrent against the launching of a nuclear attack by either. What Robert S. McNamara, secretary of defense in the Kennedy and Johnson administrations, called "mutually assured destruction" (MAD) doubtless helped prevent nuclear war. But as McNamara not long ago pointed out, a policy that truly regards nuclear weapons as a deterrent to war requires no more than a few hundred such weapons at most. Each hydrogen bomb, it must be remembered, is capable of inflicting millions of casualties, destroying structures, and making large urban areas uninhabitable. A policy of creating and deploying thousands of nuclear weapons, many of which because of their speed and precision have a first-strike capability, was a policy designed not simply to deter but also to fight and win a nuclear war. As one observer recently noted, "Virtually every new weapon added to the U.S. arsenal in recent years and every weapons system now on the drawing boards is a first-strike instrument designed to deliver a surprise attack, not to deter aggression or even to retaliate against it."[41] Insofar as such weapons could have compelled their intended victim to go on a computer-controlled launch-on-warning mode, nuclear war became more rather than less likely. For all the rhetorical attention to the deterrent purpose of nuclear weapons, the actual behavior of American leaders signified their lack of enthusiasm for so limited a purpose.

In 1977 President Jimmy Carter initiated a reappraisal of long-accepted nuclear weapons policy when he told a meeting of the Joint Chiefs that he favored slashing the U.S. nuclear stockpile to two hundred warheads, an arsenal sufficient for deterrence. The Joint Chiefs were "speechless"—but only for a moment. U.S. strategy, they advised the president, was not simply to deter attack but to attain a "war-fighting capability" that would enable us to "terminate the war on terms acceptable to the United States." President Carter was quickly convinced. The Joint Chiefs' assessment echoes the judgment of two modern students of the matter: "Deterring a Soviet nuclear attack was not the sole objective of U.S. nuclear policy, and in some sense it never had been. To the war-fighters dominating four decades of U.S. history, the chief purpose of nuclear weapons had always been to achieve superiority—to enforce a 'policy of calculated and general coercion.'"[42]

In building and testing our nuclear weapons, using them against Japan, and before the end of 1945 deploying them against the Soviet Union, American leaders made no mention of deterrence. These weapons gave us great power, a power American leaders thought sufficient to contain the Soviet Union, to coerce it into more acceptable behavior, and, if need be, to inflict on it massive punishment. *Deterrence was an after-thought*. It was a clever afterthought, designed to give the world the impression that U.S. policymakers understood, even shared its repugnance for these monstrous new weapons. These officials were largely successful in conveying precisely this impression. But the impression was false.

As retired Rear Admiral La Rocque has noted, after using nuclear weapons against Japan and counting on the nuclear monopoly to achieve "worldwide military dominance," U.S. officials only then "developed theories of deterrence to help justify our nuclear weapons." The product of cold war intellectuals, "these theories of deterrence connote restraint and a defensive attitude which helped promote public confidence in the wisdom of those in control of nuclear weapons."[43]

This early, like later, argument for deterrence attempted to camouflage the actual purposes of American leaders in creating and enlarging the U.S. nuclear arsenal. It rested on two assumptions, one inaccurate or false, the other unproven and altogether unlikely. The false assumption was Soviet superiority in manpower and conventional military strength.[44] The dubious assumption was that America's nuclear arms deterred a Red Army sweep across the Continent. Soviet war plans encompassed such an invasion, but, as our intelligence disclosed, only as a response to nuclear strikes launched by the United States and the West against the Russian heartland. As such leading American cold warriors as John Foster Dulles, W. Averell Harriman, and Bernard Baruch conceded, and as U.S. intelligence reports confirmed, the devastated Soviet Union of the immediate postwar years had neither the capacity nor the intention of invading Western Europe.[45]

After the Soviets created their own nuclear arsenal, in effect neutralizing our own, the deterrence argument was stretched by its advocates. Now they claimed that the U.S. nuclear arsenal deterred the Russians both from committing military aggression in vital regions outside Europe, and from launching a preemptive nuclear strike against the United States. It is not good enough to conjecture that the only reason the Soviets did not bomb us was their knowledge that we would bomb them in return—and to offer this conjecture in the absence of any proof. In fact, the Russians unilaterally pledged never to initiate nuclear warfare, with "every evidence," in George Kennan's words, "of meaning it."[46] More to the point, U.S. officials knew they meant it. Even before Soviet leaders made this pledge, the National Security Council in 1949 conceded that "there is ground for the belief that the Soviet Union would prefer not to use weapons of mass destruction, except in the event of prior use by others." Charles E. Bohlen, former American ambassador to the USSR, wrote in 1973 that he could "not see any circumstances under which the Soviets would embark on World War III," with conventional or nuclear weapons.[47] And while in the 1980s American public opinion, by an overwhelming three-to-one margin, supported a no-first-use pledge by the United States, the Reagan administration brushed aside the idea.[48]

President Jimmy Carter's address to the United Nations on October 4, 1977, succinctly summarizes the continuing American position since the dawn of the nuclear era: readiness to initiate the use of nuclear weapons in warfare. It is a classic use of language to try to take the sting out of, if not to camouflage, this harsh reality. "I hereby solemnly declare on behalf of the United States," the president said, "that we will not use nuclear weapons except in self-defense." Against what? Against a nuclear attack on us, among other things. Ah, but we would also use nuclear weapons, he said, against a "conventional attack" on our "territories," our armed forces, or on "our allies." This position put us at odds with the UN, which had condemned nuclear weapons as unacceptable in any circumstances.[49] President Carter's position, like that of other postwar

American presidents, affirmed the American policy of insisting that we might turn a major conventional war into a nuclear war.

One can assume that most of the nations of the world, like the ministers of the great religions, are no less opposed to aggression by conventional means than we are. They oppose a nuclear response to such aggression not because they are pusillanimous but because they believe such a response to be inhumane, inappropriate, and unnecessary. Since Soviet leaders promised they would respond to any American nuclear attack with an all-out nuclear attack of their own, thereby assuring catastrophe for all, Henry Kissinger was not the only one who thought that Europeans could not find the American policy credible, disinclined as they were to believe that the United States would risk national suicide over a Soviet or East German troop movement into West Berlin.[50]

Deterrence failed both the pragmatic and the moral tests. The threat to launch what would probably become full-scale nuclear war because of troop movements in distant places was not convincing. And threatening to initiate a nuclear attack was, as the American Catholic bishops said, itself immoral. As Raymond Perkins has written, "No one . . . would deem it morally acceptable to threaten a potential murderer's spouse and children with death in order to deter that person from committing murder. Yet this—on a vastly greater scale—is exactly what nuclear deterrence requires. The leaders of one country threaten, and propose to commit, the mass murder of the civilian population of another country in order to deter its leaders from initiating future aggression. Neither the United States nor the Soviet leadership has the moral right to threaten the lives of the people on the other side in this way."[51] Paradoxically, American leaders jeopardized the good standing of the United States in the world not by actually using nuclear weapons but by their public rhetoric promising to use them.

In sum, the concept of deterrence does not withstand close

scrutiny. It was first used, if not conceived, as a justification, a pretext, and an afterthought for a nuclear policy adopted for reasons having nothing to do with deterrence. As retired American military and diplomatic personnel have pointed out, deterrence, if sincerely intended, required no more than two or three hundred American nuclear warheads. The actual policy of building many thousands of ever more powerful and sophisticated nuclear weapons shows that American leaders had something other than deterrence in mind. American leaders do not appear to have taken their own argument seriously, counting—as obviously they could—on timid Congresses and an acquiescent media to refrain from exposing the hollowness of the deterrence thesis, and on a frightened public to be oblivious to the policy's flaws. The argument of deterrence, insofar as it was accepted by the American public, had the happy propaganda effect of offering a logical and rational defense of American nuclear policy. But it threatened to initiate the very nuclear war that most of the nations and peoples of the world strongly opposed. And if the skeptics who doubted that American leaders intended to risk national catastrophe were right, we had chosen to alienate world opinion needlessly.

In viewing with horror the unrelenting escalation of the nuclear arms race of recent years, the bishops of the American United Methodist Church denounced deterrence as a "dogmatic license for perpetual hostility" and chastised the United States for resisting nuclear arms control.[52] I am not sure the crimes of deterrence extend that far. Deterrence is, after all, only a theory. It was not deterrence that engaged the world in a frightening arms race or insisted that nuclear war is an acceptable option in resolving international disputes. Responsibility for these anxieties lies with the leaders of the nation who used the deterrence rationale. Those leaders, alas, were ours.

In opposing the growing popular call for banning The Bomb that first swept over the West in the 1950s, American leaders sought to convince other nations that the United States too favored a nuclear-free world. Ostensibly they objected only to the inadequate means for achieving it. It would have been lovely if words of agreement to ban The Bomb were sufficient to obtain that happy objective. But, as American officials patiently pointed out to supporters of the Stockholm Petition—an idea that in the 1950s enlisted millions of people behind the demand that the United States join the USSR in agreeing to outlaw The Bomb—mere words were not enough. Banning The Bomb was a noble idea, but like all worthy goals it could not be easily achieved. Complex safeguards difficult to enforce had to be put in place, assuring compliance with the measures necessary to accomplish the ban. As for the goal of outlawing The Bomb, it was indeed admirable, for certainly hydrogen bombs were dread weapons. Or so U.S. officials said—sometimes.[53]

The disingenuousness of these public protestations about nuclear weapons is revealed by the private and occasionally public observations of U.S. policymakers. Atomic Energy Commissioner David Lilienthal in 1950 deplored the "deception" in U.S. officials publicly professing support of international control of atomic bombs while simultaneously relying on them.[54] (His criticism was made not in the public press but in his private journal.) In effect, on Mondays, Wednesdays, and Fridays American leaders said one thing, telling the world that we too thought The Bomb a dreadful thing that should be outlawed, but that government statements of good intentions were insufficient. On Tuesdays, Thursdays, and Saturdays these same leaders said a very different thing. For in describing The Bomb as the Great Equalizer, as our winning weapon; in praising the Lord for giving us atomic bombs to safeguard Western civilization, as did Churchill in his Fulton, Missouri, speech; in secret advice to the U.S. Senate that a ban on The Bomb would be contrary to the interests of the United States; in building, deploying, and making detailed plans to use thousands of increasingly powerful and accurate thermonuclear bombs; in impugning the motives of "Ban the Bomb" supporters; and in insisting on reserving the right to use our bombs against a nation which had not used them against us, the leaders of the United States made clear not their abhorrence but their devotion to The Bomb. The last thing in the world that American leaders wanted was a truly effective plan for outlawing The Bomb.

NSC-68 disclosed the American government's understanding of the force of "mere words." In trying to explain why the president could not pledge to refrain from using atomic weapons "except in retaliation against the prior use of such weapons," the authors of that cold war document said, "We cannot make such a declaration in good faith until we are confident that we will be in a position to attain our objectives"—the defeat of the USSR and the overthrow of the Soviet system, with or without war. Even Ronald Reagan, who often treated words cavalierly, understood that certain words must be taken very seriously— publicly stated words, that is, that would commit the United States to repudiating The Bomb. He refused to abandon his intention of possibly using nuclear weapons against the Soviet Union.[55] The United States opposed proposals for outlawing nuclear weapons not because assurance was lacking that these proposals would be enforced, but because American leaders were unwilling to abandon the nuclear option.

U.S. reliance on nuclear weapons in executing American cold war policy raises disturbing questions about that policy. Despite the various rationalizations, making The Bomb the centerpiece of U.S. cold war strategy was an intolerable decision. In dismissing the world's objections to weapons not only capable of mass destruction but of threatening the continued existence of life on earth, the post–World War II government of the United

States abided by an amoral principle: the ends justify the means. Atomic and hydrogen bombs were a morally repulsive means, as even such cold warriors as Edward Teller, William D. Leahy, and Dwight D. Eisenhower at one time conceded.

If the motives of American leaders are inferred from their actions and from what they could expect to be the likely consequences of their actions, curbing the USSR was by no means the sole objective of American nuclear weapons policy. The fears and anxieties of an escalating weapons race were certain to create a political atmosphere congenial to perpetual cold war and world tension. Militarism and an unprecedented influence of the military and military thinking were certain to thrive in such an atmosphere. The matchless military power that nuclear weapons gave to the United States would enable it to dominate not only the Soviet Union but all other governments, friendly ones included, and pursue the hegemony that a number of anticommunist scholars believe the United States sought during the cold war.[56] One need not be an economic determinist to appreciate the lure of profits to the corporate manufacturers of nuclear weapons and their friends in the military, political, and scientific communities. Prospects so appealing to influential American leaders appear to have made them indifferent to the horrors of nuclear testing, nuclear waste, and nuclear war.

That a vision so ignoble inspired a policy so repulsive is profoundly disturbing. That the creators and supporters of such a policy resorted to deception to justify it underscores how deeply the cold war poisoned national politics. Fortunately for them—if not for most of the people and the nation—the policy was not subjected to the devastating criticism it warranted. For the cold war fostered an intellectual and political atmosphere that identified sharp critical comment of government policy with subversion, no matter how culpable or suspect the policy.

A final word must be said about the substantial numbers of Americans who after all opposed U.S. nuclear weapons policy, whether by signing petitions, sending letters, taking part in massive public demonstrations, responding to pollsters' questions, or by their actions in voting booths where, given the opportunity, they voted overwhelmingly in favor of a nuclear freeze. Washington ignored the critics, no matter how popular their criticism. Perhaps Edmund Burke was right when he said that a government, in owing constituents its talents, not its industry, need not act in accordance with the people's wishes. Yet surely a democratic government owes its citizens a respectful hearing when they make clear their views on a matter of vital importance. Not the least disturbing feature of the American government's behavior during the cold war was its disdain for public opinion in this country and in the world, on those rare occasions when the people and their religious institutions objected to U.S. policy of imposing The Bomb on human affairs.

CHAPTER VI

※

The Crusade Against 'Communist Subversion' at Home

AT the same time the United States entered into cold war against Soviet and communist forces abroad, the American government launched a campaign against the Communist party and communist influence at home. In contrast to the anti-Soviet struggle, which was essentially a government affair calling on American citizens only for their political support and tax dollars, the war on domestic "subversion" also enlisted private individuals and organizations drawn from all corners of American life to join public officials in the anti-Red crusade. As John B. Oakes, a former editor of the *New York Times*, recently observed, the effects of McCarthyism are still with us[1] eminent but "dangerous" foreign visitors are still denied entry into our country, the political activities and private lives of our greatest writers, university professors, book publishers, labor union leaders, and mainstream journalists were monitored and their actions recorded in secret government files, countries with which we are at peace continue to be off limits to American citizens. Yet the waning of the anticommunist hysteria that swept over the nation in the early years of the cold war makes

possible a detached appraisal of what historians call the second
Red Scare.

The first Red Scare in the United States followed on the heels
of the Russian Revolution in 1917 and the end of World War I
the next year. Warning that the newly formed American Communist party sought to overthrow the government and fundamental institutions of the United States, as their Bolshevik
heroes had done in Russia, Attorney General A. Mitchell
Palmer and the FBI's young J. Edgar Hoover mounted a drive
against liberal antiwar critics as well as domestic radicals,
arrested and sought to deport "subversive" aliens, and incessantly proclaimed the evils and menace of communism to the
American public. Although it planted a fear of communism that
was never entirely erased from the American mind, the first Red
Scare was short-lived and touched American life only glanc-
ingly.[2]

Modern anticommunist crusades did not begin in 1917 but go
back at least to 1848, when the young German revolutionist
Karl Marx observed that "a spectre [was] haunting Europe,"
frightening governments whether parliamentary or monarchical—
the "spectre of communism." In one of his first public addresses
to the German people after he became chancellor in 1933, Adolf
Hitler proclaimed his intention to destroy what he described as
the vile communist and Marxist agents of the Russian Bolsheviks. War to the death against communists has also been a
staple of the policies of brutal military dictatorships in the
nonindustrial world, countries in which being a well-read student or supporting free speech, trade unionism, and the rights of
the poor have been treated as indicators of membership in or
sympathy for the Communist party. The point is not that
communists are angelic. That a party or movement has been
regularly mistreated by amoral, oligarchic, and repressive regimes does not necessarily make it admirable. But the enemies
of communism have included some of the world's most loveless

states. And the proclaimed crusade against communism created the opening for a broader effort to contain dissent or opposition to official policy. Indeed, in February 1946 FBI officials launched an "educational" campaign to "influence public opinion" about the dangers of communism.

Anticommunism in the cold war United States was a pervasive but heterogeneous phenomenon. The diverse participants and activists in "the crusade" against communist subversion (FBI Assistant Director Louis Nichols described this as "the cause") formed no organized coalition. Not that all anticommunists shared common purposes. President Harry Truman and Democratic party liberals who passed anticommunist legislation could not stomach the House Committee on Un-American Activities (HUAC), whose claim to attention was its ceaseless denunciation and exposure of the Red Menace.[3] And the nation's most admired anticommunist, FBI director J. Edgar Hoover, both cooperated with and monitored the personal and political activities of prominent anticommunist liberals, notably former First Lady Eleanor Roosevelt and Democratic presidential nominee Adlai Stevenson.[4] Wisconsin Senator Joseph McCarthy's broad-gauged and unsubstantiated charges against alleged communists in the highest echelons of the American government at first earned him the covert assistance of the FBI and then, because his actions suggested he had a "pipeline" to the FBI, led Hoover to sever all assistance.[5] There were, then, anticommunists and anticommunists. And they offered a broad and disparate catalogue of reasons for destroying radical influence and containing political dissent in the United States. Yet these diverse and sometimes antagonistic groups and individuals saw eye to eye in their perceptions of the Red Menace and in their goal of exterminating it. They might disagree about tactics, but they were as one in seeking to contain "subversive" activities, however differently they defined them.

Not the least interesting feature of American cold war anti-

communism was the lack of precision in its definition of
subversion. It is not as though there were clearly discernible
communists, communist supporters, and subversives, all of
whom were demonstrably up to no good. Card-carrying members of the American Communist party were without question
Communists. But apart from a small number of well-known
party leaders, very few individuals admitted to membership.
Many people were fingered as Reds by informers before congressional committees; the problem was that this testimony was
never corroborated. Renegade Communists were known to fab-
ricate and to exaggerate Communist party strength, but their
claims were uncritically accepted since only coconspirators
could uncover the scope of the conspiracy. Persons who had
quit the party were still treated as Communists, unless they
turned informer and named names of their fellow members.[6] A
1954 U.S. Army pamphlet, *How to Spot a Communist*, stated
that a communist could be "spotted" by his or her "predisposi-
tion to discuss civil rights, social and religious discrimination,
the immigration laws, [and] antisubversive legislation."[7] Communists supposedly used "such give-away terms as 'chauvinism,' 'book-burning,' 'colonialism,' 'demagogy,' 'witchhunt,'
'reactionary,' 'progressive,' and 'exploitation.'" A security officer from naval intelligence told the newsman Elmer Davis
that "intelligent people are very likely to be attracted to communism." That these notions were pervasive was revealed in a
public opinion poll conducted by the respected Samuel A.
Stouffer. Few Americans said they had ever met a communist,
but they suspected that those "always talking about world
peace," who "read too much, who had an affinity for causes,"
who "brought a lot of foreign-looking people" into their homes,
and who, if they were white, had black friends, were Reds.[8]

U.S. Senate candidate Richard M. Nixon in 1950 equated
communism with liberalism. J. Edgar Hoover and his aides told
the country that a liberal was "inclined favorably to communist

political philosophies." Furthermore, in directing FBI agents to develop a list of individuals who might not be communists but who nonetheless represented a "potential threat in a time of emergency," Hoover cited the case of those who are "in a position to influence others against the national interest." These included, according to Hoover, "writers, lecturers, newsmen, entertainers, and others in the mass media"; and Hoover named the novelist Norman Mailer whom he described as "an admitted 'leftist.' "[9] All Martin Dies, head of HUAC, and screen actor Ronald Reagan, in his capacity as a secret informant to the FBI, needed to know was that someone was in "substantial agreement with the Communists" to be sure that he or she was a Red.[10] By this criterion it was hard to distinguish between communists and what were loosely called fellow travelers. Expert Red-spotters could evidently tell the difference. (They put one in mind of the "Jew inspector" in Max Frisch's play *Andorra* who has an uncanny knack of spotting Jews by the soles of their bare feet.)

The ultimate litmus test was a person's attitude toward the Soviet Union. Uncritical admiration and support of the USSR left no room for doubt that the admirer was a communist. A few individuals, among them Senator Robert A. Taft and the columnist Walter Lippmann, might be free of suspicion, even though they sharply criticized the cold war foreign policy inaugurated by President Truman. But FBI officials, McCarthyites in Congress, conservative journalists, and even the president believed that similar criticism signified that the critic might be an agent or dupe of Soviet communism. Indeed, Hoover feared that Martin Luther King's leadership of a movement to challenge racial segregation was influenced by communists. Opposition to the new anti-Soviet policy as a whole, or to such specific programs as the Marshall Plan, were treated by Truman administration security officials as grounds for questioning an individual's loyalty.[11]

Subversion is defined by Webster as a systematic attempt to overthrow the state. Cold warriors relied on a somewhat less precise definition, describing as subversive any individual or group said to be following the communist line or doing things or publishing books that were helpful to the Soviet Union. Since the USSR, for all its faults, unavoidably did a number of blameless things, it was all too easy to characterize the most unexceptionable behavior as subversive. During the cold war the charge of subversion was leveled cavalierly, even inviting Hoover to attempt to prevent publication of books critical of the FBI.[12]

At the height of the cold war, communists and subversives were denounced as worse than murderers. In view of the seriousness of this charge, the carelessness of the accusations is startling. Yet if respectable authors like Nelson Algren and the publisher Lyle Stuart were the subject of investigation because of their writing and publishing decisions, then every citizen had reason to fear that saying or doing things proscribed by no law, might precipitate FBI and congressional inquiries of his or her subversive activities. Subversion is too nebulous a charge to be flung at Americans who, in exercising their critical faculties, found that their viewpoints on one or more matters either coincided with those of the leaders of a foreign state or were deemed suspect by conservative congressmen, columnists, or FBI officials. The term fellow traveler was similarly flawed, available to stigmatize almost anyone, depending on the mood of the accuser. No less problematic was Martin Dies's notion that "substantial agreement with the Communists" made one a communist.

The advocacy of racial equality, pacifism, or antinuclearism; support of humanitarian and reform causes; criticisms of the FBI or Director Hoover; opposition to the containment policy—these "clues" to communist affiliation say more about the mind-set of those who gave them meaning than about communist sympathies. Even ardent cold warriors knew that some of these movements and ideas, championed as they were by Franklin D. Roosevelt, Wendell Wilkie, Winston Churchill, Mahatma Gandhi, and George F. Kennan, among others, were neither communist nor subversive. For them, anticommunism was a useful tactic to discredit policies and social movements they detested.

No indicator of communism was more unfair than the unwillingness of a former Communist to name the names of fellow party members. Insistence that the ex-Communist inform on his comrades was not evidence of current beliefs or affiliation. It was rather a police measure designed to help the state to persecute political pariahs and denigrate the coerced informer. Even if it were agreed that the state has a justifiable interest in knowing who is a communist, it would remain amoral to compel an innocent person to assist congressional inquisitors in their search for political heretics, holding over the former communist's head the threat that unless he enlists in the inquisition, he will become one of its victims. As Victor Navasky has pointed out, since HUAC already held the names of most of the communists and suspected communists it was after, its real purpose in compelling witnesses to inform was to humiliate them in a "degradation ceremony."[13]

American communists and subversives were more dangerous than common criminals, according to anticommunist crusaders, because of their beliefs and activities. In 1947 J. Edgar Hoover told HUAC that the Communist party was a "fifth column if ever there was one," working tirelessly to overthrow the American government and replace it with a tyranny installed by its Soviet masters. Spokespersons for the Truman administration agreed that American Reds were nothing more than agents and spies for the USSR. The proposed Mundt-Nixon Bill of 1948 called for the registration and what Walter Goodman has described as the effective outlawing of the Communist party because its members were engaged in the criminal activity of attempting to establish a totalitarian dictatorship under Soviet control in the United States. Undeterred by the absence of credible evidence for the accusation, HUAC in 1948 charged that communists had tried to steal American atomic secrets during World War II in order to make them available to the Soviet Union. After the Soviets exploded an atomic device the following year—and did so, according to President Truman, "without anything stolen or copied from us"—an intensive inquiry was launched to identify the Red spies who must have given the secret to the USSR. Then, when later sentencing Julius and Ethel Rosenberg to death in 1951, after a jury found them guilty of conspiring to pass atomic secrets to the Soviet Union, Judge Irving R. Kaufman declared that the evil deed these communists had done was responsible for tens of thousands of American war deaths in Korea and millions of lives that would be lost in the atomic war to come.[14]

While they were allegedly plotting to turn the United States over to the Soviet Union, American communists were simultaneously working to undermine and destroy the American way of life. According to charges made in 1950 by Attorney General J. Howard McGrath, every communist "carries in himself the germs of death for society." The godless tyranny they believed in "will always be a menace to the internal security of the United States." Since Reds were required to do battle with all "God-fearing and freedom-loving men," a "good Communist could [not] be a good American." And these dangerous subversives were everywhere—in factories, offices, butcher shops, on street corners, in private business, and even in public office where they were "undermining our government, plotting to destroy the liberties of every citizen and feverishly trying to aid the Soviet Union." Whatever jobs they held, no matter how seemingly innocuous, communists threatened the nation's security through their efforts to seduce the unwary and the gullible into subversive activity. In pondering whether communists should be permitted to teach, President Dwight Eisenhower mused that "even when teaching mathematics . . . party propagandists could substitute political symbols for apples and oranges." The thought of how they might teach political science, history, or philosophy was too frightful to contemplate.[15]

To achieve their goal of undermining American society, the communist strategy was supposedly to infiltrate important institutions and organizations, manipulating them to serve Soviet purposes. Since Reds were disciplined fanatics, they were prepared to suffer hardship, even physical attack, and when circumstances warranted to mask their sinister objectives as they performed the mundane tasks designed to demonstrate their loyalty to the trade union or other organization they sought to take over. Since their purposes were nefarious, they were always secretive, falsifying their names as well as their intentions. American communists, like the Soviet state they served, were, in J. Edgar Hoover's phrase, masters of deceit.

In pursuing their design, communists might risk life and limb, whether in organizing workers in hotbeds of antiunionism or giving direct physical as well as legal assistance to beleaguered blacks. Undeflected by threatening police presence, they had in fact organized and led demonstrations of the poor and the unemployed in the nation's cities. Everywhere they proclaimed their opposition to social injustice, racism, fascism, and war. But this seemingly praiseworthy behavior was regarded as particularly dangerous as well as deceptive. For as discerning cold warriors knew, the motives of American communists and their unwitting allies were always sinister. Here or abroad, communists were always up to no good. If at times they seemed to behave well, it was always to lull the United States and the Free World into apathy.

American communists were in fact never legion. Even during the Great Depression and the era of the so-called Popular Front, when President Roosevelt recognized the USSR, when Soviet diplomacy supported his call for collective security, and when the role played by American communists in building industrial unions was widely recognized, only once did the party win as many as 100,000 votes for its presidential candidate. As the second Red Scare gathered momentum during the early years of the cold war, and as sympathy for, let alone membership in, the Communist party came to be viewed as treasonable, the party's ranks were decimated. But cold war crusaders were quick to warn that this drastic decline in party numbers by no means diminished the communist threat. For, as Attorney General Tom Clark told the Temporary Commission on Employee Loyalty established by President Truman, "The gravity of the problem should [not] be weighed in the light of numbers, but rather from the viewpoint of the serious threat which even one disloyal person constitutes to the security of the United States." J. Edgar Hoover warned that the drop in communist numbers was significant only to "the ignorant and the apologists and the appeasers of Communism in our country, in minimizing the danger of these subversives in our midst."[16] Evidently concerned that the public might not respond to such a warning, FBI officials launched an "educational" campaign to "influence public opinion" through "available channels," relying on the cooperation of conservative reporters, columnists, and members of Congress to alert the public to the Red Menace.[17]

In sum, the leaders of the anticommunist crusade charged that communist subversives posed an unacceptable threat to American freedom and security, and that their numbers extended beyond formal membership in the Communist party to include ideological sympathizers. Zealots who had sold their souls to the atheistic and tyrannical Soviet state, they were devoted to undermining and destroying American institutions and government. To achieve their goal they would lie, cheat, spy, and commit acts of violence. Communists and their dupes were more dangerous than common criminals because they threatened the life not of this and that individual but of our entire society.

The charges against American communists and "subversives" were not based on credible evidence of criminal conduct (espionage, for example) but on membership in suspect organizations or support for controversial causes. As with some of the justifications American leaders had offered for waging cold war against the Soviet Union, great emphasis was placed on the sinister motives that lurked behind the activities of communists. Most accusations involved no alleged violation of a federal statute—the so-called Hollywood Ten, indicted for contempt of Congress, were employed as writers, actors, or producers in the film industry and could not steal (nor were they so accused) state secrets. Their "crime" was the message of the film they created. The "American way of life" that native Reds were said to threaten is a protean phenomenon that, if treated comprehensively, must include a tradition of sharp dissent, a respect for free speech, and the right—applauded by Thomas Jefferson and Abraham Lincoln—of revolution. Even when taken at face value, the charges against communist subversives do not describe a mortal threat to the United States. It was sufficient that the charges were apparently damning enough to justify extreme measures against the communist threat at home. The comforting evidence of public opinion polls demonstrated that the American people were willing to believe the worst about communists and their alleged fellow travelers.

What many doubtless regarded as the kernel of truth underlying accusations against American communists was the undeniable fact that they were uncritical admirers of the Soviet state. If to cold warriors the Soviets could do no right, to American communists they could do no wrong. Pitilessly realistic in discerning every hint or shadow of a flaw in "bourgeois society," communists were as credulous children in blinding themselves to the enormities of Soviet society. Giving total credence to Bolshevik claims that they were the vanguard of the working class, American Reds could convince themselves that allegations of Soviet wrongdoing and brutality were nothing but lies told by the capitalistic press about the glorious workers' state. If Stalin excoriated Trotskyites as vermin who had betrayed the "toiling masses," American communists thereafter treated "Trotskyite swine" as worse than lepers and murders.

It does not follow, however, that people who admire a foreign state or system, however uncritically, are therefore its agents, working to empower this state to take over their own country and its government. As J. Edgar Hoover knew, treason cannot be inferred from estimates of the likely effect of beliefs and feelings on actions; it must be proven by confirmed factual evidence of treasonable acts. Hoover did know that the Soviet Union provided financial aid to the American Communist party, and that its members acted to advance their own ideologies and those of the Soviets. But treason was another matter. Having closely investigated communist activity in the trade union movement, a modern scholar concludes that "the idea that the Communists were agents of the Soviet Union has no merit."[18]

As the head of an agency that invited the public to give it anonymous information on communist activities, and that filed and reported unverified gossip, Hoover was convinced that communists were spies who stole the American secrets that enabled the Soviet Union to make an atomic bomb several years before our leaders thought they would. In fact, as President Truman had told Secretary of State Edward Stettinius, "there was no precious secret of the atomic bomb." An English scholar reported in 1978 that "there is no documentation in the public record of a direct connection between the American Communist party and espionage during the entire postwar period."[19]

It was Julius and Ethel Rosenberg who were charged with conspiring to transmit to the Soviet Union American secrets of atomic bomb manufacture. Rosenberg had allegedly induced his wife's brother, David Greenglass, to sketch out and describe these secrets for him and for the confessed "Soviet courier," Harry Gold. Although they did not admit to being members of the Communist party, Julius Rosenberg's testimony at their trial left no doubt of his and his wife's great admiration for the Soviet Union. The jury's verdict that the Rosenbergs were guilty, the death sentence pronounced on them by the trial judge Irving Kaufman, and their subsequent electrocution on June 19, 1953, in Sing Sing prison doubtless convinced many Americans that, as prosecutor Irving Saypol told the jury, it was the Rosenbergs' "worship and devotion to the Soviet Union that led them to become traitors" and "party to an agreement to spy and steal from their own country, to serve the interests of a foreign power which today [1951] seeks to wipe us off the face of the earth."

As a result of evidence unearthed only after the passage of the Freedom of Information Act in 1974, we know what the Rosenbergs' jury could not know. Several members of the Supreme Court concluded that the Rosenbergs did not get a fair trial. The case against them was inconclusive, the crucial charges being uncorroborated by evidence. (The heavily edited FBI files, released under the Freedom of Information Act, preclude a definitive resolution of the FBI's role and the Rosenbergs' guilt.) The prosecutor's "inexcusable conduct" in the case was regarded by several Supreme Court justices as warranting a retrial. The presiding judge had worked assiduously behind the scenes to get the case; he told Roy Cohn of the prosecution team *before the trial* that he would impose the death sentence; and he met secretly on several occasions during the

trial with members of the prosecution. When Justice Felix
Frankfurter said he found Judge Kaufman's performance at the
Rosenbergs' trial "despicable," he was unaware of the remarks
later revealed by Cohn and documented in secret FBI files. For
all the FBI's strenuous pretrial publicity alleging that Julius
Rosenberg was the leader of a spy ring working to steal
American atomic and industrial secrets for the Soviet Union, the
prosecution made no such charge at the trial because there was
no supporting legal evidence for it.[20] Judge Kaufman's justification for imposing the death sentence—that the secret the Rosenbergs allegedly conspired to steal was responsible for thousands
of American casualties in the Korean War—throws light on his
mind-set: that the United States was involved in a war to the
death with the Soviet Union, and thus a death sentence was both
proper (given the magnitude of the alleged crime) and a necessary deterrent against future "subversive activities." The evidence of the "atomic conspiracy" itself was less imposing. The
Greenglass sketches, which may or may not have been given to
Harry Gold, were dismissed by our leading atomic scientists as
too inaccurate to be of "any service or value to the Russians in
shortening the time required to develop their nuclear bomb,"
and by General Leslie R. Groves, head of the Manhattan
Project, as having "minor value." Groves and Hoover saw to it
that Groves's damning statement, made to the Atomic Energy
Commission one year after the execution of the Rosenbergs,
was deleted from the published transcript of his testimony.[21]

The charge that communists were out to undermine and
destroy America's way of life was nonetheless useful and
defined the politics of the 1950s and 1960s. This charge was not
simply undocumented but, as reported in a number of recent
studies of party members' behavior by noncommunist scholars,
contradicted by a great weight of evidence. In their work with
industrial workers, farmers, blacks, the poor, and in antifascist
and antiwar organizations, American communists demonstrated

a commitment to the welfare of these groups that has impressed modern scholars as sincere. Far from trying to take over the noncommunist organizations they joined, in many instances communists turned down opportunities to assume control or to divert the activities of these organizations to Communist party purposes. As a number of historians have pointed out, some Americans became communists because they believed in "noble causes"; they did not throw themselves into causes because they were communists. And a great deal of evidence refutes the allegation that, whatever jobs they held, they used them to disseminate communist propaganda. There is no evidence that teachers who had been communists used their positions to teach or advocate communism. Blacklisted Hollywood writers charged with covering up their communist affiliations wrote *Watch on the Rhine, This Gun for Hire, Our Vines Have Tender Grapes, Mr. Smith Goes to Washington, Here Comes Mr. Jordan, Action in the North Atlantic, The Talk of the Town, Thirty Seconds over Tokyo, The Bridge on the River Kwai, High Noon, Friendly Persuasion,* and *Born Free*—not exactly tracts advocating a communist society.[22] Of course, to J. Edgar Hoover and others like him, who regarded liberalism as a stepping-stone to communism, scripts extolling community cooperation, peace, or the courage to stand up to fascistlike bullies were indeed subversive.

The allegation that communists were fanatical zealots who slavishly worshiped at the altar of Marxism-Leninism overlooks the fact that people who chose to join the party did so voluntarily out of a belief, however misguided, that the party was a heroic organization devoted to the welfare of poor and victimized people, and that the Soviet Union was truly a workers' state. They were free to join and they were equally free to leave. And they left in great numbers when they became disillusioned with the party, Marxism, Stalin, or the Soviet Union. Communists were indeed secretive. As the evidence makes clear, they had reason to be, even before the cold war, if they wished to hold on to their jobs and maintain their standing in the community. Furthermore, under the FBI's program COINTELPRO–Communist Party, after 1956 Communist members and leaders were the targets of an FBI campaign of harassment which included attempts to have them fired from even secretarial jobs in the private sector.[23]

The charge that communists' motives were always sinister was clever. Given the impossibility of reading anyone's mind, it could not be disproven. (As an eminent statistician has observed, no methodology exists or is likely ever to exist to explain why anyone does anything.) An American public, conditioned by the crisis of the cold war, was not likely to contest this charge or to think critically about its implications. This accusation speaks forcefully to the intellectual poverty of the anticommunist indictment. If it could not be disproved, neither could it be proved. When analyzed critically it puts communists in an attractive light.

People who work to improve the lot of the underprivileged, and who think that in doing so they are also helping to bring about the Good Society, are nobly motivated no matter how unrealistic their hopes, how flawed their perception of the Good Society. True, if their actions are reprehensible—and there are ideology-free standards for assessing human conduct—they will be rightly condemned. Destroying every Jew in order to purify the human race is loathsome, however sincere the assassins who act on this notion. Risking life and limb to prevent a lynching or to protect a worker who has joined a union is attractively motivated behavior, except perhaps to racists and to people indifferent to the rights and conditions of working people. Correctly assuming that in the fear and hysteria generated by the Red Scare few Americans would subject their accusations to close analysis, anticommunist crusaders led the nation to believe that communists were always guided by evil hopes.

Dr. Johnson once observed that "intentions must be judged from acts."[24] When that sensible standard was invoked, Soviet and American communists came off too well, so cold warriors simply ignored it, substituting their own reading of what was on the communist mind.

The charge that the United States was mortally threatened by the communist party, no matter how small its membership, was probably the most unbelievable element in the anticommunist indictment. Justice Frankfurter proudly asserted the he was "one of those who deems it ignominious to be awed by fear of the puny force of Communist influence in this country."[25] Yet J. Edgar Hoover seriously believed in the communist threat, and so did other high-ranking officials who yearned to educate the American public about it.

The evidence suggests that the Red Menace may have been good politics, but it was essentially a hoax. The American Communist party did have faults galore. It was undemocratically governed, its "democratic centralism" a euphemism for rule by a small elite. It tolerated no internal dissent from policies imposed from the top—"deviation" was the party's word of choice. It treated non-Stalinist Marxists disgustingly. It was both uncritical and abject in its acceptance of Soviet actions, spurious Soviet rationalizations for these actions, and every twist and turn of Soviet policy. But none of this was illegal, none of it was new, none of it was considered threatening before the cold war. And in view of the minuscule numbers and shrinking influence of the party once the U.S. government turned its ideological artillery on world communism, none of it was threatening after the onset of the cold war. But since the government's dire warnings about the Red Menace were increasingly accepted by the American people, the leaders of the anticommunist crusade felt free to mount a frenzied assault on the Great Communist Threat.[26]

*

Private citizens, singly and in groups, conservative reporters and columnists, high government officials, legislative bodies, state governors, executive agencies, and the courts played key roles in promoting the anticommunist crusade. In the process they regularly violated the law, flouted the Constitution, and offended elementary standards of fairness, decency, and morality in their zeal to demonstrate the depth of their hostility to communist subversion. The most disturbing aspect of this campaign involved the FBI's (the nation's preeminent law enforcement agency) indifference to the rule of law. FBI officials authorized (in their own words) "clearly illegal" break-ins, and then devised special records procedures to avoid complying with court-ordered discovery motions and congressional subpoenas. FBI officials also created a separate records system, called JUNE mail, to isolate "sources illegal in nature" from the bureau's central records system. When FBI Director Hoover learned that an agent attending an FBI training school had expressed the "subversive" thought that break-ins were unconstitutional, he ordered the head of the FBI's New York field office to put break-in activities on hold until an investigation established that the agents assigned to the break-in squad were not tainted by this quaint notion.[27]

In 1948 Progressive party members in Illinois were refused police protection despite being shot at, beaten, and victimized by stonings and kidnapings. In South Carolina the murderer of what he called a "nigger-lover" from Henry Wallace's Progressive party was sentenced to all of three years in jail. The governor of Ohio, in refusing to act against a mob that ransacked the home of a Communist party leader, said that "no pattern had been established" and urged the victim to "go back to Russia." In the District of Columbia a man who had invoked the Fifth Amendment was denied a license to sell furniture.

Professional wrestlers in Indiana had to take a loyalty oath. A New York woman was granted an annulment of her marriage "solely on the ground that her husband was a Communist." Federal housing was denied to "subversives" or to those who refused to sign a statement attesting their nonmembership in any organization proscribed by the attorney general. The Department of Health, Education and Welfare not only denied benefits to communists but demanded refunds from them. The Social Security Administration for a time terminated old-age and survivors' insurance benefits to Reds who had made compulsory payments to the program; the Veterans Administration acted similarly toward communists and their "sympathizers." The Hollywood American Legion in 1952 offered a letter of "clearance" only to suspects who agreed to denounce and repudiate all past Communist party or "front" associations; appear before HUAC and make "full public disclosure of past Communist front activities by identifying all those responsible . . ."; join organizations that [were] "actively . . . combating Communism; publicly condemn Soviet imperialism; and promise not to do it again."[28] The Cincinnati National League baseball team demonstrated its Americanism by changing its name from Reds to Redlegs. (All fans know that when the team was formed shortly after the Civil War it took the name Red Stockings. How and why it became the Cincinnati Reds might have been an interesting research problem for HUAC and the FBI.)

In violation of state statutes prohibiting the practice, private corporations maintained blacklists of "subversive" workers. Lockheed Aircraft in 1946 fired eighteen employees for whom it claimed to lack "sufficient proof as to their loyalty." The CIO joined the crusade by expelling communists, as did the AFL. The catalogue of outrages committed against "subversives" is too long to be cited here. It is unsurprising.

An atmosphere of fear and hysteria breeds irrational behavior, infecting even persons of unusual learning, intellect, and reputations for tolerance and liberalism. In a 1951 newspaper column attacking several prominent noncommunist critics of the Red Scare and official cold war policy, Professor Arthur Schlesinger, Jr., conceded that "none of these gentlemen is a Communist." Unfortunately, Schlesinger continued, none of them "objects very much to Communism. They are the Typhoid Marys of the left, bearing the germs of infection even if not suffering obviously from the disease." (The adverb left open the possibility that perhaps secretly they did after all suffer from the "disease.") Schlesinger bemoaned Hollywood's "particularly favorable climate for the spread of communism," and wrote scathingly of the "fellow-travelling, ex-proletarian ... film hacks" there who "refused to own up to their political beliefs before a committee of Congress." He did criticize that committee (HUAC) for its failure to distinguish anticommunist "liberals from fellow-travellers."

Norman Thomas, leader of the American Socialist party, claimed that communists were "either too foolish or too disloyal to democratic ideals to be allowed to teach in our schools." Sidney Hook, earlier a procommunist philosopher, during the Red Scare praised HUAC for "educating the public on the dangers presented by the Soviet fifth column" in America. The liberal Americans for Democratic Action in 1948 published ads in a number of newspapers listing the names of contributors to the Progressive party and names of the organizations to which they belonged. The *New York Times*, after accepting an ad from the Communist party in March 1947, adopted a policy of refusing ads from organizations called subversive by the attorney general. At its national convention in 1949 the National Education Association adopted a report stating that membership in the Communist party "and the accompanying surrender of intellectual integrity, render an individual unfit to discharge the duties of a teacher in this country." Ellen Schrecker has reported the numerous dismissals of professors by the nation's great universities, not for having done anything improper in or out of class but for not answering questions about their beliefs.[29]

Government at all levels joined in the holy war. Sheriffs and local police departments conducted illegal surveillance of suspected subversives, maintained secret files on them, and manhandled and permitted others to manhandle them. In May 1956 the Supreme Court ruled unconstitutional a provision of the New York City charter permitting the summary dismissal of employees who invoked the Fifth Amendment privilege against self-incrimination. Before that decision the city had fired many teachers and other employees. A New York state law of 1949 required public school administrators to investigate every employee and to fire all those who belonged to "subversive organizations" appearing on a list drawn up by the state board of regents. In Maryland a Subversive Activities Act of 1949 called for dissolving and confiscating the property of organizations deemed subversive by a state court. A Massachusetts law of 1951, outlawing the Communist party, called for a three-year prison term for party members and those who knowingly provided it a meeting place. By 1955 more than forty states had criminalized membership in organizations that "advocated violent governmental change."[30]

The most important—because most influential—campaigns against "communist subversion" were directed by agencies of the national government. Before it was stopped by a Supreme Court decision in 1954, the army for years gave less than honorable discharges to "subversives," depriving them of all benefits. Making a soldier culpable were such activities as hiring a lawyer in an automobile liability case who was said to have favored peace with the Soviet Union. Another soldier was accused of having a father who had expressed an open mind about communism. Still another was charged because his mother-in-law was said to be subversive. Nor were such cases atypical.[31] The National Security Agency was a marvelously effective surveillance organization which used state-of-the-art equipment to alert the United States to just about every movement, sound, and event transpiring in the USSR. From 1947 to 1975 its computers recorded every cable sent overseas by Americans. Between 1967 and 1973 it intercepted and distributed to the CIA, the FBI, and other intelligence agencies every communication by the fifteen hundred Americans on its "watch list."[32] Not to be outdone, the Internal Revenue Service kept its own secret "watch list" of about eleven thousand " 'extremists' or radicals." The acuity of the list's compilers is nicely indicated by its inclusion of Joseph Alsop, Shirley MacLaine, U.S. Senators Ernest Gruening and Charles Goodell, Coretta King, and *Playboy* magazine.

The National Security Council was created in 1947 to advise the president on matters relating to the international struggle against Soviet communism. But it too paid attention to the Red Menace at home. One part of "Dropshot," its March 1949 plan for an atomic attack on the Soviet Union, was a section on internal security. It called for "scrutinizing, curtailing, and counteracting to the fullest extent possible, the open and clandestine activities of communists and other subversive groups, whether party members or not." The only thing left to the imagination was whether "fullest extent possible" might mean "with extreme prejudice." A few years later President Eisenhower, after chastising Chief Justice Earl Warren for the Supreme Court's errant ways under his direction, told Warren that he favored killing all communists. That was a mite more dramatic than Ike's 1954 State of the Union message demanding that communists be deprived of citizenship.[33]

The leading roles in the war on subversives, however, were played by HUAC and the FBI, sometimes acting in concert, sometimes independently of each other. A leading student of the two agencies concluded that whatever its official purpose, the actual intent of HUAC "was not to investigate subversive activities but to disseminate information already known to the FBI," information acquired through the bureau's domestic intelligence operations.[34] That the House Committee's performance was bizarre is not surprising in view of its membership. HUAC's first chairman, Martin Dies, who came to hate the New Deal as well as the communism with which he equated it, was widely regarded in Congress as unprincipled and erratic. One committee chairman was sent to federal prison for pocketing salary payments to persons whom he falsely claimed worked in his office. Another was a virulent anti-Semite who charged publicly that almost all Jews—he called them "kikes"—were communists. Two other members were open racists who later joined the John Birch Society. A HUAC staff director was a private consultant to a group seeking to prove that black Americans were genetically inferior.[35] These questionable models of democratic principles pounded the pulpit, warning that our government would survive only if "Christianity remained firm in the hearts of the people" and if we were able to fend off the "four horsemen of autocracy"—communism, Nazism, fascism, and New Dealism. In fact, HUAC focused almost exclusively on the Red Menace. The committee paid many of its witnesses and conceded that it was prepared to "wrongly accuse" innocent persons if necessary.

Critics questioned the legislative purpose of HUAC's activities, and for good reason. Its chief activity was to hold circuslike public hearings designed to put on the public record the names of "subversives" furnished by the FBI and "cooperative witnesses" (information that the committee already had before its hearing), and to destroy the reputations of "unfriendly witnesses" who "pleaded the 5th" rather than turn informer.[36] The near disappearance of the Communist party ultimately induced Congress in 1975 to let HUAC expire. The most interesting explanation of the committee's demise was offered by President Ronald Reagan. It was due, he said, to the power of the Soviet

Union to make it "unfashionable to be anticommunist" in the
United States by the late 1970s.[37]

Even in the 1930s, when G-men were tracking down John
Dillinger and other most-wanted thugs, J. Edgar Hoover directed the FBI to gather information on "subversive activities."
When the cold war transformed the Soviet Union into the
"enemy" of the United States, the agency swiftly turned its
attention to the communist threat. But the FBI did not simply
collect information. Since much of the information it collected
was either illegally obtained or involved noncriminal activity
(homosexuality or infidelity, after all, were not federal offenses), FBI officials soon sought other means to use this
information. Despite claims that FBI files were confidential, in
the 1950s FBI Director Hoover authorized a series of dissemination programs and a formal liaison relationship with the Senate
Internal Security Subcommittee. Having informally provided
information to reporters and columnists since the early 1940s,
Hoover authorized a mass media program in 1956 whereby
derogatory personal and political information on "subversive"
individuals and organizations was leaked to reliable reporters
(reliable because they shared the FBI's agenda and would not
disclose the FBI's assistance). Under another program, the FBI
leaked information about "subversives" to the nation's governors in order to ensure the dismissal of these individuals from
state agencies, notably public universities. Having collected
information on homosexuals since 1937, the FBI disseminated
information on alleged homosexuals to officials in the executive, legislative, and judicial branches and to universities and
police agencies. The FBI's formal liaison program with the
Senate subcommittee was intended to help discredit "subversive" witnesses and publicize the Red Menace. In view of
the dubious nature of the evidence that agents fed into the
bureau's files—raw, hearsay, undocumented, what one historian
calls "fantasies [that] filled millions of pages," dossiers that

"mingled fiction with facts," and agents' own falsehoods and distortions—the disseminated information was equally dubious. The agency depended heavily on—and paid handsomely for— the uncorroborated stories told it by renegade communists, some of whom were notorious perjurers. In a particularly bizarre sequence, Harvey Matusow, one of its chief informers, on whose testimony the FBI had depended heavily in trials of communists, later recanted and confessed to having perjured himself many times as a government witness. The government then proceeded to charge that his confession was perjury! And the FBI and the Senate Internal Security Subcommittee sought to prevent publication of Matusow's book about his suborned perjury. Nor was Matusow the sole recanting perjurer who was so treated.[38]

The catalogue of FBI improprieties and illegal actions during the cold war is substantial. It induced perjury, furnished secret evidence to friendly witnesses, and suppressed evidence embarrassing to the prosecution of "subversives," most brazenly in the cases of the Rosenbergs and Alger Hiss. In the latter case, which became a *cause célèbre*, the bureau helped HUAC, several congressmen, and above all Richard M. Nixon to convince the nation that Hiss, a respected government official, had been a communist spy who had stolen and delivered to the Soviet Union important U.S. strategic secrets. The FBI withheld information from defense attorneys and the court about Whittaker Chambers, Hiss's accuser, including Chambers's homosexuality and testimony to the FBI in 1946 that contradicted his testimony during Hiss's trial. Hoover's men helped in the preparation of Chamber's testimony which was used to secure a conviction.[39]

The bureau blackmailed officials and harassed and sought to discredit radical activists. Agents illegally wiretapped, bugged, opened mail, and broke into homes and offices. They manufactured false letters and other materials designed to embarrass or

destroy its chosen enemies. Among the subversives on whom
the FBI maintained secret files were W. H. Auden, Nelson
Algren, Truman Capote, William Faulkner, Ernest Hemingway,
Sinclair Lewis, Theodore Dreiser, John Steinbeck, Thornton
Wilder, Thomas Wolfe, Tennessee Williams, and other of the
nation's greatest writers.[40] The practice of monitoring political
activists (who may also be writers) continues. In 1956 the FBI
introduced a new departure—COINTELPRO, or counterintelli-
gence programs—to "expose, disrupt, misdirect or otherwise
neutralize" groups and individuals that Hoover found "opposed
to the national interest." The bureau now sent operatives into
left-wing, civil rights, black nationalist, and other organizations
to act as *agents provocateurs*; this included seeking to incite
others to commit violent acts designed to destroy the infiltrated
organizations and in some instances literally to destroy their
leaders. Using the bureau's lavish propaganda apparatus to fill
the press, the airwaves, and movie screens with glowing versions of the FBI's heroic feats, ruining the reputations of its few
critics, and not so incidentally promoting its own image, Hoover
and the FBI rode roughshod over communists, subversives,
radicals, civil rights reformers, and individuals and groups that
incurred the director's wrath. A hint of criticism or a whispered
question about Hoover's sexual proclivities was sufficient to
bring intimidating visits by agents.

The most notorious anticommunist was the junior senator
from Wisconsin, Joseph McCarthy. An opportunist who in 1946
spoke admiringly of Joseph Stalin's sincerity and peaceful
intentions, while condemning politicians who sought to "pick
up votes by attacking Russia," McCarthy shortly discovered the
political gold in anticommunist politics. He did so with a
vengeance. Starting with his famous speech on February 9,
1950, in Wheeling, West Virginia, in which he falsely claimed
to have in his hand the names of 205 known communists in the
State Department, McCarthy went on to make himself the idol

of the anticommunist right, a heroic anticommunist zealot to the American public, and by his bullying tactics an object of fear and ultimately a source of embarrassment to more genteel antisubversives. Holding nothing sacred, McCarthy charged the U.S. Army, General George C. Marshall, President Eisenhower, and lesser lights with playing the communist game. He led a Senate committee whose hearings denounced subversives and those effete types in high places who supposedly were unwitting dupes of the Communist party, and he won the attention of the American public.

McCarthy struck terror in the hearts not only of "subversives." President Eisenhower, in what was not his finest moment, withheld a statement praising his wartime superior, General Marshall, out of fear of provoking McCarthy. The Wisconsin senator induced self-respecting men in the press to hold their tongues, certainly to guard their words. As a *New York Times* editor wrote shortly before McCarthy's star fell, "If McCarthy should drop dead today [December 23, 1953] he would still have worked a fairly profound change in the American intellectual atmosphere that will take us a long time to recover from."[41] These words were prescient. McCarthy did die shortly after he suffered what was in effect his political death when the Senate censured him in 1954. His excesses, his sneering demeanor, the brutality he displayed on national television as he harassed high army officials, the political enemies he made in his reckless charges, the concern he aroused among influential cold war eminences worried that he was giving anticommunism a bad name, and the opportunity he afforded more fastidious cold warriors to display their admirable liberalism by turning on this repulsive figure—all combined to do him in.

McCarthyism may have been publicly reviled by cold war liberals. Yet for all its unique extremism, it captured well the essential recklessness and mendacity of the anticommunist crusade. As a number of modern scholars have shown, McCarthyism was prefigured, some of its most dismaying features anticipated, by the Truman administration.[42]

One is tempted to say that President Truman set the stage for McCarthyism, both by word and by deed. But this would not do justice to the ambiguity of his actions. Distancing himself from the anticommunist lunatic fringe and thus evoking the support of anticommunist liberals, Truman from time to time spoke scathingly of HUAC, of informers such as Chambers and Elizabeth Bentley, of McCarthy, and of all those anticommunist demagogues who spread the false charge that domestic communism posed a serious danger to American security. In 1948 he and his attorney general, Tom Clark, "accused HUAC of irresponsibly attempting to inflate the communist danger for political purposes." The leading student of the Truman administration's treatment of the communist issue at home finds this "a remarkable performance for a president who had relied upon frightening the country with the communist threat during his campaign for foreign aid" a year earlier, and whose attorney general had "cooperated fully with [and] publicly praised [HUAC] for promoting popular concern about domestic communism." Alan Barth, editorial writer for the *Washington Post*, thought it "a little thick to hear [Truman] Administration spokesmen denounce Senator McCarthy for imputing guilt by association" when agencies "operating under presidential order had for two and one half years been condemning men on grounds of 'sympathetic association' with organizations arbitrarily called 'subversive' by the attorney general."[43]

After firing Henry Wallace from his cabinet in the fall of 1946 for opposing the new cold war foreign policy, Truman proceeded to link Wallace and the Progressive party that nominated Wallace for president in 1948 with the Communist party. Truman warned that the Reds and their stooges were "becoming a national danger...a sabotage front for Uncle Joe Stalin." These accusations were based on advice from White House counsel Clark Clifford that the president should red-bait Wallace, his new party, and all critics of the Truman Doctrine and our anti-Soviet foreign policy. (Twelve years later, after Martin Luther King and Roy Wilkins challenged his public statement that communists were "engineering the student sit-downs at lunch counters in the South," Truman conceded that he had no proof for his allegation. "But I knew," he said, "that usually when trouble hits the country the Kremlin is behind it."[44]) In a bravura performance in 1950, Truman in the same speech warned on the one hand of the acute "threat of the [international] communist movement, directed from a central source and committed to the overthrow of democratic institutions throughout the world," and on the other, of the danger of "unwise or excessive security measures" and "undue" restrictions on civil liberties. In a 1946 speech to the Chicago Bar Association, Tom Clark urged lawyers "vigilantly to police their own ranks" by censuring and casting out lawyers who in defending communist clients were doing the devil's work.[45]

The Truman administration's most important contribution to the anticommunist crusade was the president's Executive Order 9835, establishing the Federal Employee Loyalty Program. Issued on March 21, 1947, just nine days after he made his Truman Doctrine speech declaring cold war on international communist subversion, the order compelled roughly two and a half million people to undergo new security checks. It covered federal civil servants, the military, local and state government workers, and industrial workers whose employers had defense contracts with the government. By 1957 the order's proof of loyalty had become more demanding and covered more than ten million people. Disloyalty was defined as "sympathetic association with any organization, association, movement, group or combination of persons designated by the attorney general as totalitarian." In practice this meant that one's past as well as present beliefs, activities, and associations were to be investigated. Appointive security officers, some of whom equated "intellectuals" with subversives, were empowered to make assessments that determined an employee's fate. Presidents Truman and Eisenhower claimed that accused persons had the right to face their accusers, a right they said was honored. The claim was false. Ninety-four percent of the persons dismissed were not confronted by prosecution witnesses. Supreme Court Justice William O. Douglas observed that a "hearing at which the faceless informers are allowed to present their inspired rumors and yet escape . . . cross-examination is not a hearing in the Anglo-American sense." On the basis of what the American Jewish Congress described as the uncorroborated testimony of informers who were "scandalmongers, crackpots, and personal enemies," people were fired for such offenses as signing petitions to place the Progressive party on the ballot; having the "wrong" books in their personal libraries; criticizing monopolies, the Marshall Plan, or the loyalty order itself; and advocating equal rights for "coloreds" or attending interracial meetings.[46]

The most notorious feature of the loyalty order was the power it gave the attorney general to create a list of disloyal or subversive organizations. Membership in or association with any of them was ground for investigation and possible dismissal. Attorney General Clark needed to answer to no one in placing on his list organizations that he found objectionable for any reason. No criteria were stipulated, no opportunity presented for a group to challenge its inclusion on what was treated by the media as a list of subversive organizations. As Clark admitted, such a listing was "a little bit contrary to our usual conception of democratic process." But that gave him little pause. He disseminated the list widely, using it to ruin the reputations of those who reputedly had associated with any of the organizations listed. The stated purpose of the list was to furnish security officers with relevant, not necessarily public, information. Its actual purpose, to judge from the actions of Clark and his successors as attorney general, was to expose, stigmatize, and therefore neutralize organizations critical of the government's cold war policy or the Red Scare. The very existence and reputation of the list also had a salutary effect on the behavior of organizations concerned about their reputations. Indeed, Clark told HUAC that "our strategic objective must be to isolate subversive movements in this country from effective interference with the body politic."[47] Publishing and publicizing the attorney general's list was one way to achieve that objective.

Nothing better illustrates President Truman's motives with regard to Executive Order 9835 than what he said after he promulgated it: "Well, that should take the Communist smear off the Democratic Party!"[48] It didn't quite work out that way. True, HUAC approved of the order, with even the anti-Semite and anti–New Dealer John Rankin joining in the applause. But unrelenting anticommunists in both parties did not let up in what they found to be the profitable political game of denouncing the Truman administration for softness on communism.

Liberal congressional Democrats often expressed their disdain for Senator McCarthy and McCarthyism. Yet such of their stalwarts as Senators Paul H. Douglas of Illinois, Harley M. Kilgore of West Virginia, Frank P. Graham of North Carolina, Herbert H. Lehman of New York, and Estes Kefauver of Tennessee in 1950 proposed a bill that in times of "national emergency" would put subversives in concentration camps and detain without trial anyone in the Communist party after January 1, 1949. Moderates and liberals might hold their noses at HUAC's excesses, but they scarcely flinched from joining in the great witch-hunt. Even before the cold war began, Congress had in 1940 passed the Smith Act, which provided for the deportation of "subversive aliens" and made it a crime "to teach and advocate the overthrow of the United States Government by force and violence." But starting in 1947, when President Truman declared the equivalent of war on international communist subversion, Congress over the next seven years proposed more than fifty anticommunist bills. Laws were passed that some congressmen, including Senator Hubert H. Humphrey of Minnesota, had not even read. Humphrey proposed making Communist party membership a crime.

The Taft-Hartley Act of 1947 prohibited certification of labor unions as bargaining agents with employers until the union officers had filed affidavits that they were not communists. Organized labor, for all its opposition to some of the provisions of the new law, swiftly complied. The CIO, built largely through the efforts of organizers who were communists, soon expelled unions whose opposition to the cold war and whose other actions were too often in accord with communist objectives. The Mundt-Nixon Bill of 1948 (it was never passed) not only called for the registration of the Communist party and "front organizations" named by the attorney general but proposed to make it a crime to attempt to establish in this country a totalitarian government under foreign domination. Since that is precisely what the government accused communists of doing, the bill in effect would have outlawed the party.[49] In 1950 Congress passed the McCarran Internal Security Act which defined the American Communist party as a Soviet-controlled organization "whose purpose it is, by treachery, deceit, infiltration into other groups, espionage, and sabotage, to establish a Communist totalitarian dictatorship" in the United States and throughout the world. Proclaiming that party membership did not constitute per se a crime, the act nevertheless defined as "unlawful" precisely the acts it charged American communists with committing.

The McCarran Act established a subversive activities control board to be appointed by the president, whose five members were empowered to determine which "communist action" and "communist front" organizations were to register with and have their names published by the attorney general. Aliens with dangerous ideas who "displayed" writings advocating communist doctrines, were to be barred from the United States. In practice this kept the country free of visitors who were critical of nuclear weapons, who had traveled in Eastern Europe, who belonged to scientific organizations which had "subversive" members, or who were peace activists. That some of the persons excluded were Nobel laureates or admired artists, writers, and diplomats—noncommunists all—availed them nothing. Supplementing the McCarran Act was Public Law 637, the Communist Control Act, passed four years later by Congress and opposed only by Senator Kefauver. It formally outlawed the Communist party and stripped it of all rights.[50]

It is a modest tribute to the American judiciary that, alone among the three branches of government, in some instances it resisted the anticommunist hysteria. Particularly after the late 1950s the courts asserted that the First and Fifth Amendments were still in effect in the United States. In 1950 the Supreme Court ruled against HUAC's attempt to charge with contempt witnesses who pleaded the Fifth Amendment. And a federal court held that the Justice Department had not been able to justify placing on the attorney general's list a group working for Soviet-American friendship. But also in that year the U.S. Court of Appeals for the District of Columbia ruled that while firing a federal worker in the absence of due process ran "counter to every known precept of fairness to the private individual," it was nevertheless justified by the "present world situation." The Supreme Court upheld the ruling.[51] In a not atypical decision the California Supreme Court in 1955 found Communist party membership "of itself cause for dismissal [since] a Communist employee could be assumed to be dedicated to the 'practice of sabotage.'" There was no single instance of such sabotage, but this was no problem for a court that was obviously unmoved by the Holmesian dictum that the life of the law is not logic but experience. The most important and perhaps the most egregious judicial behavior occurred in the 1949 Smith Act trial of national Communist party leaders, *Dennis et al. v. U.S.*

In 1943 the high court in *Schneiderman v. U.S.* had found that the American Communist party "desired to achieve its purpose" of a socialist America "by peaceful and democratic means." It was "as a theoretical matter" that the party justified the use of force and violence, but only to prevent an attempted forceful overthrow of the government after the party had obtained control in a peaceful manner. That decision upheld Charles Evans Hughes's view that guilt could not be "attributed to the holding of an opinion or to mere intent in the absence of overt acts." But in *Dennis* the Court, now headed by Truman appointee Fred Vinson, found otherwise. The Communist leaders had been accused of violating the Smith Act and had been found guilty by a jury, one of whose members had said before the trial, "I'm going to hang those Commies." The trial had been marked by what Justice Frankfurter later described as unjudicial and biased behavior toward the defendants and their attorneys by the trial judge, Harold Medina. No evidence was adduced that the Communist leaders had advocated the overthrow of the government by force and violence. The judge and jury instead found convincing the inspired testimony of a paid informer and onetime party leader, Louis Budenz, that the Red chieftains spoke "Aesopian language" which masked their illegal intentions. They were not charged with having expressed such intentions, not even in the veiled manner described by Budenz, but rather with having conspired to express them at some future time. As Supreme Court Justice Hugo Black observed, finding people criminal for purportedly planning to publish "certain ideas at a later date" was "a virulent form of prior censorship of speech and press which . . . the First Amendment forbids." But Black's was a dissenting opinion, joined only by Justice William Douglas. The Vinson Court upheld the conviction. And lower courts upheld the convictions of hundreds of lower-echelon party leaders in Smith Act trials marked by bias and perjured testimony.[52]

Black's concluding observations turned out to be prescient. "Public opinion being what it now is," he said, "few will protest the conviction of the Communist petitioners. There is hope, however, that in calmer times, when present pressures, passions and fears subside, this or some later court will restore the First Amendment liberties to the high preferred place where they belong in a free society."[53] When the Warren Court six years later ruled in *Yates v. United States* that advocacy, in order to be criminal under the Smith Act, must be actual advocacy of future illegal action, convictions of state and national Communist party leaders were overturned. But by that time the cold war message had been thoroughly absorbed by the American public. Communism was anathema. Dissent was dangerous.

The cold war Red Scare almost totally wiped out the American Communist party and destroyed whatever influence it might earlier have had. It instilled in the American people a fear both of communism and of saying or doing anything that might be construed as a sign of sympathy for communism or insufficient hostility to it. It fostered conformity and helped create the "silent generation" of the 1950s. It induced respected institutions and their leaders—universities, trade unions, the arts, publishers, the media—to rid their ranks of individuals who only yesterday had been acceptable. These people were banished not because the quality of their work had suddenly deteriorated but because they had committed the sin of attending the wrong meetings, signing the wrong petitions, having the wrong friends. When a government policy was too flagrantly absurd or hateful, critics took pains to proclaim that it had to be opposed in the interests of more effectively waging war on communist subversion. Certainly that was the line taken by many anticommunist liberals in their condemnation of escalating American involvement in Vietnam.

In the civil rights struggle, many activists, particularly among the young, brushed aside the communist issue as irrelevant. Yet Martin Luther King felt compelled to dump an aide who had been a communist. And many supporters of the movement explained that such action was necessary in order to compete successfully with the Soviet Union in the struggle for the "hearts and minds" of men and women between the Free World and the communist world.

In suggesting that criticism of capitalism was a communist game, the Red Scare effectively insulated our economic system and its inequities from the challenges that had been leveled against it by populist reformers for generations. Socialism became a dirty word, antimonopoly faintly suspicious. The crusade created a political atmosphere conducive to the growth of right-wing influence, an atmosphere congenial to the rise of men whose chief claim to prominence was their ability to exploit the nation's fear of communism. It was an atmosphere, too, in which patriotism was misdefined as uncritical approval of government foreign policy actions, no matter how unjustified, illegal, or brutal the actions.

The consequences of the cold war Red Scare, many of which could have been anticipated, throw light on why the United States mounted its campaign against "communist subversion." President Truman's remark that his loyalty order should take "the Communist smear off the Democratic Party" makes clear that his concern was political advantage rather than internal security. Scary rhetoric about the domestic Red Menace doubt-less convinced many people that the threat was real. Most of the men who employed this bombast, however, had every reason to know how insignificant and ever diminishing were communist numbers and influence. They indeed sought to destroy the Communist party and communist influence, to make commu-nism and the prospect of socialist revolution frightening to the American people. But in view of the remote possibility of communist ascendancy in this country, American leaders had other, political objectives when they cried out against the Red Menace. Above all, by stigmatizing criticism of government cold war actions and policy as communist inspired, if not subversive, they sought to discredit such criticism.

To wage cold war successfully abroad, American leaders felt it necessary to stifle criticism of their cold war policy at home. The anticommunist crusade also assured that if war did break out between the U.S. and the USSR, no sounds of criticism would be heard on our shores.

Different members of the anticommunist coalition had diverse axes to grind. The crusade enabled ambitious and amoral men to appeal to the public, to bash not only subversives but also major party opponents for their suspicious lack of zeal in fighting the Red Menace. It enabled champions and apologists for capitalism and inequality to smear reform and reformers as utopian—a charge that laid all visions of the Good Society at the door of the wicked Karl Marx. It permitted those who were particularly strident and unscrupulous to achieve great power as towers of anticommunist rectitude before whom all America trembled. It provided a bonanza to persons who, having once been Commu-nist party members, could now find fame and modest fortune for informing about party activities before congressional commit-tees and to the FBI. Anticommunist liberals evidently hoped to win acceptance by demonstrating that they too sought to destroy hateful communism. The legions of Americans who joined the crusade because they believed what leaders in and out of government told them about the communist threat, did so out of a sense of patriotic duty, combined with a legitimate concern to free themselves from any hint of suspicion about their own loyalty.

The crusade against domestic communist subversion was not what it seemed. It was launched and pursued not because of danger at home but because of the cold war abroad. To extract from the American people massive tax monies and uncritical political support, cold war leaders organized a domestic campaign designed to convince the American public that a menacing fifth column had to be exposed, fought, and exterminated at home. An atmosphere of hysteria and fear was precisely what was needed to assure that America's cold war foreign policy would be spared a critical analysis.

CHAPTER VII

✿

Covert Operations Against International 'Communist Subversion'

THE chief means the United States relied on to wage the cold war against international "communist subversion" was intervention, usually secret, in the affairs of governments throughout the world. The organization responsible for carrying out the great majority of these interventions was the Central Intelligence Agency. And the authority for such interventions did not derive from the legislation creating the CIA but from secret directives issued by presidents.

Although its career has been shrouded in secrecy, a great deal of information about the CIA's behavior has come to light in recent years. Former CIA directors, retired CIA officers, congressional investigating committees, presidential commissions, scholars, journalists, and other writers have presented a mass of evidence on the CIA's actions at home and abroad.[1]

In exploring the significance of the CIA's cold war career, I offer not a comprehensive survey of its history but a discussion of several important questions. They concern the disparity between the tasks assigned the CIA by law and the tasks it actually performed; the behavior of presidents and Congresses in dealing with the agency; its activities in countries and against individuals and groups that were clearly noncommunist; its treatment of American citizens; the effect of its behavior on the constitutional system of checks and balances; and the implications of the CIA's performance for a democratic society.

The CIA was established by the National Security Act that Congress passed in the summer of 1947 and President Truman signed into law. The act replaced the War and Navy departments with the Department of Defense, and created a National Security Council to advise the president on matters relating to "national security," and a Central Intelligence Agency to coordinate and possibly collect foreign intelligence information. In addition to advising the NSC "on matters concerning such intelligence activities... as relate to national security" and making "recommendations to the NSC for the coordination of [the] intelligence activities of various government departments and agencies," the new law called for the CIA to "correlate and evaluate intelligence relating to the national security," to arrange "dissemination of such intelligence within the government," to "perform for the benefit of the existing intelligence agencies additional services" that the NSC determined were "more effectively accomplished centrally," and, finally, "to perform such other functions related to intelligence affecting the national security as the NSC may from time to time direct."[2] There was not one word in the law about covert operations. Allen W. Dulles, in urging creation of a central intelligence agency, had spoken only of the need for a centralized intelligence analysis agency, independent of the service-oriented agencies of the State, War, and Navy departments.

The "other functions" clause was not an elastic provision, empowering the agency to engage in secret operations of any sort. Rather, it confined the CIA to other functions that were related to intelligence. As Smith Simpson of the State Department observed, "If language means anything, that clause authorized the CIA to engage in [additional] intelligence activities"; it "did not mean and was not intended" to justify or cover up clandestine "subversive activity."[3]

When the CIA began almost immediately after its creation to perform actions that bore no relationship to intelligence or intelligence gathering, it did so despite the conclusion of its general counsel, Lawrence Huston, that the National Security Act had not authorized the agency to carry out such operations. Were the agency to do so, Huston pointed out, the president would have to convince Congress to amend the act. Disregarding Huston's advice, the National Security Council at its very first meeting in December 1947 directed the CIA "to undertake a broad range of covert activities to prevent a Communist victory in the [forthcoming] Italian elections," and to finance the creation of a noncommunist trade-union movement in France. In addition, the CIA began a series of psychological warfare operations in Eastern Europe. According to William Colby, a later director of the CIA, the NSC in 1947 had the sudden "stroke of ingenuity" to interpret the "other functions" clause as justification for "the clandestine, subversive operations needed now. The matter was put to Truman. He agreed."[4] Certainly the president raised no objection to the NSC directive of the following June (1948), setting up a covert action organization with what former CIA director Richard Helms's biographer calls the "typically euphemistic name of the Office of Policy Coordination." This authorization defined covert actions as operations related to "propaganda, economic warfare, preventive direct action, including sabotage . . . demolition and evacuation measures; subversion against hostile states, including assistance to underground resistance groups, and support of indigenous anti-Communist elements in threatened countries of the Free World."[5] With the passage of time, presidents and their national security advisers greatly expanded the CIA's repertoire of covert actions.

President Truman soon showed, however, that he had a selective memory. In a nationally syndicated column in 1953 he observed that "the last thing we needed was for the CIA to be seized upon as something akin to a subverting influence in the affairs of other people," thereby "casting a shadow over our historical position." Truman expressed the hope that the CIA be "restored to its original assignment as the intelligence arm of the President and that its operational duties be terminated." Had he somehow forgotten its original assignment to perform those covert operations that would "prevent a Communist victory" in Italy, undercut communist influence in France, and prevent the consolidation of communist regimes in Eastern Europe? Ten years later, after the Bay of Pigs fiasco, Truman complained that the embarrassments "we have experienced are in part attributable to the fact that this quiet intelligence arm of the President had been so removed from its intended role of gathering, coordinating, and disseminating intelligence."[6] One would hardly suspect from these public denunciations that it was Truman who shortly after the CIA was created gave it a "charter to conduct small-scale" covert operations.

What had Congress intended the CIA's role to be? Was it not to be a spy agency confined to analyzing and collecting intelligence? That indeed was the role assigned by the language of the National Security Act. But the agency almost immediately strayed from that limited function to assume an operational rule, and its resort to covert operations derived exclusively from secret NSC directives.

The evidence suggests that in 1947 Congress and the president chose to interpret the law setting up this new executive agency in a way that would hide from public view one of its intended purposes—what many in and out of the agency would later describe as its most important purpose.[7] As Daniel Patrick

Moynihan recently reminded his colleagues in the U.S. Senate, "Intervention in the internal affairs of another nation is a violation of the U.N. Charter, the Charter of the Organization of American States, and is simply a violation of law."[8] Since the CIA's covert operations constituted precisely such illegal intervention, it is understandable that public officials who regularly professed their devotion to the rule of law would feel it impolitic to disclose that they had decided not to seek legislation amending the original statute.

In the post-Watergate age Senator Howard Baker and other influential leaders have taught us to think that the absence of "smoking gun" evidence somehow absolves high officials from blame or legal culpability for illegal acts. The absence—at least to this point—of evidence disclosing that Truman and the Congress might have said, "Let's set up an agency that the people will think deals only with intelligence but which we will see to it performs illegal acts around the earth," leads some to conclude that the president interpreted the "other functions" clause as providing sufficient authority. And the CIA, as some presidential apologists have reminded us, did at times act as a "rogue elephant," going off on its own, embarrassing presidents no end with its strange antics, an agency simply out of control. A concern for secrecy, and a desire to safeguard the president from responsibility for operations that went awry, resulted in a records procedure of "presidential deniability." Those who think it cynical to question these plaintive executive cries of ignorance should be advised that it is the higher cynicism to accept presidential disclaimers that are so self-serving. What could be more cynical than the stipulation which the NSC tacked on to its June 1948 directives describing the scope of CIA covert operations—that these operations should be "so planned and conducted that any United States government responsibility for them is not evident to unauthorized persons and that, if uncovered, the U.S. government can plausibly disclaim any responsibility for them."[9]

This secret admonition by the president's chief advisory body puts one in mind of Shakespearean monarchs carefully refraining from direct calls for the assassination of persons they want out of the way, even as they cry out, "Where are the truly loyal aides who would rid the king of his enemies?" The demand for "plausible deniability" was tacit admission that the president and the NSC knew they were directing and would in the future direct the CIA to take outrageous actions which no decent government could publicly countenance.

Plausible deniability also masked an intent to mislead both Congress and the public, and undermine accountability. Furthermore, what is plausible to some may not be to others. The essential point is that through such a disclaimer, if illegal CIA actions were exposed, the presidents who ordered them could be free of legal responsibility for the criminal behavior. The trick that presidents and their CIA operatives swiftly mastered was to create a network of secret government operatives, ordinary citizens, private organizations, and dummy corporations or CIA-sponsored, -financed, and -manned enterprises whose people would, if caught out, insist on their nongovernmental status. No matter how implausible were such denials, the very assertion of them would suffice to get the president off the hook, legally. In the era of the cold war, accusations of deception could be shrugged off because they could not be proven.

If the CIA's early leaders can be believed, "before 1955 covert operations were approved in a haphazard way," responding to the limited policy goals of the Truman administration. By 1955 covert operations had become part of the presidential arsenal, offering the dual benefit of undermining hostile governments without the risk of public discovery. This required an entirely different setup to ensure that agency proposals complied with the overall policy objectives of the president. Accordingly, in May 1955 President Eisenhower authorized a special NSC group, the 5512 Committee, was set up "to provide final approval for all covert operations which the CIA considered large, important, or sensitive enough to require White House approval."[10] As the Senate committee investigating the CIA later disclosed, the existence of such a group, composed of prominent officials close to the president, was no assurance they would approve or even be cognizant of every CIA operation. But if the agency had a certain leeway, the fact is that the CIA was the operational arm of the executive branch. Whether a president believed in hands-on supervision or in looking the other way, he was responsible for the CIA's actions, no matter his management style. President Richard M. Nixon did not have to participate in secret meetings working out in detail the schemes that would wreck the Chilean economy in the early 1970s. It was enough that he directed his subordinates to make that economy "scream."[11] It did not diminish his responsibility that he left the dirty work to the CIA. Richard Helms had a point when he later said, "It was not the Agency's job to make policy. If you don't like what it did, talk to the men who issued the orders." Helms's biographer rightly observed, "The CIA and its director serve the President alone [and] one could infer pretty accurately what the President wanted by paying attention to what the CIA did."[12] Neither President Truman nor his successors were surprised that the CIA engaged in covert activities nowhere mentioned in U.S. law.

Nothing in Congress's behavior at the time it passed the National Security Act in 1947 or afterward indicated any awareness that the CIA was more than an espionage agency. In 1949 Congress exempted the agency from federal laws regarding disclosure of its personnel and their titles, functions, and salaries. The stated rationale reflected an appreciation of the need for espionage, not covert operations. The 1949 act gave the CIA director what leading scholarly authorities on the agency call the "staggering and unprecedented power to spend money without regard to the provisions of law and regulations relating to the expenditure of government funds. It granted him the unique right to spend the hundreds of millions of dollars in his secret annual budget simply by signing his name." He could also bring one hundred aliens secretly into the country, "outside of the immigration laws."[13] The CIA budget was made so secret that not even Dean Rusk, when he was secretary of state and a statutory member of the NSC, ever saw it. That privilege was confined to the president and "two or three specially cleared people in the Bureau of the Budget."[14] Congressional willingness to permit the CIA huge secret expenditures, like congressional authorization permitting the director of intelligence secretly to bring Nazi war criminals into the country, invited presidents to rely more and more on covert operations, confident that Congress as a body (and not simply a reliable minority who would support the president) could not monitor questionable CIA operations. Indeed, when he opposed legislation designed to create a joint congressional oversight committee in 1956, Senator Leverett Saltonstall first claimed that the Armed Services Committee already provided sufficient oversight. Then he described the nature of that oversight: "It is not a question on the part of CIA officials to speak to [the Armed Services Committee] ... [but] our reluctance ... to seek information and subjects which I personally, as a member of Congress and as a citizen, would rather not have."

In its report on the CIA's illegal covert operations within the United States, however, the Rockefeller Commission in 1975 concluded that "while Congress [had] established special procedures for review of the CIA and its secret budget," the CIA had not as a general rule received detailed scrutiny by the Congress, apparently because members of the subcommittee charged with the review had "many other demands on their time."[15] If the commission's explanation for congressional nonscrutiny was charitable, its conclusion was unassailable. For the very congressional leaders who were chiefly responsible for oversight of the CIA had adopted the stance, "in effect, 'we don't watch the dog. We don't know what's going on, and furthermore, we don't want to know.' "[16] Even after revelations of CIA abuses in 1975–1976, Stansfield Turner, who was appointed by President Jimmy Carter to be director of the CIA, "had not even been obligated to report all its covert operations" to Congress and in fact reported very few of them. Congress's sole reform, instituted in 1974 and then modified in 1980, simply required the president to certify to congressional committees that CIA covert operations were consistent with national security interests. This requirement of written findings did not, however, call for notification "prior" to the proposed covert operation, only that such notification be "timely." Not surprisingly, when he authorized the sale of arms to the fundamentalist government in Iran in January 1986, President Ronald Reagan decided not to notify the House and Senate intelligence committees, as required by the 1980 Intelligence Oversight Act.[17] Such was the norm. When senatorial mavericks like Mike Mansfield in 1955 or Eugene McCarthy eleven years later attempted to push through measures providing real congressional oversight of the CIA, presidential and agency opposition helped induce the Senate to reject these attempts by margins of better than two to one.[18] It seems no accident that the very senators whom the Senate designated to oversee the CIA were almost invariably disinclined to exercise such oversight, preferring rather to let the agency go its own way, unrestrained by Congress.

Senator John Stennis, who in the early 1970s was chairman of the Senate committee for CIA oversight, confessed, "You have to make up your mind that we are going to have an intelligence agency and protect it as such, and shut your eyes some and take what is coming." In view of this attitude, shared by Senator John L. McClellan who headed another committee

charged with the oversight function, it was no wonder that CIA
director William Colby praised them for "faithfully and patrioti-
cally protecting the CIA from public prying."[19] Before Watergate, Senator Richard Russell had been chairman of the Senate
Armed Services Committee which, together with McClellan's
appropriations committee, had "oversight authority" over the
CIA. He had very great power over the agency but he exercised
that power to "preserve the security and autonomy of the
CIA." Since he told the CIA director that "there were certain
CIA operations he'd rather not even know about," it is scarcely
surprising that Russell helped quash congressional attempts to
institute real oversight of the agency. Senator Henry ("Scoop")
Jackson, who in 1973 used his great influence to deflect an
investigation of the CIA by a Senate foreign relations subcommittee, doubtless spoke not for himself alone when he "report-
edly made the comment that in his view the CIA Oversight
Committee had the responsibility of protecting the CIA."[20]

    Before Watergate, Congress "neither knew nor wanted to
know" what the CIA was up to. Many congressmen of course
knew what readers of the public press knew, but had no way of
knowing whether in Cuba and Central America, and in Chile,
the Congo, Iran, and elsewhere, the CIA and other agencies of
the United States government had engaged in hostile acts
against foreign states with which the United States was at peace.
Just as "plausible deniability" might provide a formal shield of
alleged noninvolvement by the executive branch in operations of
its choosing, so congressional ignorance of the specific details
of CIA operations could provide a shield of congressional
innocence regarding CIA actions that went awry or were flagrantly illegal. Theoretically responsible for overseeing the
behavior of an agency it had created to perform intelligence
activities for the nation, Congress chose rather not to perform
this duty—and to encourage the CIA to get away with murder.
When the Senate voted 68 to 17 at the time of Watergate to

defeat a bill that would have "forbidden the CIA any function beyond pure intelligence," it demonstrated its continuing approval of CIA covert operations.[21]

The public revelations of President Nixon's misuse of the intelligence agencies to serve his own political purposes compelled Congress to take some action, if only to assure public opinion that the legislative branch was prepared to prevent similar future misdeeds. The Senate Select Intelligence Committee, headed by Frank Church of Idaho, set out to discover, among other concerns, why the United States had mounted covert action programs; what roles had been played by the different intelligence agencies in conducting covert operations and how presidents had overseen them; whether the operations were lawful or had violated the "rights of Americans"; and whether the national interest justified the actions that had been taken. The committee's final report, based on an "extensive review of documents" and testimony, provided invaluable chapter and verse on the CIA's activities (as well as those of the FBI and the NSC). But even as it conducted its investigation and prepared its findings, the Church Committee disappointed those in the Senate and elsewhere who hoped for a tough critical appraisal of CIA misbehavior. It did not explicitly ask whether the CIA's actions were ethical and legal, and whether the president alone should authorize covert operations to destabilize and overthrow foreign governments. Liberal Democratic senators on the committee, Walter Mondale, Philip Hart, and Gary Hart, were critical of its final report for giving too much ground to the "ridiculous demands" of the White House. Nonetheless, the committee decided not to promote legislation to prohibit the recurrence of these abuses; instead it chose tighter congressional oversight. Even this limited goal was set aside owing to the demands of the 1976 presidential campaign (and Church's last-minute but unsuccessful candidacy for the Democratic presidential nomination). Not even CIA director William Colby could dissent from the committee's conclusion that "the United States should maintain the capability to react through covert action [in] extraordinary circumstances involving grave threats to American security."[22] And reflecting Congress's continued acquiescence to "national security" considerations, the House of Representatives voted in January 1976 not to make public the findings of its intelligence committee, findings sharply critical of the CIA's illegal operations.

The chief legislative result of the Church Committee's investigation of the CIA was the creation of permanent oversight committees by both houses of Congress. Then, in 1980, Congress enacted the Intelligence Oversight Act, requiring the president to authorize in writing all major covert operations and in "timely" fashion to notify the Senate and House Intelligence committees of this decision. While the act called for fuller and more regular disclosure of particular covert actions by the executive to the Congress, as well as closer collaboration between the two branches, in practice little changed. Ex-CIA heads Colby and Stansfield Turner applauded the post-Watergate oversights for actually strengthening the CIA.[23] After Watergate, as before, few Congressmen knew or wanted to know what the CIA was secretly doing, while those charged with oversight continued to act more like protectors than overseers of CIA behavior. In 1981 Barry Goldwater assumed the chairmanship of the Senate oversight committee, following Republican victories in the 1980 Senate races, and based his oversight action on the stated belief: "I don't think it's any of our business." But since oversight of sorts there had to be, Goldwater appointed as his staff director a former high-ranking CIA official. The former staff director of the House subcommittee on oversight said of the appointment, "With [Senator Goldwater] as chairman of the Senate Intelligence Committee holding the door, the fox suddenly found himself in the henhouse. The CIA had achieved one of its more notable penetrations."[24] After serving as vice-chairman of the Senate committee from 1981 through 1984, Senator Daniel Patrick Moynihan concluded that "the CIA got what it wanted." Most of his colleagues agreed with him that the Senate oversight committee "came to be an advocate for the agency it was overseeing."[25]

The 1980 modification of the Hughes-Ryan Act of 1974 reveals how disinclined Congress was to have too many of its members know too much about clandestine CIA operations. The number of senators and representatives to be briefed under the Intelligence Oversight Act was reduced from about sixty to fewer than forty in the Senate and House oversight committees. Under what a president might declare were "extraordinary circumstances affecting vital interests of the United States," briefing could be confined to eight congressional leaders. And if a president decided that his constitutional prerogatives might be violated or the protection of "sources and methods" jeopardized, he need not inform Congress in advance of his authorization for covert action. Where a president chose not to give prior notice to Congress, all he needed to do was "submit a separate statement explaining why he considered the delay essential to national security."[26]

The record of congressional performance does not speak with crystal clarity. Some congressmen were strongly opposed to covert operations. And yet the evidence is clear enough. For more than twenty-five years after it established the CIA, Congress chose to avoid inquiring into the agency's clandestine operations. The congressional performance suggests that Congress approved the principle that the CIA should engage in covert operations of the president's choosing.

As to what Congress had in mind when it passed the National Security Act, its behavior immediately after President Truman signed the bill into law leaves the distinct impression that Congress approved what came after, though it may not have known what was coming. The notion that the CIA's covert operations were the result of a serendipitous "sudden stroke of ingenuity" that opened the eyes of the agency's leaders only after it was created—*immediately* after it was created—is not terribly persuasive. As CIA directors were fond of saying, the agency did not think for itself. It did not make policy. It did what it was told. The NSC, to which the CIA was directly responsible, gave it the order first to engage in covert actions in Italy, France, and Eastern Europe, and subsequently to continue them around the globe. The NSC at its very first meeting could speak so unhesitatingly as it did, ordering the CIA to perform acts nowhere authorized in the National Security Act, because it knew its directive had the approval of the president.

Since the CIA also performed intelligence functions, precisely as the 1947 law required it to do, it is not quite appropriate to charge that the National Security Act was written to be broken. But in mounting dramatic and drastic programs not mentioned in that act, the agency's subsequent actions revealed that the leaders of the United States government had engaged in a covert operation of their own.

The Church Committee had also concluded that "CIA intelligence was not serving the purpose for which the organization had been created—informing and influencing policymaking."[27] The indictment does not do justice to the agency. The CIA's intelligence reports were at times brushed aside because the facts they revealed were uncongenial or even embarrassing to presidential administrations, but this was hardly the fault of the agency. By one means or another, CIA agents did obtain sensitive information about Soviet political, economic, and military plans—true intelligence. At least some CIA reports simply followed the facts wherever they led, even contradicting inaccurate presidential assertions about such matters as Soviet military and nuclear weapons strength. The agency's findings more than once refuted President Reagan's charges of Soviet violations of nuclear weapons treaties. Yet, more revealingly, CIA director George Bush agreed to appoint "Team B" after "Team A's" report on Soviet military capacity and intentions was so disappointing to American hawks. Director Colby's boast that American intelligence was "comprehensive enough to assure that we catch the Soviets at any attempt" to achieve nuclear superiority by cheating on arms agreements was well founded (though it was the intelligence activities of the Defense Department and above all of the National Security Agency that were primarily responsible).[28] A problem was that CIA intelligence was not always what it seemed.

Just as the FBI's "investigations" often produced inaccurate information, so-called CIA intelligence was not always the accurate information that true intelligence must be. Rather it was uncorroborated surmise which seemingly confirmed the preconceptions of White House policymakers. A longtime CIA officer charged that rather than report facts about the Third World that were at odds with a president's propaganda line, the agency "broadcasts false propaganda" that "transforms reality" to fit preconceptions shaped by the cold war. Given the difficulty of piercing the closed society of the Kremlin, much "low-level information collected by CIA officials was second or third hand" and therefore of doubtful reliability. So an "analyst could make of it just about anything he wanted to," exaggerating or downgrading the Soviet threat, depending on whatever distortion was given by high-level officials in the agency and the White House.[29] However the CIA's mixed intelligence performance is assessed, from the 1950s through the 1970s its chief activity was covert operations. As director Richard Helms's biographer has reported, the agency and its director not only "serve the President alone," but the CIA is the "docile tool of violence which allowed American presidents to engage in acts of gross intervention and even of war, free of the restraints imposed by the Constitution."[30]

The CIA's current notoriety stems from the revelations about its covert operations in foreign countries. But in violation of its charter and at least since 1953, it also began to engage in covert actions at home and against American citizens in the United States. To help carry out its underground activities, the agency used part of its mysterious budget to recruit and subsidize American as well as foreign individuals and organizations. These included banks and industrial corporations, publishing houses, newspapers and magazines, journalists and writers, colleges and universities, intellectuals and scholarly researchers, students and student organizations, trade unions, and leaders of the women's rights and other important movements. Those who accepted CIA monies in effect agreed to render services to the agency in return. Such transactions were kept secret because the CIA obviously sought to use its grantees as a cover. And the recipients of such funds sought, understandably, to keep the relationship secret. Scholars and writers, whose proper function is to report truths about whatever topics they treat, including the behavior of their own government and its agencies, compromised themselves by agreeing in effect to refrain from speaking truth about the piper who paid them. As the anticommunist authors of an admired text on the agency—which they called the "invisible government"—observed, "the liaison between the universities and the CIA" raised questions about "the intellectual objectivity of American scholars."[31]

The Church Committee investigation disclosed that hundreds of universities and individual professors had collaborated with and performed clandestine services for the CIA. The nation's preeminent universities, including Harvard, Yale, Columbia, Georgetown, MIT, and Michigan State, helped the agency recruit American and foreign students to become agents, collaborated with CIA officers, published foreign policy studies propagating the CIA line, trained the South Vietnamese and other nations' police in "internal security," and performed various undercover missions.[32] The eminent anticommunist political scientist Hans J. Morgenthau charged that "by making it appear that the voice of government were the voice of truth," scholars who worked secretly for the CIA were committing a "treason of the intellectuals" that did inestimable harm to the nation.[33]

In what the Church Committee called "an attempt to lay an intellectual foundation for anti-Communism around the world," the CIA sponsored seminars by speakers from the Christian Anti-Communist Crusade and the John Birch Society and subsidized thousands of books and publications. If Praeger was essentially a CIA publishing house, Doubleday also bowed to CIA demands. The agency successfully pressured a bureau chief of *Time* magazine in 1965 to prevent a cover story on *The Invisible Government*, the book by David Wise and Thomas B. Ross that laid bare some of the CIA's covert operations. A CIA agent became an editor of *Encounter*, the British journal of anticommunist intellectuals, and another became publisher of the liberal *New Republic*. The mighty *New York Times* several times played the CIA's game. On one occasion the agency induced Arthur Hays Sulzberger, publisher of the *Times*, to keep its correspondent in Central America, Sidney Gruson, out of Guatemala until after the CIA had helped overthrow the Arbenz government in that country. Later the agency prevailed on the *Times*'s reporter Seymour Hersh to defer to CIA director Colby's request that he neither write nor speak of what he knew about a "deep-ocean CIA project." When Thomas Jefferson said better a press and no government than a government and no press, he of course had in mind a press that was independent of government, honest and fearless enough to report and condemn government's misdeeds. The third president would have turned over in his grave at the information reported by Carl Bernstein in 1977 that more than 810 American journalists had secretly carried out assignments for the CIA.[34]

In addition to using for its purposes such diverse institutions and individuals as the Mafia, Gloria Steinem, First National City Bank, Grace Shipping Lines, George Meany, Walter Reuther and Irving Brown of the AFL-CIO, missionaries and religious leaders, ITT, Pan American, and Chase National Bank, the CIA secretly set up its own supposedly private companies.[35] Wise and Ross reported a quarter of a century ago, "Overseas the CIA operates principally under embassy cover and commercial cover. In several corners of the world, the CIA operates what appear to be small business concerns but which are really covers." And in the United States, too, the CIA was "deeply involved in many diverse, clandestine activities . . . in at least twenty metropolitan areas . . . appear[ing] in many guises and under many names. . . . On university campuses and in the great urban centers of America, the foundation, the cultural committee, the emigré group, the Cuban exile organization, the foreign-affairs research center, the distinguished publishing house specializing in books about Russia, the steamship company, the innocent-looking consulting firm," served as arms of the invisible government.[36]

From 1967 to 1973, under its code name Operation CHAOS program, the CIA engaged in covert operations against hundreds of thousands of American citizens, operations that violated the National Security Act's ban against CIA "internal operations."[37] Responding to revelations early in the second Nixon administration that had raised public suspicions of these agency transgressions, CIA director James R. Schlesinger in May 1973 directed CIA employees to "come forward with anything the CIA might have done which exceeded the limits of the Agency's charge." This order and other congressional investigations revealed the range of the agency's domestic activities: secret drug-testing programs, involvement in the Nixon administration's illegal domestic intelligence plan, "training programs for local police departments," a "program to recruit counter-intelligence agents, . . . the mail interception program," a burglary, bugging of American journalists, and improper "contacts with the Watergate burglary team." Even more questionable overseas activities were publicized, including "involvement in assassination plots against Trujillo, Diem, and Castro," as well as Congolese leader Patrice Lumumba and Chilean general Rene Schneider.[38] The public was put on notice of illegal CIA activities at home by Seymour Hersh's story in the *New York Times* on December 22, 1974. The three-column front-page headline read, "Huge CIA Operation Reported in U.S. Against Anti-War Forces, Other Dissidents in Nixon Years," and the story that followed attributed its allegations to "well-placed government sources." CIA director Colby at first called Hersh's revelations a "distorted concocting of partial truths." But the follow-up congressional and presidential (Rockefeller Commission) investigation confirmed that the agency had indeed violated its charter and had committed an even wider range of offenses against American citizens in the United States than Hersh had reported.

The Rockefeller Commission, in its report on CIA activities within the United States, began by ticking off the initial "public charges" against the agency. These included "large-scale spying on American citizens in the U.S. . . . , keeping dossiers on large numbers of American citizens, aiming these activities at Americans who have expressed their disagreement with various government policies." They were "supplemented by [other charges], including allegations that the CIA had intercepted and opened personal mail in the United States for twenty years; had infiltrated dissident groups and otherwise intervened in domestic matters; had engaged in illegal wiretaps and break-ins and had improperly assisted other government agencies" in such violations.

Although the Rockefeller Commission had no objection to the

CIA accumulating an "information base on domestic dissident activities in order to assess fairly whether the activities had foreign connections," it did conclude that the CIA's Operation CHAOS was "improper" because it "exceeded what was reasonably required to make such an assessment." More disturbing was the fact that the CIA's own memoranda indicated it knew that "its activities were improprieties." Beginning in 1967 and continuing at an accelerating rate during the years of the Nixon administration, the CIA created secret dossiers on thousands of American citizens at home and abroad as its agents infiltrated "dissident" organizations. The agency's files contained the names of more than 300,000 individuals and organizations, all entered into a computerized index.[39]

In the careful language of the Rockefeller Commission, the CIA's cooperation with the Nixon administration's invasion of Daniel Ellsberg's privacy, after he revealed the "Pentagon Papers" on the Vietnam War, "was not related to the performance by the Agency of its authorized intelligence function and was therefore improper." So was its assistance to former CIA agent, White House consultant, and Watergate conspirator E. Howard Hunt, and its failure to cooperate fully with ongoing investigations following Watergate.[40]

In its own more thorough investigation, the Church Committee found that the CIA had created a secret "computer bank" of 1.5 million names from its illegal program, begun in 1953, of opening the letters and otherwise tampering with the mails of American citizens. In the years 1972–1973 alone the agency opened and photographed millions of items of mail between the U.S. and the Soviet Union. Although since 1958 the FBI had known of these violations, and CIA officials were well aware of the criminal nature of their mail tampering, the program continued at least until 1973. Those victimized included congressmen, religious leaders, even a president (ironically, Richard Nixon), as well as peace activists and those who corresponded with the "wrong" countries. The Rockefeller Commission also uncovered instances of illegal CIA physical surveillance of Americans, including wiretaps, buggings, and improper use of tax records. According to CIA director Richard Helms, when President Johnson was told about the mail interception program "and some other things that were going on," Johnson "just nodded and said something along the line of, 'but be careful, don't get caught.' "[41]

Among the CIA's diverse clandestine surveillance of American citizens, close tabs were kept on Bernard Gwertzman of the *New York Times* and other investigative reporters, purportedly to uncover leaks of sensitive intelligence material. While Director Colby thought "this operation not patently illegal," he did expect that a "political uproar would embroil the CIA if this operation were ever exposed." Even though the CIA's "own analysts had concluded repeatedly that anti-[Vietnam] war activists and other domestic protesters were free of foreign control," the agency lent itself to Nixon's wish "to know what his domestic opponents were up to so that he might anticipate, harass, frustrate, and discredit them," and it expanded and refined the CHAOS program, started in 1967 during Johnson's presidency, "to break an opposition which Nixon found inconvenient."[42]

The CIA subjected hundreds of unwitting Americans to experiments with a variety of drugs. The Rockefeller Commission described as "clearly illegal" the CIA's administration in the 1950s of LSD to "persons who were unaware that they were being tested." But this commission, so sympathetic to the agency's mission, found that only "a few" of the CIA's drug activities were "improper or questionable," that after the inspector general's "discovery of these events" in 1963, "new stringent criteria were issued" and ostensibly followed, "prohibiting drug testing by the CIA on unknowing persons."[43] In congressional testimony in 1975, CIA officials claimed that all drug testing programs had been ended in 1967. But in the 1970s CIA agents were spiriting men away from bars and experimenting on them with various drugs. The agency failed to give the Church Commission this evidence because it had been conveniently destroyed. In 1977, however, the agency managed to uncover evidence showing that the scope of this program was far greater than the characterization provided to the Church Committee. The committee did discover that one CIA drug experiment on an unwitting subject had resulted in the man's death, covered up by the agency. And the CIA admitted to the Senate committee "that it had conducted drug experiments on hundreds of unwitting American citizens by hiring prostitutes to lure them into apartments, feed them drugs and seduce them so their activities could be filmed secretly for later viewing by pseudoscientists of the CIA's Office of Technical Services."[44]

Despite the Rockefeller Commission's assurance that such "improper invasions upon the rights of Americans" would not be "permitted to happen again" by the nation's political leaders,[45] they did happen again. President Reagan's December 4, 1981, Executive Order 12333, entitled "United States Intelligence Activities," had the effect, according to a longtime CIA agent, of giving the agency "the right to conduct its illegal operations in the United States." Reagan's followup Executive Order 12356 of April 2, 1982, entitled "National Security Information," "limited the public's access to government documents, thereby increasing the CIA's ability to hide from public scrutiny" its illegal behavior in the United States and abroad.[46] Congress acquiesced in this new departure, exempting the agency's "operational files" from the disclosure provisions of the Freedom of Information Act. As the *New York Times* observed, the new authority granted the CIA opened the door to "intrusive intelligence activities in the United States." Without identifying themselves, CIA agents could now interview Americans about their foreign travel, order physical surveillance of

Americans abroad, authorize covert actions in the United States, and open without warrant the mails of selected Americans.[47]

The CIA's covert domestic operations against citizens of course violated the laws and the Constitution of the United States. That the agency's illegal activities had in many cases been directed, tolerated, and then unreported by presidents of the United States indicates that our chief executives have not lived up to their responsibilities under the Constitution. That Congress also made no attempt before 1975 to uncover such CIA and presidential malfeasance points to the disconcerting conclusion that the executive and legislative branches of the United States government were indifferent to the agency's lawless secret actions against American citizens. In recommending no punishment for what it admitted were the CIA's many illegal assaults on the rights of Americans, the Rockefeller Commission fulfilled the prediction of skeptics that a body composed mainly of friends of the CIA would whitewash the agency. According to CIA director Colby, after his "second or third appearance [before the commission], Vice-President [Nelson] Rockefeller drew [him] aside into his office and said in his most charming manner: 'Bill, do you really have to present all this material to us? . . . Nobody here is going to take it amiss if you feel that there are some questions you can't answer quite as fully as you seem to think you have to.' " Colby interpreted the commission chairman's comments to mean that "Rockefeller would much prefer [me] to take the traditional stance of . . . drawing the cloak of secrecy around the Agency in the name of national security."[48]

The CIA's major efforts, in any event, were devoted to the outside world. The Church Committee reported that between 1961 and 1965 the agency conducted several thousand covert-action projects through which it "developed a worldwide infrastructure of individual agents or networks of agents in a variety of covert" activities. CIA operations were indeed worldwide, performed in countries hostile, neutral, and friendly. For even if a foreign country was "freedom-loving" or at least anticommunist, there was no assurance it would remain so, and its citizens might support policies detrimental to U.S. interests. Neutral or nonaligned nations could, if neglected, fall into the enemy camp. And governments sympathetic to the Soviet Union were an unacceptable threat to American freedom and security and were therefore priority targets of CIA penetration. The catalogue of countries receiving CIA "attention" therefore ranges over all the continents. A partial list includes Germany, the Soviet Union and its East European satellites, Korea, the Chinese People's Republic, Taiwan, Vietnam, Cambodia, Laos, Thailand, Sudan, Egypt, Syria, Burma, Indonesia, Pakistan, Afghanistan, Iraq, Cuba, Guatemala, Nicaragua, Costa Rica, Honduras, El Salvador, Guyana, Jamaica, the Dominican Republic, Zaire, Ghana, Iran, Chile, Greece, Brazil, and Angola. And of course the CIA did more than set up an infrastructure or network of agents. The range of its covert operations was impressively wide and fascinatingly amoral.

Among its ventures the CIA, in close cooperation with military intelligence, protected and covered up for Nazi war criminals who had been responsible for wiping out entire Jewish communities in the Soviet Union. Intent on using Nazi officers for spying and sabotage operations in the USSR and in Eastern Europe, CIA and other American officials lied about and falsified the records of Nazi officers, spirited them into the United States—in at least one case in the uniform of an American officer—and by conferring citizenship on some of them, made them "virtually immune from deportation." Nazi and other U.S. agents sent into the Soviet Union to commit sabotage suffered what our ambassador to the USSR called "an enormous fatality rate," but this did not discourage the agency from continuing the project. During the years of the Truman administration, what one investigator calls the CIA's "private army" of Nazi war criminals from Belorussia and Eastern Europe launched an undeclared war against the Soviet Union. Under Eisenhower the agency authorized uprisings in all the cities of the USSR and Eastern Europe and had the president's approval for detailed plans to seize strategic buildings, overpower Soviet garrisons, blow up roads, bridges, and rail lines, and overthrow the Soviet state. Explaining why incontrovertible evidence of participation in Nazi war crimes was not regarded as "derogatory information," one CIA official recently said that since "Nazism was regarded as anti-communist... information that a person was a Nazi was not derogatory."[49]

Nor did CIA officials have compunctions about dealing with drug kingpins and overloads. Since the CIA "valued the intelligence [on leftist organizations] that drug dealers could collect," it kept secret the identities and Latin American connections of leaders in the heroin and cocaine traffic. The authoritative account of the "politics of heroin" in Southeast Asia reports that, "practicing a ruthless form of clandestine *realpolitik*, [CIA] agents made alliances with any local group willing... to stem the flow of 'Communist aggression.'... American diplomats and agents have been involved in the narcotic trade at three levels:... allying with groups actively engaged in the drug traffic; abetting the traffic by covering up for known heroin traffickers...; and active engagement in transport of opium and heroin. It is ironic," the author concluded, "that America's heroin plague is of its own making."[50]

The CIA had access to massive funds which permitted secret expenditures that Congress neither regulated nor wished to know of. This made bribery one of the CIA's most important tools, not only for buying valuable intelligence but for inducing foreign nationals and political leaders to promote American

objectives. In 1958 the agency offered President Miguel Ydigoras Fuentes a half-million American dollars cash if he would
withdraw as a candidate for president of Guatemala. Ydigoras,
who later permitted the CIA to use his country for a secret
training area for the Cuban exiles who were to attack the Bay of
Pigs, admitted this on national television. Thirteen years later
the U.S. offered General Du-ong Van ("Big") Minh three
million dollars, in this instance to remain on the ballot as a
candidate for the presidency of South Vietnam, so that we could
say that the agency favorite, Nguyen Van Thieu, had not won
without a fight. CIA director Colby tells how in the early days
of the cold war he was authorized "to fill the back seat of [his]
Fiat with millions of lire and pass them on to Italian voters
through his 'outside agent,' an ostensible student." Five years
later American money was dispensed freely to recruit mobs to
demonstrate against the Mossadegh government in Iran. Gamal
Abdel Nasser, Egypt's leader, was given three million dollars in
a valise for services the U.S. hoped he would render. The
agency actually kept tabs on politicians and leaders throughout
the world for signs of their interest in receiving graft or in
gaining "personal economic advantage" from officeholding, so
that when the time came for the CIA "to select which man it
wants to push for higher office in some foreign government,
bribability is obviously considered an asset." Although not the
norm, the CIA was willing to regard corrupt foreign politicians
as fitted for national leadership. The agency also induced
private corporations such as Northrop and Lockheed to shell out
millions of dollars to anticommunist leaders and their rela-
tives.[51]

Disinformation was another CIA tactic. In their range of dirty
tricks agency officials demonstrated considerable ingenuity. At
home, as the Church Committee discovered, the CIA used its
operatives who worked in major press organizations to plant
false stories. In one instance CIA agents prepared a leaflet,

purportedly written by the communists and reporting that "South Vietnamese were to be sent to China to work on the railroad," that duped syndicated columnist Joseph Alsop into writing a column about it. An agency operations officer later disclosed that the CIA harassed all groups which opposed American policy, for whatever reason, and treated them as "propaganda fronts" for the Soviet Union.[52] Among their lies and dirty tricks in Ecuador and Peru, CIA agents distributed a phony list of persons who allegedly "received payments from the Cuban Embassy totalling about $15,000 annually." Ironically the CIA's agents were describing as an outrageous piece of Cuban behavior precisely the sort of behavior the agency engaged in. An article written by CIA people in Uruguay was passed off as the work of a Communist party leader, appearing in the press as an ad boasting that Soviet and Cuban embassies in Mexico City, Buenos Aires, and Montevideo were directing "current insurgent movements in Venezuela, Honduras, Peru, Colombia, Argentina, Panama, and Bolivia." The American press dutifully gave much space to a White Paper prepared by the Reagan administration purportedly showing that the international communist conspiracy was aiding and arming guerrillas in El Salvador. This action is interesting not so much because the agency prepared a fraudulent document but because the administration knew it to be fraudulent. The CIA station in Angola put out false stories about Cubans and Soviets committing rapes and other atrocities. In Thailand a CIA officer sent the prime minister a letter "purportedly from a Communist leader... the object being to stir up dissension among the party's chiefs." When in this case the forgery was discovered, furious students in Bangkok denounced the agency's interference in their country.[53]

In view of the enormity of its consequences, the CIA's performance in Indonesia was one of its most important acts of disinformation. The former Notre Dame All-American Ralph

McGehee explains that after twenty-five years working for the agency, he wrote his exposé because he "had to do something to fight the terrible things [he] had seen the CIA do." Not the least terrible were the false stories planted by the CIA in the Indonesian press, among them a tale that communist women had mutilated six army officers allegedly killed by "leftist plotters" in 1965. CIA propaganda accompanying gruesome photos of the dead officers was used by Indonesian General Suharto as justification for "cleaning out" the Indonesian Communist party. What McGehee calls "this cynically manufactured campaign," featured in all the newspapers, "was designed to foment public anger against Communists and set the stage for a massacre." A massacre indeed followed, in which estimated deaths "ran from one-half million to more than one million people," as "suspects" of all ages and entire villages were ruthlessly destroyed. "To conceal its role in the massacre of those innocent people," McGehee writes, "the CIA in 1968 concocted a false account of what happened. . . . At the same time that the Agency [published this fraudulent book, *Indonesia 1965: The Coup That Backfired*] . . . , it also composed a secret study of what really happened. . . ."[54]

Planting delayed-action bombs in heavily populated areas, contaminating the food and fuel supplies of "unfriendly" countries, arming and training and of course financially rewarding antigovernment "irregulars" to act as *agents provocateurs* and disrupt, undermine, and overthrow governments—including democratically elected noncommunist governments—are among the CIA's inventory of tactics. Philip Agee explains why he and other agents quit the agency when they could no longer stomach "how much suffering it was causing, [the] millions of people all over the world [that] had been killed or had their lives destroyed by the CIA and the institutions it supports."[55]

That CIA officials were indifferent to the consequences of their efforts to promote U.S. cold war policies is demonstrated by their reliance on torture and assassination. In 1956 the agency helped set up the notorious police force of Cuban dictator Fulgencio Batista, the Buro de Repression Actevidades Communistas (BRAC), "famous for its brutal methods of torture." Together with Massad, the Israeli intelligence service, the CIA, as one of its chief officers acknowledged, organized and trained SAVAK, described by one American investigative reporter as a "torture-happy Iranian security organization that kept the shah in power" for more than a quarter of a century. Agee further recounts how his conversation with the chief of police in Montevideo had been interrupted by the cries of a prisoner being tortured in police headquarters. CIA agents also financed the construction of provincial interrogation centers in each of South Vietnam's forty-four provinces, while "torture tactics [were employed] against suspected Viet Cong." According to Philip Roettinger, a former CIA agent in Guatemala, the agency trained the Guatemalan police in torture and murder.[56]

In studying crime, scholars refer to a "dark figure" never included in statistical surveys—crimes that go unreported. No one knows precisely the dark figure of CIA assassinations. What is known is that CIA directors and other high officials, at times under the direction of the President of the United States, have plotted the secret murder of at least four heads of foreign states (Lumumba, Castro, Trujillo, Diem) and other individuals. The Church Committee gathered incontrovertible evidence on CIA-planned assassinations; the Ford administration tried to prevent publication of evidence on American-directed murders that would "provide the Soviet Union with an unparalleled propaganda weapon." Whether or not all CIA assassination planning has been disclosed, former President Lyndon B. Johnson's 1971 interview is suggestive—"We were running a damn Murder Incorporated in the Caribbean."[57]

In the case of Cuban President Fidel Castro, the CIA did not simply make one effort at assassination; it bungled efforts spanning a four-year period. Not the least scandalous feature of this plotting was the agency's offer to pay a sum of six figures to Mafia hands to kill the Cuban leader; it was not patriotism but Castro's 1959 confiscation of their gambling interests that made this offer attractive. Two of the gangsters had been intimate with the very woman whom the Church Committee reported became the mistress of President John F. Kennedy. Some of the methods approved for assassinating Castro were so bizarre that they give the impression of a Keystone Cops outfit, too incompetent to execute successfully its sinister but unrealistic plans. Strengthening such an impression was the CIA's failure to get rid of Colonel Nasser, Ho Chi Minh, and Walter Ulbricht, among others, whom the agency considered assassinating or inducing foreign agents to assassinate. The impression that the CIA was too error prone to get rid of the foreign leaders on its "hit list" is misleading. For the agency played a crucial role in the deaths of Ngo Dinh Diem, Patrice Lumumba, Salvadore Allende, and Che Guevara, to name some of its better-known victims.

Under Secretary of State Douglas Dillon told the Church Committee that President Eisenhower believed Patrice Lumumba (of the former Belgian Congo) was a "very difficult person . . . to deal with" and therefore "very dangerous to the peace and safety of the world." In the wake of Belgium's grant of independence to its former colony, the Eisenhower administration feared that Lumumba's popularity would lead the new nation into the communist camp and influence other anticolonial movements on the African continent. But shortly before Lumumba was assassinated, the U.S. embassy had reported on July 26, 1960, that he "is an opportunist and not a Communist." (That availed Lumumba little, no more than it helped Arbenz in Guatemala, Mossadegh in Iran, Allende in Chile, Goulart in Brazil, Bosch in the Dominican Republic, Nkrumah in Ghana, Diem in South Vietnam, or Sukarno in Indonesia—

noncommunists all, their governments overthrown in plots hatched by the CIA.) Three weeks later our ambassador to the Congo was urging the preparation of a coup to remove Lumumba. The following years, as the CIA deputy director of operations Richard Bissell admitted to the Church Committee, the agency conducted "feasibility studies" of how to assassinate Lumumba while its office of technical services experimented with different poisons for doing the job. Director Richard Helms's subsequent order to destroy all records of CIA tests of "specific poisons to be used in killing Lumumba" assured, at least for the moment, the "plausibility" of the American government's denial of involvement in the assassination of the leader of the Congo.[58]

Nor did the CIA shrink from considering the assassination of some Americans, such as CIA operatives who had gone sour. The agency denied that such executions were policy; if they did occur they were supposedly "exceptional." One CIA officer did not know whether the policy was ever carried out, but he did recall being instructed at the agency's Camp Peary, Virginia, training center that "on occasion it's been necessary to physically eliminate someone who was a threat to the Agency." A CIA officer told Thomas Powers that "low-level" assassinations, like the orders to perform them, would not "ever get into the files."[59]

After he heard from CIA director William Colby of the agency's role in the secret assassination of foreign nationals, Senator Church told reporters, "It is simply intolerable that any agency of the government of the United States may engage in murder." Intolerable, no doubt. Yet for all the sincerity of the few politicians who expressed horror at American involvement in secret murder plots, the fact remains that CIA officials were involved in precisely such plots. For CIA officials had no compunctions about the killing of what they called communists. In South Vietnam the agency's Operation Phoenix disposed of tens of thousands of "suspects." Apprised of the murder of numerous suspected subversives by right-wing death squads in El Salvador, an American official in 1981 observed that "the CIA didn't mind what was going on so long as they were killing Communists."[60] As for the actual wars the agency launched, in all fairness the credit—if that is the appropriate term—for them belongs properly to the presidents who ordered them, not the agency that carried them out.

In a variation on the Machiavellian argument that the ends justify the means, the (Herbert) Hoover Commission appointed by President Eisenhower to make recommendations concerning the appropriate tactics for waging cold war stated in 1954 that since it was "now clear that we are facing an enemy whose avowed object is world domination by whatever means and at whatever cost . . . hitherto accepted norms of human conduct do not apply. If the United States is to survive, longstanding American concepts of 'fair play' must be reconsidered. We must learn to subvert, sabotage, and destroy our enemies."[61] The commission kept secret from the American people the admittedly "repugnant policy" it approved. While the U.S. government had already overthrown noncommunist governments and would continue after 1954 to overthrow and remove with "extreme prejudice" the leaders of many more, evidently it had doubts about the persuasiveness of its argument that these victims of our policy were truly "enemies" out to destroy us. Since such covert operations were kept secret from the American people, American leaders need not offer public justifications for these operations. The unspoken premise was that U.S. policymakers could do whatever they wished to whomever they wished.

Several retired American officials have concluded that the

nation's top national security officials acted on the assumption that the United States has "an inherent right—a sort of modern Manifest Destiny—to intervene in other countries' internal affairs"; they had assumed the "self-appointed role as the dominant arbiter of social, economic, and political change," above all in the "awakening regions of Asia, Africa, and Latin America."[62] Impressed by the close ties the agency invariably had with upper-class wealth in the Third World and by the great influence large American corporations had in determining which foreign governments had to be destabilized or overthrown, Philip Agee concluded that the CIA was "nothing more than the secret police of American capitalism, plugging up leaks . . . so that the shareholders of United States companies operating in poor countries can continue enjoying the rip-off." By "national security" American leaders meant "the security of the capitalist class in the United States, not the security of the people . . . Our government support for corruption and injustice in Latin American flow[ed] directly from the determination of the rich and the powerful in the U.S., the capitalists, to retain and expand their riches and power." To John Stockwell, the agency's close ties with the "official communities of the host country," the police chiefs and the "economic elite" they serve, led the CIA to "share their resentment" of reformers and "revolutionaries who threaten the status quo."[63]

The CIA did characteristically cozy up to the elite in the countries it penetrated. This does not, however, prove that the agency's chief purpose was to promote the interests of American capitalists, or that those interests were paramount in every instance. Life was more complicated than that. CIA officials did not have a mind of their own. The agency was the action arm of the chief executive, and agency officials took their marching orders from the president's national security advisers. The men giving those orders thought in terms of larger political and economic interests, all interrelated in their thinking. At the same time, in the interest of maintaining the plausible deniability of the CIA's superiors, presidents and their senior advisers purposefully remained ignorant of the details of agency covert operations designed to destroy organizations, governments, and individuals in targeted countries. They were willing to accord the CIA much leeway in determining the precise tactics of punishment for "hostile" governments or their leaders. Former NSC executive secretary James Lay admitted to the Church Committee in 1975 that "If extremely sensitive matters were discussed at an NSC meeting, it was sometimes the practice that the official NSC minutes would record only the general subject discussed without identifying the specially sensitive subject of the discussion. In highly sensitive cases, no reference to the subject would be made in the NSC minutes."[64]

The CIA did succeed in achieving the cold war objectives of the various presidents between 1947 and 1991. Since those objectives appear to have included the destabilization and overthrow of a great number of governments of diverse ideological persuasion, the CIA's record has been impressive. It also scored dramatic intelligence coups, particularly in ensnaring Soviet defectors, commissioned important and accurate studies on a variety of strategic matters, and on occasion displayed enough detachment to prepare reports that its directors knew would displease the administration in power. The great problem, of course, concerns the validity of the CIA's objectives, the extent to which pursuing them truly served the national interest, and above all the abhorrent and illegal tactics used by CIA officials to accomplish the agency's assigned mission. However one appraises these objectives, the effects of the CIA's actions on the constitutional balance of power among the branches of the American government must be a matter of concern to all who are troubled by "executive tyranny" or the "imperial presidency." For Congress abandoned both its power of the purse and its involvement in the execution of foreign policy.

Thoughtful people in and out of government, including such anti-Soviet eminences as former Secretary of Defense Robert Lovett and the former high-level official in the World War II OSS, David Bruce, came to think that CIA "covert action was not worth the risk, money, and manpower involved," that the nation would be better off without them.[65] But that counsel was rejected. Even in the wake of the recent revelations of presidential corruption of the agency, the Senate overwhelmingly voted down a proposal to bar future covert operations. As underscored first by the so-called Iran-Contra affair and then by Iraqgate, Presidents Reagan and Bush continued to rely on secrecy and duplicity to advance controversial policy objectives.

By their continuing support of the CIA's illegal interventions in foreign countries with which the United States was at peace, cold war presidents displayed an indifference to international law and a readiness to act as the world's political censor and policeman. They were unwilling to permit the continued existence of governments they found unacceptable, and at the same time sought to conceal those decisions from public scrutiny. The CIA's performance indicated that while various presidents hoped to overthrow the Soviet government, their larger purpose was to shore up anticommunist governments throughout the world or destabilize radical nationalist leaders. This containment policy was based on strategic and economic objectives and viewed with alarm the influence of militant unionists, socialists, revolutionaries, and even independent nationalists who were unwilling to bow to American demands. If need be, it might be necessary to end the lives as well as the influence of "dangerous subversives."

CHAPTER VIII

✿

The Consequences of America's Cold War Policy

The ultimate test of policy is its consequences. This chapter puts the cold war policy of the United States to that test. Since the effects of a policy continue to unfold even after the policy has achieved its main purposes or has been abandoned, what follows is necessarily an interim report. Consequences unforeseen at this moment are likely to make their appearance later. But whatever the future may hold, the results to date of U.S. cold war policy and the means employed to implement it have been substantial, and may in some cases prove to be irreversible. The effects of the cold war and of the U.S. role in it have been felt all over the world.

Robert Burns was right when he wrote that the best-laid plans of mice and men go "aft agley." American leaders appear not to have anticipated some of the most important consequences of the foreign policy they pursued after the end of World War II. But the great majority of consequences appear not only to have been unsurprising but to have been sought by American policymakers.

*

The most baneful effect of this anti-Soviet policy is the unprecedented insecurity it brought to the United States. For the first time in the nation's history it could be almost destroyed and most of its people killed in a matter of minutes by weapons against which we had no effective defense.[1] And it was our own doing that brought us to this condition. True, a massive nuclear arsenal would enable American leaders to wipe out any nation that attacked us. But the resulting mutual destruction would be of little comfort to the few irradiated survivors, for all of Herman Kahn's assurances that they would be a hardy breed, capable of wonders. President John F. Kennedy at one point doubted that the expenditure of hundreds of billions of dollars on nuclear and conventional arms had increased U.S. security at all. In fact, the nuclear weapons buildup, and the Soviet buildup it evoked, seriously undermined our security. Many thousands of misreadings of radar and frightening superpower confrontations threatened nuclear holocaust, by accident or design.[2] American leaders neither hoped nor planned for this state of affairs, but it might have been anticipated had they given more serious thought to the likely results of their nuclear policy.

Yet another consequence of official cold war policies was the great fear and anxiety that swept over the world at the dread of a nuclear holocaust. There is no way of measuring precisely the emotional pain suffered by a generation trained to "duck and cover," but there is no reason to doubt that nuclear nightmares left psychic scars in their wake.

The manufacture and above all the testing of nuclear bombs has had a deleterious and perhaps irreversible effect on the environment, poisoning the earth, the waters, the air, the atmosphere, and causing untold injury and death to plant, animal, and human life. We have not to this point learned how to dispose of nuclear wastes.[3]

To those who would argue that nuclear bombs, however awful their effects, were simply the latest progression in the history of weapons development and therefore not chargeable to the cold war, evidence says otherwise. President Truman's use of the atomic bomb in adopting a tougher stance toward the Soviets, and our questionable plan for control of atomic weapons, proposed to the United Nations, indicates that we aggressively seized this new weapon for policy ends.[4]

Morally questionable presidential actions to implement their cold war policy, including an ardor for nuclear bombs, destruction of Vietnam, and the CIA's less than secret involvement in the assassination of foreign leaders, aroused strong anti-American feeling in many countries of the world. Senator Frank Church believed that the CIA's covert operations had "destroyed the moral leadership of [the United States] throughout the world. . . . Resistance, hostility, and hatred toward the United States—much of it stems from our covert operations."[5]

Most satisfactory to the United States in international affairs was the collapse of the Soviet Union. Responding to what he felt was the excessive self-praise of President George Bush in claiming credit for bringing about the demise of the USSR, George Kennan has argued that the Soviet implosion was due to internal strains and weaknesses that had been developing over time in that vast and complex nation. Yet it seems beyond doubt that American post–World War II actions played an important role in hastening the dissolution of the Soviet order and the fall of the Communist party both in the USSR itself and in the satellite states of Eastern Europe. The amazing inefficiency and backwardness of an economy bypassed by the technological revolutions of the postwar decades were of course instrumental in undermining the Soviet Union. But the great economic strain imposed on the Soviets by an arms race that we promoted, the havoc that American-sponsored covert operations spread throughout the Soviet empire, the cold war tensions that induced the Soviet government to tighten already onerous internal controls and restraints—all contributed to the fall of the Marxist-Leninist state.

Yet these policies also accounted for at least three million Asian deaths in Southeast Asia, the wounding of millions more, the destruction of much of the Korean countryside, and the utter devastation of Vietnam, on which more bombs were dropped than on all the belligerents combined in World War II. In Korea and in Southeast Asia, American leaders made war on nations that had neither attacked nor threatened to attack the United States. Absent the cold war and absent a theory that political victories for Communist or communist-supported parties anywhere were Soviet-directed and therefore unacceptable to the United States, there would not have been wars in Korea, Vietnam, Laos, and Cambodia. Reliance on carpet bombing, napalm, Agent Orange, search-and-destroy missions, body counts, and Operation Phoenix, which killed many thousands of unarmed "communist suspects" in a war Presidents Johnson and Nixon chose to wage, were the assured results of these very tactics.[6]

Bloodbaths in Indonesia, the Congo (now Zaire), Angola, Iran, Guatemala, El Salvador, Chile, Brazil, and Argentina; the killing of hundreds of thousands of peasants, students, trade unionists, priests, and nuns; the wiping out of entire villages by right-wing governments, police forces, militias, secretive death squads, many of them financed and trained by and in the United States—these were other consequences of our cold war policy. A cynical Latin American noted that they had been "killing 'communists' there for centuries." American policymakers approved such executions, insisting however that they not be publicized. In Guatemala, for example, after the CIA had helped overthrow the government of Arbenz Guzman, when anti-communist Colonel Enrique Diaz balked at enforcing the American ambassador's order to kill the communist suspects on his proscription list, Diaz was quickly dumped and replaced by a more cooperative officer.

Many noncommunist Third World governments were overthrown as a result of cold war policy, and in some cases their leaders were assassinated. Among the victims were Mossadegh in Iran, Arbenz Guzman in Guatemala, Lumumba in the Congo, Diem in South Vietnam, Allende in Chile, and Sukarno in Indonesia. Castro of Cuba was not among their number, but not for want of American efforts. American leaders also promoted the civil wars that during the era plagued the Philippines, El Salvador, Nicaragua, Angola, and Peru. In Central America and elsewhere in the Third World, brutal dictatorships that came to power commanded the support of native oligarchs, large American corporations, and an American government that in many instances instructed the despots in torture and terror. The shah's notorious SAVAK which terrorized post-Mossadegh Iran, was the beneficiary of such American assistance.[7]

In an address he gave at the University of Pennsylvania in 1962, historian Arnold Toynbee likened the United States to Rome in the days of empire, everywhere the champion of the rich against the poor and the enemy of popular revolutions.[8] Invariably American policies supported wealthy oligarchs against the peasant masses from whose ranks, after all, came communist "suspects," thus doing the bidding of such corporations as the United Fruit Company, which profited mightily from its vast landholdings and the low wages it paid peasant labor in the Central American banana republics it dominated. We resisted reforms that threatened the profit margins of American investors in the Third World, acquiesced in the heroic looting of the national treasury of Zaire by despot Joseph Mobutu, and poured arms and financial aid into countries ruled by our favored elites rather than assisting the beleaguered poor. In all these ways American policies helped perpetuate the poverty and inequality that reigned in the non-industrial world.[9]

Capitalistic economies able to buy American products and absorb American investments were restored by the Marshall Plan and by other U.S. economic policies put in place after World War II in Central and Western Europe.[10] Since a condition of American aid was the ouster of communists from governing positions in countries seeking U.S. assistance, the exorcising of longstanding leftist influence in the life and politics of the Western democracies was another consequence of our cold war policy. It was perhaps unsurprising that the vacuum created by the retreat of the left was ultimately filled by an invigorated right that could function well in a political climate defined by anticommunism.

The earth's surface was pockmarked with American air bases, war planes armed with hydrogen bombs, and the military personnel called for by the treaties and alliances the United States entered into with nations on almost every continent. Since these agreements were designed to meet "indirect aggression" and internal subversion as well as to confront the Soviet Union or, as in Asia, Red China, one of their not insignificant effects was to prevent change in the status quo or, in exceptional cases like the Dominican Republic, the accession to power of democratically elected governments.[11]

Our cold war leaders brushed aside international law and traditional restraints on the use of force against nations with which we were at peace. The United States intervened in the affairs of other countries, resorting to sabotage, demolition, assassination, and out-and-out warfare. The Founders of the nation had regarded war as a barbaric institution, to be entered into only in case of an attack or threatened attack on our country. When he became secretary of state, Daniel Webster expressed the hope that the War of 1812 would be our last war. War, he observed, should be rejected as an instrument of national policy because "the spirit of the age ... demanded that civilized nations settle their differences by conciliation [and] moral precept rather than by narrow advantage."[12] But during the cold war our leaders became as children of Clausewitz, willing to embrace war as a perfectly acceptable means of conducting foreign policy. In Korea and Vietnam the United States embarked on major if undeclared wars.

Almost one hundred thousand American troops died and hundreds of thousands were wounded in the wars we fought in Asia. Our leaders regretted these casualties. Yet in choosing to make war on distant countries of difficult terrain, occupied by well-armed and strongly motivated hostile troops, surely they knew that much American blood would be spilled.

Korea, as Secretary of State Dean Acheson had indicated early in 1950, was outside the American defense perimeter. In Vietnam, as *The Pentagon Papers* made amply clear, both our civilian and military leaders told a plethora of lies, the better to justify an appallingly destructive war. This war became increasingly unpopular despite the rationale which Presidents Johnson and Nixon intoned about fighting for freedom, preventing falling dominoes, and demonstrating our trustworthiness and devotion to honor, suggesting that the American people had by the late 1960s come to reassess the assumptions of the containment policy.

At home our cold war policy and our means of implementing it have profoundly affected American society. In making ourselves the greatest military power in the history of the world, we achieved the "swollen military establishment" that George Washington warned was the greatest threat to "republican liberties." In his own farewell message, President Dwight Eisenhower urged the nation to guard against the acquisition of unwarranted influence by the "military-industrial complex." As he noted, "this conjunction of an immense military establishment and a large arms industry" was "new in the American experience." It had already made its influence felt in "every city, every statehouse, every office of the federal government."[13] Nor did the process slacken after the general left the White House. The growing military-industrial complex was sustained by the emergence of a broad constituency in favor of a policy that generated military crises and the massive military outlays thought necessary for dealing with them successfully. This coalition for ever more arms included millions of relatively well-paid "defense" workers, the great arms manufacturing corporations such as General Dynamics, Rockwell, Litton Industries, Raytheon, the Bechtel Corporation, and Grumman, and the small army of congressmen unusually sensitive to the wishes of the Pentagon and above all to the interests of the giant defense contractors located in their communities and states. That Senator Henry "Scoop" Jackson of Washington state was sometimes described as "the senator from Boeing" indicates that the readiness of politicians to do the bidding of the great arms suppliers was widely known. It was no accident that a United States bristling with weapons and led by a government strongly influenced by the corporations that made the weapons and the military who ordered them, was prone to resort to force in its response to international issues. Ironically, the end of the cold war and the reduction of defense expenditures brought a severe economic recession to regions (most notably southern California) that had profited from the location of the aerospace industry.

One of the cold war's worst effects on American economic life was to undermine a "free market" economic system. From the world's leading industrial state in 1945, powered by superior technology, the United States by the 1990s had lost its technological advantage over its cold war allies Japan and Germany. This decline was the inevitable by-product of a cold war economy in which, by 1988, more than 65 percent of all federal research and development was allocated to defense. In contrast, only .5 percent of such federal expenditures went to environmental protection and .2 percent to industrial development. Defense spending played an increasingly important role in the economy, rising from $13 billion in 1947 to $300 billion in 1990. These massive expenditures helped saddle the United States with a huge national debt—the federal deficit swelled from $59.6 billion in 1960 to more than $300 billion in 1991, while for the same period the national debt increased from $914.3 billion to approximately $4 trillion. Excessive government spending on the military shortchanged the domestic economy, precisely as President Eisenhower had warned it would. Hospitals, schools, and houses went unbuilt because we built bombs, war planes, and tanks instead. As John Kenneth Galbraith and Michael Harrington observed, the nation's infrastructure deteriorated during the cold war era. Bridges sank into disrepair or collapsed, city streets buckled, millions of people went underfed and unhoused. The nation's array of social, economic, educational, and medical problems went underfunded because of the government's commitment to military production. And the level of the resulting deficit made it economically and politically impossible for the Clinton administration to undertake educational, housing, and health care programs needed to address the festering social and economic inequities left unattended during the cold war years.[14]

Seymour Melman, David Calleo, and other American economists conclude that the nation's overemphasis on military production has had strongly negative effects on the economy, impairing the ability of our manufacturing sector to compete in international markets. Ironically, Germany and Japan, our defeated enemies in World War II, whose economies were brought back to life by American dollars, purchases, and investments, surpassed us in rate of economic growth and in the quality and reputation of their manufactured products, while devoting a much smaller percentage of their wealth to the military budget than had the United States. This disparity in military expenditures largely accounts for the superior performance of their domestic economies, their more favorable balances of trade and payments, and their smaller national debts than ours.[15]

An important but unanticipated by-product of the cold war was the racial integration of the armed forces ordered by President Truman in 1948. The struggle for the "hearts and minds" of people in an overwhelmingly nonwhite world was an important factor in inducing the Truman administration to put an end to racial segregation in the armed forces. Poverty and lack of equal opportunity drove young black Americans to join the military in such great numbers that by the time of the Vietnam War they were represented in the infantry in a far higher proportion than their numbers in the population. Mixed blessing and social safety valve though it turned out to be, the barring of racial segregation in a crucial area of American life expanded democracy in the nation—in this instance democratizing the institution of death in battle.

The cold war had even more far-reaching effects on the nation's political values and beliefs. Before the ascension of Mikhail Gorbachev and the breakup of the USSR that followed soon after, the American people had come to regard the Soviet Union as an evil empire responsible for almost all the world's problems. Communism was regarded not simply as wrong-headed but malevolent. As a system it was inefficient, doomed to failure because contrary to human nature; as a theory it was monstrous, sacrificing the individual to the state and destroying the human spirit. Communists came to be regarded precisely as J. Edgar Hoover, the House Committee on Un-American Activities, and Senator Joseph McCarthy described them: traitors who spied and committed subversive activities ordered by their Soviet masters, fanatics whose every waking moment was devoted to undermining American institutions and ultimately overthrowing the American government by force and violence.[16]

Marxism became anathema to most Americans. It might interest intellectuals for its scope and its appraisals of the power of wealth and private inheritance in human affairs; or iconoclasts for its implicit denunciation of inequity and exploitation; or poor people for its promise of a just society free of poverty. But it was the FBI, CIA, HUAC, and McCarthyite appraisals of Marxism as inhumane and fallacious that took hold in cold war America.[17]

Radicalism, other ideologies calling for thoroughgoing reform, even liberalism became suspect because of the supposed affinity of their proponents for Marxism. J. Edgar Hoover, Joseph McCarthy, and Richard M. Nixon sought to educate the American people to the idea that liberalism was the starting point on the road to communism. Utopianism of any sort became suspect—and these themes informed the apocalyptic warnings of several influential conservative scholars. Socialism, of the democratic or any other variety, was stigmatized as a social and economic order that inevitably paved the way to a totalitarian political order.

The cold war constricted the parameters of the political debate, making suspect the sharp criticism of capitalism or of its malpractices. Eleanor Roosevelt might deplore our cold war policy for having time and again led the nation to the brink of disaster, as she did in 1958 without being branded a communist subversive.[18] But other critics of our policy who did not enjoy her eminence could not afford the luxury of such public criticism—nor, as FBI files fully document, was such caution paranoiac.

Capitalism was increasingly exalted, not only as the most productive and efficient economic system but as the only economic order compatible with freedom and democracy. The inequality and inequity, the corruption, the unpredictable course of the business cycle that have permeated the history of capitalism in the United States were no longer central issues in

national politics, as they had been since the 1890s. During the
cold war years they were treated as minor blemishes when they
were not ignored. A great increase in the prestige of businessmen paralleled the rise in the reputation of the capitalistic
system over which they presided. Lee Iacocca, the head of
Chrysler, was for a time regarded as an almost certain winner in
any presidential contest he might decide to enter (for either
major party), and not for his mastery of statecraft. He had, after
all, run a giant corporation which met huge payrolls. No longer
were big business executives damned as robber barons, malefactors of great wealth, greedy monopolists, or the "sons of
bitches" that President Kennedy's father told him businessmen
were.

Needless to say, the strikingly favorable impression of business leaders in an America witness to the declining productivity
and competitiveness of its manufacturing sector, worsening
imbalances of trade and payments, huge fortunes made through
manipulations of a stock market become, it seemed, little more
than a gambling ring, and half of its giant defense contractors at
one point under indictment or investigation, was based less on
solid achievement than on a changed climate of opinion. The
sharp criticism of American corporate business practices contained in the many volumes produced by the U.S. Senate's
Temporary National Economic Committee in the New Deal era
would have been regarded as suspiciously radical if not subversive during the cold war.

One of the more ironic consequences of the cold war has been
a growing suspicion of and hostility toward the media and the
Congress. The nation's most influential molders of public opinion are widely regarded as too aggressive and critical of government actions. Yet, as Ben Bagdikian and other close students of
the subject have noted, the nation's most powerful newspapers,
magazines, and radio and television networks dutifully repeated
and approved the government line on cold war issues. And

when Congress became more assertive in the late 1970s, conservatives represented this trend as threatening the national security because of its insistence on accountability. Explaining why he had lied to Congress in 1986, NSC aide Oliver North said the choice he confronted was "lies or lives." Most of the public was made to believe that even faint criticism of government policy was unacceptable because it was helpful to the "enemy."[19]

Cold war America redefined democracy. In their public explanations of what the cold war was about, American leaders described it as a struggle to defend democracy and freedom against a totalitarian threat. But when a democratic election abroad seemed likely to bring the "wrong man" to power, as in Vietnam in 1956, U.S. officials used their influence to scuttle that election. Countries ruled by oppressive military regimes friendly to the United States were propped up. When democratically elected governments did things sufficiently displeasing to U.S. policymakers, as did Iran in 1953, Guatemala in 1954, the Dominican Republic in 1965, and Chile in 1973, we helped overthrow them, putting military dictatorships in their place. Henry Kissinger's classic remark that we could not let Chile go "communist" because of the irresponsibility of the Chilean people captures well the increasingly prevalent American attitude: democracy is fine as long as it produces results that national security advisers find acceptable. While this view has occasioned little criticism from an American public inclined to live with the most curious explanations offered by our cold war leaders, it is in fact profoundly undemocratic. Those who talk of their love of democracy but who favor it only selectively, show not a love of democracy but only their awareness that professing such love is politic.

The most democratic government must permit leaders leeway to do what they think right. Yet political leaders in a democracy owe a decent respect to the people's wishes, particularly when these wishes concern life-and-death matters. Polls and local and state elections established that between 80 and 90 percent of the American public favored the cessation of nuclear weapons production and testing by the U.S. and the USSR as well as a no-first-use policy for the American government. Governmental indifference to popular sentiment on so crucial an issue displayed something other than respect either for the people or for democracy.[20]

Cold war presidents described as democracies regimes which were voted into power in elections patrolled by the military, elections in which voting was not by secret ballot and nonvoting was suspect.[21] Non-Marxist scholars put little stock in democratic electoral procedures that are in place in countries lacking independent media, countries in which an oligarchy and its military servants preside over massive poverty and drastic inequality, and employ violence and terror to assure that whatever the outcome of this or that election, the wealth and power of the oligarchic elite will not be diminished.

Patriotism has come to be widely misdefined in the wake of the cold war. The dictionary defines it as love of country. As the generation of Washington, Jefferson, and the Adamses knew, love of country is not synonymous with love of government. When government misbehaves or pursues bad policy. "real" patriotism takes the form of open criticism of the government's actions, no matter how risky or harmful such criticism may be to one's reputation. Courage may be required of real patriots because government's power to shape public opinion is so great that it can transmute stupid into seemingly wise policy and stigmatize criticism of policy as unpatriotic if not treasonable.[22] Cold war America has treated patriotism as a kind of blind, Ramboesque nationalism, according to which patriots offer uncritical, even enthusiastic approval of government actions against foreign states, no matter how illegal, cruel, and amoral the actions.

The American way of life, whose defense against communist subversion spiced so much cold war rhetoric, has also taken on new meaning. In fact the concept is broad and inclusive, for it describes a complex and often discordant reality. But during the cold war it was stripped of the irreverence, the suspicion of business and ill-gotten gains, the pacifism, the sharp dissent, the sympathy for foreign revolutions that had come to be an important part of the American tradition.

The American people have acquiesced in the remarkably arrogant behavior of its government during the cold war. While the details of most clandestine activities were kept from public view, the broad outlines of many covert operations were known. Nor did the media and the public question whether the CIA or other government officials were involved in publicized coups or assassinations of foreign leaders. Nor were complaints heard about the tendency of presidents to resort to force on their exclusive authority in defense of what they called our vital interests. In effect, Congress's power to declare war was set in abeyance.

These interests have been ever more elastically defined during the cold war and in its aftermath. Time was when, in accord with the principles admired by our Founding Fathers, our vital interests were peace, security against foreign invasion, and a prosperity that was most surely achievable through trade and commerce on equal terms with all willing nations. No longer. America's cold war leaders acted on the unspoken premise that the struggle against communist subversion somehow created an imposing new catalogue of interests so important as to justify illegal actions in order to safeguard and secure them. These allegedly vital interests required us to prevent a number of unacceptable circumstances: elected procommunist or insufficiently anticommunist regimes; the toppling of pro-American governments, no matter how undemocratic and repressive; the loss or unavailability to us of foreign resources which we had grown accustomed to having on our own terms; the emergence anywhere of political movements our leaders adjudged as hostile or threatening.

Almost all shades of influential American opinion in and out of government have come to regard U.S. accessibility to Middle Eastern oil, under terms to which we have become accustomed, as an American interest so vital that war would be justified in order to maintain it. We are saying in effect that we will not permit a foreign people to take control of their own resources if the United States has come to depend on getting those resources under terms of our choosing, and if we have reason to fear that the new regime may change these terms or, worse, shut off the supply. So bizarre a notion goes largely unremarked in the contemporary United States. Under international law a nation does have the right, after all, to do what it will with its own products and natural resources, no matter how much these goods are coveted by any other nation. Pursuing the cold war has evidently accustomed American leaders and the public alike to feel that whatever Uncle Sam wants anywhere on earth, Uncle Sam has the right to get, and by whatever means he thinks necessary.

It would be unrealistic to expect a great power cheerfully to forgo foreign raw materials important to its economy. Yet international as well as moral law do forbid the use of force by one state to compel another to part with or sell at reasonable price what it does not wish to. In such a circumstance, a law-abiding nation has no alternative but to pay the higher price, find a substitute source for the material in question, or adapt and modify its own economic processes and domestic behavior.

Equally arrogant is our tendency, very much a child of the cold war, to treat uncongenial developments within foreign countries as threats to our vital interests, justifying a forceful American response. This mind-set seems certain to involve the nation in the future, as in the past, in costly, unnecessary military adventures inimical to the interests of most American citizens.

The political mood as well as the workings of the nation's political process have been altered by the cold war. The left lost whatever influence it had in politics and in the trade union movement and was in full retreat in the intellectual life of the nation. The right, particularly the anticommunist right, was ascendant. The voice of the right was heard as never before on radio and television talk shows on major networks in prime time; the ideas of the right were expressed in editorial pages, widely syndicated newspaper columns, and in the councils of the Republican party. Anticommunism and anti–New Dealism; unquestioning support of unconstitutional wars and illegal interventions abroad as well as a continuing nuclear weapons build-up; hostility toward government spending for the poor and needy, toward government interference with the business of profit-making, toward abortion and what neoconservatives called the liberal agenda—these were the central themes of right-wing argument. Also an object of suspicion were special interests, once identified with big-money groups, now redefined as labor, consumer, and old people's organizations.

The new political atmosphere was conducive to the rise of men whose chief claim to preferment rested largely on their shrewd exploitation of the nation's fear of communism. Senator Joseph McCarthy had played the anticommunist game dramatically but so indiscriminately as to irritate influential leaders. Richard Nixon and Ronald Reagan were much more effective, playing the anticommunist card more cleverly and therefore more enduringly than McCarthy. Our other cold war presidents may not have been as politically single-minded as Nixon and Reagan, but with perhaps one exception they sought to demonstrate their fervent anticommunist convictions. Senator Truman, responding to the German invasion of the Soviet Union in 1941, argued that the United States should not choose sides but rather welcome the bloodletting between the two totalitarian regimes. Eisenhower favored killing Reds and approved the execution of Ethel Rosenberg, about whose guilt security officials had doubts until the moment of her death. Presidential candidate Kennedy found the Soviet internal order an unacceptable threat; during the televised presidential debates of 1960 he performed the special feat of redbaiting Richard Nixon over Nixon's insufficiently belligerent stance toward the communist threat posed by Castro's Cuba. Senator Lyndon Johnson thought the proper way of fighting the Korean War was to drop hydrogen bombs on Russia, the "real enemy."

That ambitious candidates for the highest office evidently thought it useful if not indispensable to take such positions indicates the power anticommunism had assumed in cold war America. Fear of being perceived as soft on communism led the Democratic party and some of its most liberal leaders to support an executive order that permitted the firing of government workers on the basis of undocumented charges made by "faceless informers," pass anticommunist laws they had not read, assume an anticommunist stance at least as strident as that taken by Republicans, wage the cold war no less relentlessly than their Republican opponents, and support hot wars against countries allegedly governed by communists or procommunists.

Freedom was a designated casualty of our cold war policy. Dissent was inhibited. Thinking thoughts that were branded criminal thoughts by J. Edgar Hoover and a succession of attorneys general induced people to avoid thinking the unthinkable, then to deny they ever harbored such thoughts. Since the effective cold war Red Scare convinced the American public that Hoover and William Buckley, not Sartre and O'Casey, were right about communism and communists, and that both the theory and its practitioners were criminal, the exorcism of the freedom to think whatever one wished about communism was not regarded as a limitation on freedom at all. It was not the intellectual merits of ardent cold warriors' arguments that enabled them to carry the day on this matter but the understandable fear that to challenge their arguments risked ruin. The point is not that communism was an intellectually meritorious theory but that an idea was branded "poisonous, off limits" and so accepted by the public out of fear.

The cold war United States denied American citizens the freedom to visit or do business with foreign countries with which we were at peace but which the State Department designated out of bounds. Cold war America barred—and the United States continues to bar—admired foreign visitors, Nobel laureates among them, from entering this country because of their past associations, sympathies, or thoughts.

Another political casualty of the cold war has been the people's "right to know." The Freedom of Information Act passed in the wake of the Watergate scandal did make a significant dent in the federal government's policy of withholding from public and scholarly scrutiny records and files bearing on individuals and organizations. But federal agencies have responded to requests for information grudgingly, charged stiff fees for what they disclose, and blacked out much material to safeguard national security and the methods employed by intelligence agencies to obtain information—and, in a supreme irony, because the release of this information would violate rights of privacy. The Reagan administration outdid all its predecessors in extending the catalogue of restricted materials.[23]

The cold war has effected a serious alteration in the constitutional balance of power between the executive and the legislative branches of the federal government. Presidents have arrogated to themselves powers that under the Constitution fall within the province of Congress. That Congress has chosen to acquiesce in the diminution of its constitutional power to make war, participate in the making of foreign policy, and control the budget tells interesting things about cold war Congresses and about their courage.

In 1935 the Supreme Court ruled the National Recovery Act unconstitutional on the grounds that Congress could not delegate to the president a power that is Congress's alone, the power to regulate interstate commerce. No court has challenged Congress's de facto delegation to the president of the more important power to declare and make war or to conduct covert operations. Presidents had of course drawn the country into wars before the outbreak of the cold war. These were small-scale conflicts. In Korea as in Vietnam, American presidents sent into battle massive forces, hundreds of thousands of American troops. Congressional declarations of war were bypassed not because of a lack of time for Congress to assemble but because of a lack of congressional will to assemble and face up to its constitutional responsibility. Suggestions that an imperial presidency led us into wars that Congress might have refused to declare ignore the complicity of cold war Congresses in their own constitutional degradation. As for the vaunted War Powers Act passed by Congress in 1973, not only have presidents ignored it but, as Walter LaFeber has pointedly observed, the act, "in reality, gives the President the power to wage war for sixty days without congressional approval, a power that the founders wisely did not give the chief executive in 1787."[24] In the nuclear age sixty days can be a lifetime. Nor was Congress any more willing to address another component of presidential warmaking powers, the secret authorization of covert operations. Unwilling even after the Church committee revelations to enact a legislative charter for the CIA, Congress in effect permitted the CIA, an agency that serves the executive branch, to make foreign policy on the spot, to function as an "invisible government," and to have access to a secret budget over which Congress has no real control.[25]

The cold war's effect on the national mood and the values of the American people cannot of course be measured, since the realm of the intangible is beyond the reach of quantitative analysis. There are, however, clear indications that our leaders' policies have indeed affected our feelings. Historians have discerned a great fear that hovered over the land, fear of nuclear war, fear of communism, fear that misbehavior might be misconstrued as evidence of sympathy for communism. Since men and women in the media were unusually well informed and relatively intelligent, fear seems best to explain their uncritical acceptance of governmental enormities, of official explanations for outrageous actions. One result of widespread fear of saying the wrong thing was what John B. Oakes, former editor of the *New York Times* editorial page, called a great silence in the aftermath of the McCarthyism practiced not only by the junior senator from Wisconsin but by his critics in the Oval Office and on Capitol Hill.[26] Teachers and professors remarked the silent generation of students who moved quietly toward their diplomas, degrees, and the jobs that beckoned to young people who did not make waves. Crucially important policies hammered out by small groups of insiders who seemed impervious to popular feelings, as was clearly the case in the formation of our nuclear weapons policies, induced public apathy. The lies intoned by government sources in describing and trying to justify questionable and illegal actions could not but foster cynicism. And public acquiescence in American atrocities in Iran, Chile, Vietnam, and elsewhere in the Third World betokened the increasing moral callousness of the American people.

EPILOGUE

✿

The Legacy
of the
Cold War

THE cold war was an international crisis, but it was also more than that. After 1945 U.S. policymakers identified the Soviet Union as a hostile state threatening U.S. economic and strategic interests. But this threat was not represented as a direct attack on the United States. Reflecting a shift in defining the American role in international affairs, the objective of U.S. policy was not to promote "national defense." This pre–cold war term reflected a limited conception, confined to repulsing direct attacks on the United States, and captured in the principles of the so-called Neutrality Acts of 1935–1937. Instead the new objective was "national security," a cold war term that reflected the need for open-ended commitments and the capability of anticipating and responding to political and military changes anywhere in the world.

What's more, the Soviet Union was not perceived as another great power, having the economic resources and military capabilities to challenge U.S. interests. As fully captured in National Security Council memorandum No. 68, the Soviet threat was of a different sort—an orchestrated conspiracy directed from the Kremlin, bent on world domination. To contain this threat

and preserve American liberty required appropriate responses—
necessitating the ability to react immediately and without tip-
ping off adversaries to U.S. intentions and capabilities. On the
one hand this required that presidents commit troops into military combat without securing a congressional declaration of
war. On the other hand U.S. policymakers had to anticipate
future threats and at an early stage destabilize hostile movements or governments. Thus, in contrast to President Wilson's
1917 and President Roosevelt's 1941 actions, Presidents Truman
(in 1950) and Johnson (in 1965) could not afford the luxury of a
dilatory congressional debate over a request to declare war. At
the same time presidents since Truman relied on the CIA to
conduct covert operations, whether to prevent a Communist
electoral victory in Italy in 1948, to overthrow the noncommunist Mossadegh government in Iran in 1953, to shore up the
Diem government in South Vietnam after 1954, or to promote
the ouster or assassination of Diem in 1963.

One legacy of the cold war, then, is a more powerful presidency, less and less accountable to Congress or to public
opinion. Policy decisions that formerly might have been rejected
as immoral (assassination), illegal (Operation CHAOS), or contradicting the president's public stance (negotiating with and
selling arms to Iranian fundamentalists in 1986) could be safely
pursued. This sense of immunity encouraged what former Senator J. William Fulbright characterized as an "arrogance of
power" on the part of presidents—the belief that a desired
policy result could be readily achieved, *and* a conviction that
Congress could not be trusted to act in the national interest.

But not only presidents were emboldened to act unilaterally
and secretively. Bureaucrats, whether an Oliver North or a
J. Edgar Hoover, were encouraged to assume the mantle of
savior of the Republic. Convinced that the ends justified the
means, these cynical officeholders devised sophisticated records
procedures to immunize their activities from public scrutiny.

Thus, if Hoover in 1942 had devised a crafty "Do Not File" procedure to hide his authorization of "clearly illegal" break-ins, North in 1986 devised a "do not log" procedure to ensure that his communications with his superior, John Poindexter, were not recorded in the NSC's highly classified central records system.

Nor were the cold war's adverse effects confined to the conduct of foreign policy. The perception of a sinister communist subversive threat also required the unleashing of the FBI at home. Combating the communist conspiracy required the intensive monitoring of the activities of American communists as well as those individuals and organizations whom communists might have sought to influence. The targets of FBI surveillance ranged across the political spectrum. The secretive nature of the conspiracy further required the resort to intrusive but illegal investigative techniques. Nor was the FBI's primary mission to prosecute "subversives" suspected of violating the Espionage Act of 1917 or the Smith Act of 1940. The need for advance intelligence first led to the collection of massive amounts of noncriminal information (about both political activities and immoral conduct) and then to more efficient and effective attempts to contain "dangerous" individuals and organizations. As part of a quest to define the parameters of permissible political conduct, FBI officials disseminated derogatory information to like-minded congressmen and media.

The need to contain communism required as well a massive increase in defense spending and the targeting of investment and engineering skills in the research and production of increasingly sophisticated weaponry. The unprecedented and spiraling increase in defense spending had inflationary consequences, creating a situation where industries and geographic regions became dependent on defense contracts. It also diverted capital investment and engineering expertise from the production of commodities that could compete in the world market. Conservatives in

1947–1948 might have railed against the adverse consequences for a free-market economy of the proposed Truman Doctrine and the Marshall Plan, but these criticisms were soon abandoned. The end of the cold war in 1989–1991 brought a severe economic recession to Connecticut and California.

Not surprisingly, the end of the cold war and the U.S. victory over communism did not provoke the public celebration that followed the end of World Wars I and II. American leaders and the public seem unsettled by this long-desired victory, wary of the future in a post–cold war world, and uncertain about the priorities that should inform future domestic and foreign policy. What should be the U.S. role in the post–cold war world? What should be the respective roles of the president, the intelligence agencies, the Congress, the media, and the public in defining national policies and priorities? Is there a need to enact legislative charters defining the role and authority of the intelligence agencies? What policies should be adopted to convert from a wartime to a peacetime economy and promote the changes essential to competing in a global economy? Is there a need to amend the Freedom of Information Act and revise executive classification orders in order to ensure fuller public access to information about the plans and purposes of executive agencies? The answers to these questions will define the legacies of the cold war.

NOTES

I. American Cold War Policy

1. John Lewis Gaddis, *Strategies of Containment: A Critical Appraisal of Postwar American National Security Policy* (New York, 1982).

2. The containment policy and its likely effects were spelled out in Kennan's famous "Mr. X" article, "The Sources of Soviet Conduct," *Foreign Affairs* 25 (July 1947), 566–582. In the previous year his "long telegram" to the State Department had a profound influence in directing the United States' opposition to Soviet communism. See Daniel Yergin, *Shattered Peace: The Origin of the Cold War and the National Security State* (Boston, 1977), 168–171.

3. Good studies of American support of despotic anticommunist regimes include Walter LaFeber, *Inevitable Revolutions: The United States in Central America* (New York, 1983); LaFeber, *America, Russia, and the Cold War, 1945–1990* (New York, 1991); Thomas G. Paterson, *Meeting the Communist Threat: Truman to Reagan* (New York, 1988); Gaddis, *Strategies of Containment*; Raymond Bonner, *Waltzing with a Dictator: The Marcoses and the Making of American Policy* (New York, 1986); and Richard J. Barnet, *Intervention and Revolution: American's Confrontation with Insurgent Movements Around the World* (New York, 1972).

4. Michael J. Hogan, "American Marshall Planners and the Search for European Neocapitalism," *American Historical Review* 90 (February 1985), 44–72; Hogan, *The Marshall Plan* (New York, 1987): David Calleo, *The Imperious Economy* (Cambridge, Mass., 1982); and Jonathan Kwitny, *Endless Enemies: The Making of an Unfriendly World* (New York, 1984).

5. Richard J. Barnet, *Roots of War: The Men and Institutions Behind U.S. Foreign Policy* (New York, 1972); Ronald Brownstein and Mina Easton, *Reagan's Ruling Class: Portraits of the President's Top Officials* (Washington, D.C., 1982); Philip H. Burch, Jr., *Elites in American History*, 3 vol. (New York, 1981); and Edward Pessen, *The Log Cabin Myth: The Social Backgrounds of the Presidents* (New Haven, 1984).

6. Barnet, *Roots of War.*

II. The Foreign Policy Principles of a Democratic Republic

1. For a coherent statement of the Founding Fathers' foreign policy beliefs see Felix Gilbert, *To the Farewell Address: Ideas of Early American Foreign Policy* (Princeton, 1961).

2. The address is presented in Victor Hugo Paltsits, ed., *Washington's Farewell Address . . .* (New York, 1945), an invaluable book which also contains the preliminary drafts of the address and an informed account of contemporary and later questions that arose concerning the famous message. All subsequent quotations from the paraphrases of the address are drawn from Paltsits's book.

3. I have discussed at length the criticisms leveled at the address and the implications of its principles for American policy, in "George Washington's Farewell Address, the Cold War, and the Timeless National Interests," *Journal of the Early Republic* 7 (Spring 1987), 1–25.

4. Harold W. Bradley, "The Political Thinking of George Washington," *Journal of Southern History* 11 (November 1945), 469–486.

5. Thucydides, *The Peloponnesian War*, trans. by Richard Crawley (New York, 1951), 15, 33, 40, 46–49, 50, 65–67, 80–81, 104–106, 118, 189, 253, 440, 509.

6. In *Federalist* 34 Hamilton wrote, "We ought to try the novel . . . experiment in politics of tying up the hands of government from offensive war founded upon reasons of state. . . ."

7. On August 21, 1787, Mason told the Constitutional Convention, "Providence punishes national sins by national calamities."

8. Henry Kissinger said in December 1969, "We have no permanent enemies; we will judge other countries, including Communist countries . . . on the basis of their actions and not on the basis of their domestic ideology." Cited in Gaddis, *Strategies of Containment*, 284. As will be made clear in the chapter that follows, many influential American policymakers disagreed.

9. Nathan Schachner, "Washington's Farewell," in Burton Ira Kaufman, ed., *Washington's Farewell Address: The View from the Twentieth Century* (Chicago, 1969), 149.

10. David F. Healy, *The United States in Cuba, 1898–1902: Generals, Politicians, and the Search for Policy* (Madison, Wisc., 1963); David H. Burton, *Theodore Roosevelt: Confident Imperialist* (Philadelphia, 1968); Dana G. Munro, *Intervention and Dollar Diplomacy in the Caribbean, 1900–1921* (Princeton, 1964); E. Berkeley Tompkins, *Anti-Imperialism in the United States: The Great Debate, 1890–1920* (Philadelphia, 1970); Barbara Tuchman, *The Proud Tower: A Portrait of the World Before the War, 1890–1914* (New York, 1966); Paul A. Varg, *The Making of a Myth: The United States and China, 1897–1912* (East Lansing, Mich., 1968); George F. Kennan, *American Diplomacy: 1900–1950* (Chicago, 1951); Richard Hofstadter, *Social Darwinism in American Thought, 1860–1915* (Philadelphia, 1945); Rubin F. Weston, *Racism in U.S. Imperialism: The Influence of Racial Assumptions on American Foreign Policy, 1893–1946* (Columbia, S.C., 1972); and Robert L. Beisner, *Twelve Against Empire: The Anti-Imperialists, 1898–1900* (Chicago, 1985).

11. Gilbert, *To the Farewell Address*, 123.

III. American Justifications for Waging the Cold War

1. Yergin, *Shattered Peace*, 285; Edward Herman, "The Mass Media: Adversary or Servant of State Power," paper presented to the City University of New York, March 16, 1987.

2. *Foreign Relations of the United States* (hereafter *FRUS*): *The Conference at Washington and Quebec, 1943* (Washington, D.C., 1970), 624–625; Lloyd C. Gardner, Arthur Schlesinger, Jr., and Hans J. Morgenthau, *Origins of the Cold War* [Morgenthau essay] (Waltham, Mass., 1970), 79; Vilnis Sipols, *The Road to Great Victory: Soviet Diplomacy 1941–1945* (Moscow, 1984), 194; Vojtech Mastny, *Russia's Road to Cold War: Diplomacy, Warfare, and the Politics of Containment, 1941–1945* (New York, 1979); Yergin, *Shattered Peace*, 56, 82; Francis L. Loewenheim, H. D. Langley, M. Jones, eds., *Roosevelt and Churchill: Their Secret Wartime Correspondence* (New York, 1975), 202; Winston Churchill, *The Second World War* (Boston, 1948–1953), IV, 588; Hans J. Morgenthau, *In Defense of the National Interest: A Critical Examination of American Foreign Policy* (New York, 1951), 167.

3. A good example of this pattern is provided by the breakup of the anti-Napoleonic alliance after Waterloo and the resultant tensions that quickly arose among the coalition members who had defeated Bonaparte.

4. Documentation of this point can be found in too many publications to cite here. Sources I have relied on include Yergin, *Shattered Peace*; LaFeber, *America, Russia, and the Cold War*; Paterson, *Meeting the Communist Threat*; Diane Shaver Clemens, *Yalta* (New York, 1970); John Lewis Gaddis, *The United States and the Origins of the Cold War* (New York, 1972); Adam B. Ulam, *The Rivals: America and Russia After World War II* (New York, 1971); Melvyn P. Leffler, "The American Conception of National Security and the Beginnings of the Cold War: The United States, Turkey, and NATO, 1945–1952," *Journal of American History* 71 (March 1985), 807–825; Gardner, et al, *Origins of the Cold War*; and Robert L. Messer, *The End of an Alliance: James F. Byrnes, Roosevelt, Truman and the Origins of the Cold War* (Chapel Hill, 1982).

5. All of the publications cited in note 4, as well as others not cited here, address the question, if for the most part implicitly.

6. William A. Dorman, "The Media: Playing the Government's Game," *Bulletin of the Atomic Scientists* 41 (August 1985), 118–125; Herman, "Mass Media"; Edward Herman and Noam Chomsky, *Manufacturing Consent: The Political Economy of the Mass Media* (New York, 1988): Edwin R. Bayley, *Joe McCarthy and the Press* (Madison, Wisc., 1981); Ben Bagdikian, *The Media Monopoly*, 3rd ed. (Boston, 1990).

7. On the influential role of presidential adviser Clark Clifford in persuading the Truman administration to equate criticism of U.S. cold war policy with pro-Soviet subversion, see Richard M. Freeland, *The Truman Doctrine and the Origins of McCarthyism: Foreign Policy, Domestic Politics, and Internal Security, 1946–1948* (New York, 1971). See too Athan Theoharis, *Seeds of Repression: Harry S. Truman and the Origins of McCarthyism* (Chicago, 1971); and Theoharis and John Stuart Cox, *The Boss: J. Edgar Hoover and the Great American Inquisition* (Philadelphia, 1985).

8. Yergin, *Shattered Peace*, 270, 338; *Defense Monitor* 12, No. 3 (1983), 5; Adam B. Ulam, *Expansion and Coexistence: The History of Soviet Foreign Policy*, 1917–1967 (New York, 1968), 403–404.

9. Melvyn P. Leffler, "Adherence to Agreements: Yalta and the Experiences of the Early Cold War," *International Security* 11 (Summer 1986), 88–89, 115, 122; Yergin, *Shattered Peace*, 81.

10. Leffler, "Adherence to Agreements," 84–122; Yergin, *Shattered Peace*, *passim*; Paterson, *Meeting the Communist Threat*; LaFeber, *America, Russia, and the Cold War*; Ulam, *Expansion and Coexistence*; Gaddis, *United States and the Origins of the Cold War*; Mastny, *Russia's Road to Cold War*.

11. Clemens, *Yalta*; Charles L. Mee, Jr., *Meeting at Potsdam* (New York, 1975); Bruce Kuklick, *American Policy and the Division of Germany: The Clash with Russia over Reparations* (Ithaca, 1972); Leffler, "Adherence to Agreements," 104–106.

12. Leffler, "Adherence to Agreements," 109–110.

13. Yergin, *Shattered Peace*, 279–283; Lawrence Wittner, *American Intervention in Greece, 1943–1949* (New York, 1982); John Iatrides, *Revolt in Athens: The Greek Communist "Second Round," 1944–1945* (Princeton, 1972).

14. On American leaders' recommendation of a military invasion of Italy if the Communists won the national elections, see Thomas Powers, *The Man Who Kept the Secrets: Richard Helms and the CIA* (New York, 1979), 30. See too Freeland, *Truman Doctrine and the Origins of McCarthyism*, 173.

15. Yergin, *Shattered Peace*, 183–190; Leffler, "Adherence to Agreements," 111–113; Clemens, *Yalta*, 246.

16. The letter is cited in Robert H. Ferrell, ed., *Off the Record: The Private Papers of Harry S. Truman* (New York, 1980), 80. See too Gaddis, *United States and the Origins of the Cold War*, 336–337; Melvyn Leffler, "Strategy, Diplomacy, and the Cold War," *Journal of American History* 71 (1985), 807–825.

17. Gregg Herken, *The Winning Weapon: The Atomic Bomb in the Cold War, 1945–1950* (New York, 1980); Martin J. Sherwin, *A World Destroyed: The Atomic Bomb and the Grand Alliance* (New York, 1975); P. M. S. Blackett, *Fear, War, and the Bomb* (New York, 1949).

18. Mastny, *Russia's Road to Cold War*, 260, 282, 287; Ulam, *The Rivals*, 109; Yergin, *Shattered Peace*, 103, 177, 243, 275, 276, 367, 371–373, 400.

19. The quoted material is in Yergin, *Shattered Peace*, 242–244, 263, 264–270, 275–276, 351, 367, 371–372. See also Gardner, et al, *Origins of the Cold War*, 24, and the address by Admiral Gene La Rocque to the annual meeting of the American Academy of Political Science in 1983, *Defense Monitor* 12, No. 3 (1983), 1.

20. On the CIA's reliance on these versions of Marxism-Leninism, Soviet leaders, and the Soviet internal order in their orientation lectures to new agents, see Ralph W. McGehee, *Deadly Deceits: My 25 Years in the CIA* (New York, 1983), 8–10. See too Mastny, *Russia's Road to Cold War*, 260, 306, 312; LaFeber, *America, Russia, and the Cold War*, 151; Paterson, *Meeting the Communist Threat*, 199; Robert Scheer, *With Enough Shovels: Reagan, Bush, and Nuclear War* (New York, 1982), 42, 172; Göran Rystad,

Prisoners of the Past? The Munich Syndrome and Makers of American Foreign Policy in the Cold War Era (Lund, Sweden, 1982), 45–47; Gardner, et al, *Origins of the Cold War*, 4.

21. LaFeber, *America, Russia, and the Cold War*, 53.

22. Matthew A. Evangelista, "Stalin's Postwar Army Reappraised," *International Security* 7 (Winter 1982–1983), 110–138; Andrew Cockburn, *The Threat: Inside the Soviet Military Machine* (New York, 1983); David Holloway, *War, Militarism, and the Soviet State* (New York, 1981) and *The Soviet Union and the Arms Race* (New Haven, 1983); Ulam, *Expansion and Coexistence*, 403–404, 414; Leffler, "Strategy, Diplomacy, and the Cold War," 811; *Defense Monitor* 12, No. 3 (1983), 5; Yergin, *Shattered Peace*, 270, 380; Paterson, *Meeting the Communist Threat*, 45–47.

23. Cited in Barnet, *Roots of War*, 100.

24. Herken, *Winning Weapon*, 268, 152, 157, 160–161, 163–164, 167, 170, 171, 175, 176, 178, 264–265.

25. Evatt's statement is cited in Mark Oliphant, "Three Men and the Bomb," *Bulletin of the Atomic Scientists* 45 (March 1989), 41.

26. Yergin, *Shattered Peace*, 238; Herken, *Winning Weapon*, 268.

27. Herken, *Winning Weapon*, 185, 171. For Oppenheimer's excitement about the Gromyko proposal, see Oliphant, "Three Men and the Bomb."

28. Cited in Thomas G. Paterson's 1968 doctoral dissertation, "The Economic Cold War," in turn cited in Barnet, *Roots of War*, 161.

29. Clemens, *Yalta*, 259; Leffler, "Adherence to Agreements," 98–99, 115–119, 122–123; Morgenthau, *In Defense of the National Interest*, 110–111.

30. The quoted statements are cited in Leffler, "Adherence to Agreements," 95, 97. See too Clemens, *Yalta*, 288, 290; Edward R. Stettinius, *Roosevelt and the Russians: The Yalta Conference* (Garden City, N.Y., 1949), 295–303; Morgenthau essay in Gardner, et al., *Origins of the Cold War*, 89, 102; David Horowitz, *The Free World Colossus: A Critique of American Foreign Policy* (London, 1965), 38; Yergin, *Shattered Peace*, 64, 85, 89, 98–99, 160; Churchill, *Second World War*, VI, 581–582; Sipols, *Road to Great Victory*, 247–248; and Gaddis, *United States and the Origins of the Cold War*, 135, 173–174.

31. Ulam, *Expansion and Coexistence*, 429. DeGaulle's view is cited in Gar Alperovitz, *Atomic Diplomacy: Hiroshima and Potsdam* (New York, 1967), 233.

32. Gaddis, *United States and the Origins of the Cold War*, 173. See too David Caute, *The Great Fear: The Anti-Communist Purge Under Truman and Eisenhower* (New York, 1978), 43; Leffler, "Adherence to Agreements," 96.

33. Morgenthau, *In Defense of the National Interest*, 154, and essay in Gardner, et al, *Origins of the Cold War*, 88. Deutscher is cited in Horowitz, *Free World Colossus*, 92.

34. Leffler, "Adherence to Agreements," 102.

35. Mee, *Meeting at Potsdam*, 290; Yergin, *Shattered Peace*, 143, 146.

36. Cited in Morgenthau essay in Gardner, et al, *Origins of the Cold War*, 98.

37. Gaddis, *United States and the Origins of the Cold War*, 134, 137, 202; *FRUS 1945*, V, 252–255, cited in Sipols, *Road to Great Victory*, 260; Ronald W. Pruessen, *John Foster Dulles: The Road to Power* (New York, 1982);

Herken, *Winning Weapon*, 138, 206, 277; Charles E. Bohlen, *Witness to History, 1929–1969* (New York, 1973); John Prados, *The Soviet Estimate: U.S. Intelligence Analysis and Russian Military Strength* (New York, 1982), 7; Ulam, *Rivals*, 109; Yergin, *Shattered Peace*, 213.

38. Clemens, *Yalta*, 269, 28; Leffler, "Adherence to Agreements," 103–106, 114; Yergin, *Shattered Peace*, 95, 114, 231–232, 363.

39. The diplomat is cited in Gaddis, *United States and the Origins of the Cold War*, 243. Mosely, *The Kremlin and World Politics* (New York, 1960), is cited in Sipols, *Road to Great Victory*, 191.

40. Yergin, *Shattered Peace*, 232, 330–331, 366–367, 373, 385; Thomas D. Lairson, "Revising Post-Revisionism: Credibility and Hegemony in the Early Cold War," paper presented at the University of Wisconsin Conference on Rethinking the Cold War, October 18–20, 1991, Madison, 30; Hogan, *Marshall Plan*, 32–45; Walter Isaacson and Evan Thomas, *The Wise Men* (New York, 1986), 386–418; Scott Jackson, "Prologue to the Marshall Plan: The Origins of the American Commitment for a European Recovery Program," *Journal of American History* 65 (March 1979), 1043–1068.

41. Yergin, *Shattered Peace*, 369–388.

42. Cited in Yergin, *Shattered Peace*, 291–292. See too Theodore Draper, "Falling Dominoes," *New York Review of Books* 30 (October 27, 1983), 10.

43. John Iatrides, "The United States and Greece, 1945–1963: Politics of Alliance and Penetration," cited in Yergin, *Shattered Peace*, 288–289; Wittner, *American Intervention in Greece, 1943–1949*.

44. Churchill's comments are cited in Yergin, *Shattered Peace*, 295.

45. Powers, *Man Who Kept the Secrets*, 30; Kerkev, *The Winning Weapon*, 236–23.

46. Cited in Sipols, *Road to Great Victory*, 142.

47. Freeland, *Truman Doctrine and the Origins of McCarthyism*, 173; David Wise and Thomas B. Ross, *The Invisible Government* (New York, 1964).

48. Cited in Leffler, "Adherence to Agreements," 112.

49. Clemens, *Yalta*, 246; Yergin, *Shattered Peace*, 180, 189, 191, 269; Isaac Deutscher, *Stalin: A Political Biography* (New York, 1967), 581; Gary Hess, "The Iranian Crisis of 1945–1946 and the Cold War," *Political Science Quarterly* 89 (March 1974), 117–146.

50. Ferrell, *Off the Record*, 80.

51. Leffler, "Strategy, Diplomacy, and the Cold War," 809.

52. Churchill, *Second World War*, V, 336; Ulam, *Expansion and Coexistence*, 430–431; Leffler, "Strategy, Diplomacy, and the Cold War," 813, 824; Jonathan Knight, "American Statecraft and the 1946 Black Sea Straits Controversy," *Political Science Quarterly* 90 (Fall 1975), 451–475; Yergin, *Shattered Peace*, 234.

53. Leffler, "Adherence to Agreements," 111–112, 107.

54. *Ibid.*, 110–111. See too Sherwin, *A World Destroyed*; Herken, *Winning Weapon*; and Alperovitz, *Atomic Diplomacy*.

55. Leffler, "Adherence to Agreements," See too Akira Iriye, *The Cold War in Asia: A Historical Introduction* (Englewood Cliffs, N.J., 1974).

56. En-Hao Gao, "The Origin of the Cold War: The Founding of the United Nations," City University of New York Master's Essay, 1992; Clemens, *Yalta*, 216; Yergin, *Shattered Peace*, 103; *FRUS: The Conference at Malta and Yalta*, 714, 723, cited in Sipols, *Road to Great Victory*, 228–229.

57. McGehee, *Deadly Deceits*, 8–10.

58. Caute, *Great Fear*; Stanley I. Kutler, *The American Inquisition: Justice and Injustice in the Cold War* (New York, 1982).

59. See Rystad, *Prisoners of the Past?*, for a persuasive and well-documented critique by an eminent Swedish [anti-Soviet] scholar of American attempts to equate Marxism-Leninism and the USSR with Hitlerism and Nazi Germany.

60. Edward H. Carr, *Socialism in One Country, 1924–1926* (London, 1964).

61. Stalin's letter is cited in Sipols, *Road to Great Victory*, 49. Eisenhower's statement is cited in Horowitz, *Free World Colossus*, 163.

62. Kennan, "The United States and the Soviet Union, 1917–1976," *Foreign Affairs* 54 (July 1976), 682.

63. Morgenthau, *In Defense of the National Interest*, 239–240.

64. Scott Pious, "No First Use: Having It Both Ways," *Bulletin of the Atomic Scientists* 42 (January 1986), 10–11.

IV. Treating the Soviet Union as the Enemy

1. Cited in Gaddis, *United States and the Origins of the Cold War*, 303–304.

2. Gaddis, *Strategies of Containment*, 229; Yergin, *Shattered Peace*, 22; Herken, *Winning Weapon*, 106; *The Progressive*, August 1983, p. 14.

3. Professor Martin J. Sherwin, whose knowledge of the matter is unsurpassed, agrees with my appraisal of the significance of General Groves's comment. Sherwin told me (February 6, 1992) that in view of Groves's key position and great influence as the man who "stood astride the civilian/scientific management and the military use of the product" created by the Manhattan Project, his words have a force that has not been fully recognized.

4. Roy Cohn of the prosecution reports that Kaufman told him even before the trial of the Rosenbergs began that he was going to sentence Julius Rosenberg to death. *The Autobiography of Roy Cohn*, ed. by Sidney Zion (Seacaucus, N.J., 1988), 77.

5. Bruce Cumings, *The Origins of the Korean War: Liberation and the Emergence of the Separate Regimes, 1945–1947* (Princeton, 1981); John Halliday and Bruce Cumings, *Korea: The Unknown War* (New York, 1988).

6. LaFeber, *America, Russia, and the Cold War, 1945–1990*, 97.

7. Paterson, *Meeting the Communist Threat*, 52.

8. Cited in Herken, *Winning Weapon*, 333–334.

9. Seymour Hersh, *Price of Power* (New York, 1983), 26.

10. See "U.S. Objectives with Respect to Russia," NSC 20/21, August 18, 1948, cited in Herken, *Winning Weapon*, 275–276.

11. *Ibid.*, 287.

12. Walter and Miriam Schneir, *Invitation to an Inquest* (New York, 1983), 432.

13. Gaddis, *Strategies of Containment, passim.*

14. President Reagan's statement was published in a May 1982 UPI dispatch; cited in Scheer, *With Enough Shovels,* 7. Shultz's statement appears in the *New York Times,* October 19, 1982.

15. *United States v. Greathouse,* cited in Charles Warren, "What Is Giving Aid and Comfort to the Enemy?" *Yale Law Journal* 27 (January 1918), 331–347.

16. *Monongahela Insurance Co. v. Chester,* 43 Pa., 491, 493; *Grinnan v. Edwards,* 21 W. Va., 347, 357.

17. *United States Code Annotated,* Title 50, "War and National Defense."

18. Warren, "What Is Giving Aid and Comfort to the Enemy?" 333.

19. Rusk's statement is in *Executive Sessions of the Senate Foreign Relations Committee (Historical Series),* Vol. XIII: *Eighty-Seventh Congress, First Session,* 1961. Pt 1 (Washington, D.C., 1984), cited in *Journal of American History* 72 (September 1985), 457.

V. Nuclear Bombs for Freedom

1. What the author calls this "vile remark" is cited in Martin J. Sherwin, "The Atomic Bomb and the Origins of the Cold War," *American Historical Review* 78 (October 1973), 945–968; Sherwin, *A World Destroyed,* 221.

2. *Encyclopaedia of the United Nations and International Agreements* (Philadelphia, 1985), 574–575; *The Catholic Almanac* (Huntington, Ind., 1986), 213–214; Theodore Draper, "Nuclear Temptations," *New York Review of Books* 36 (June 19, 1984), 42–48. In private, Truman had conceded that The Bomb was not a military weapon but one "used to wipe out women and children and unarmed people." Cited in David Lilienthal's *Diaries* and in Barnet, *Roots of War,* 33.

3. Harvey Wasserman, N. Solomon, Robert Alvarez, and Eleanor Walters, *Killing Our Own: The Disaster of America's Experience with Atomic Radiation* (New York, 1982); Dr. H. Jack Geiger, "Civil Defense: A Myth," *New York Times,* Op-ed page, February 8, 1982.

4. Dr. Abrams's statement is in the *New York Times,* October 22, 1982. A handful of the thousands of nuclear weapons in the then superpowers' arsenals could inflict such damage.

5. Edward Teller to Leo Szilard, a letter cited in Sherwin, *A World Destroyed,* 217–218.

6. David Alan Rosenberg, "American Atomic Strategy and the Hydrogen Bomb Decision," *Journal of American History* 66 (June 1979), 62–87. Rosenberg, who was a consultant to the Naval Research Advisory Committee of the Office of the Secretary of the Navy, reports that the president decided to make the atomic bomb the "centerpiece of future American strategic planning" before the Soviets exploded their first atomic device and before he ordered the building of a hydrogen bomb.

7. The statement in the pastoral letter on nuclear weapons drawn up by the

National Conference of Catholic Bishops by Archbishop Roach, president of the conference and Cardinal Bernardin, chairman of the committee that drafted the pastoral letter, appears in the *New York Times*, April 10, 1983, section 1, 15.

8. In his famous "iron curtain" speech at Fulton, Missouri, on March 5, 1946, Winston Churchill said that God had given the capacity to make the atomic bomb to the United States. One need hardly guess as to which satanic force shortly afterward gave the power to the evil empire.

9. Joseph Rotblat, "Leaving the Bomb Project," *Bulletin of the Atomic Scientists* 41 (August 1985), 17. See too Sherwin, *A World Destroyed;* Alperovitz, *Atomic Diplomacy;* Blackett, *Fear, War and the Bomb;* Richard Rhodes, *The Making of the Atomic Bomb* (New York, 1986).

10. See Chapter 4.

11. Alperovitz, *Atomic Diplomacy.*

12. Yergin, *Shattered Peace*, 115–116.

13. *Bulletin of the Atomic Scientists* 42 (January 1986), 56–57; Alperovitz, *Atomic Diplomacy*, 237–238; Barton J. Bernstein, "A Postwar Myth," *Bulletin of the Atomic Scientists* 42 (June/July 1986), 38–46; Robert L. Messer, "New Evidence on Truman's Decision," *Bulletin of the Atomic Scientists*, 41 (August 1985), 50–56; Rufus E. Miles, Jr., "Hiroshima: The Strange Myth of Half a Million Lives Saved," *International Security* 10 (Fall 1985), 121–140.

14. Miles, "Hiroshima," 140.

15. Rotblat, "Leaving the Bomb Project," 16–19.

16. Sherwin, *A World Destroyed*, 3, 193, 197–198, 222, 237; Alperovitz, *Atomic Diplomacy*, 229, 240, 242.

17. Alperovitz, *Atomic Diplomacy*, 237–238; *Bulletin of the Atomic Scientists*, 42 (January 1986), 56–57.

18. Rosenberg, "American Atomic Strategy and the Hydrogen Bomb Decision," 75; Alperovitz, *Atomic Diplomacy*, 200; Herken, *Winning Weapon*, 221.

19. In an interview with Leslie Gelb of the *New York Times* in 1983, Marshal Nikolai V. Ogarkov, chief of the Soviet general staff at the time, said it would be impossible to limit a nuclear war; "inevitably such a war will extend to all-out war." Cited in Draper, "Nuclear Temptations," 42–48. Draper pointed out that most Americans and almost all Europeans agreed with the Soviet general's view, as did the pastoral letter of the American Catholic bishops.

20. Sherwin, *A World Destroyed*, 217–218. The scientists who have participated in the Star Wars project explain their involvement in terms strikingly similar to those used by Teller; William J. Broad, *Star Warriors: A Penetrating Look into the Lives of the Young Scientists Behind Our Space Age Weaponry* (New York, 1985).

21. Alperovitz, *Atomic Diplomacy*, 200; T. H. Etzold and John Lewis Gaddis, eds., *Containment: Documents on American Policy and Strategy, 1945–1950* (New York, 1978); Michael S. Sherry, *Preparing for the Next War: American Plans for Postwar Defense, 1941–1945* (New Haven, 1977), 201, 205, 212–215; Anthony Cave Brown, ed., *Dropshot: The United States*

Plan for War with the Soviet Union in 1957 (New York, 1978); Michio Kaku and Daniel Axelrod, *To Win a Nuclear War: The Pentagon's Secret War Plans* (Boston, 1986); Herken, *Winning Weapon*, 222.

22. Howard Ball, *Justice Downwind: America's Atomic Testing Program in the 1950s* (New York, 1986); Herken, *Winning Weapon*, 121, 244, 288, 293; Etzold and Gaddis, *Containment*, 361–364; Rosenberg, "American Strategy and the Hydrogen Bomb Decision," 307; Rosenberg, "U.S. Nuclear Strategy: Theory and Practice," *Bulletin of the Atomic Scientists*, 47 (March 1987), 20; and Bryan Johns, "Sixty Seconds over Moscow," *The Progressive*, 47 (August 1983).

23. Herken, *Winning Weapon*, 317. Barnard Gwertzman, "Nuclear Arms: A Cool, Candid Debate," *New York Times*, July 14, 1983, A20, cites the records of the NSC meeting that appear in *FRUS, 1952–1954*.

24. Carol Cohn, "Sex and Death in the Rational World of Defense Intellectuals," *Signs* 4 (Summer 1987). Cohn "SLICK'EMS, GLICK'EMS, Christmas Trees and Cookie Cutters: Nuclear Language and How We Learned to Pat the Bomb," *Bulletin of the Atomic Scientists*, 43 (June 1987), 17–24.

25. On the overwhelming opposition of the American people to our first use of The Bomb, recorded in many responsible polls, see "Voter Options on Nuclear Arms Policy," Public Agenda Foundation and the Center for Foreign Policy Development, cited in Scott Pious, "No First Use: Having It Both Ways," 11.

26. Wiesner's observations are recorded in his public address on the nuclear arms race at Hunter College in New York City on April 12, 1983, and in his essay "The United States: A Militarized Society, *Bulletin of the Atomic Scientists*, 41 (August 1985), 105. Kennan's views are stated in his *Proposal for International Disarmament* (Washington, D.C., 1981). Bethe's remarks, originally published in *Science*, November 1982, are reprinted in *The Progressive*, February 1983, 30. See too Andrew A. Stern, *How Much Is Enough? Decision Making in the Nuclear Age* (Valligo, Calif., undated), which cites statements by prominent government scientists about the cavalier way in which presidential administrations decided to accelerate the nuclear arms race; and Sherwin, *A World Destroyed*, 126–127.

27. The president's press conference is cited in the *New York Times*, May 14, 1982, A16. McGeorge Bundy, George F. Kennan, Robert S. McNamara, and Gerard Smith, "Nuclear Weapons and the Atlantic Aliance," *Foreign Affairs*, Spring 1982, 753–768.

28. *The Progressive*, January 12, 1988, 12.

29. When Weinberger testified to the Senate Foreign Relations Committee on April 29, 1982, Senator Charles Percy asked him, "Would you rather have at your disposal the U.S. nuclear arsenal or the Soviet nuclear arsenal?" Weinberger answered, "I would not for a moment exchange anything, because we have an enormous edge in technology." Cited in *Defense Monitor* 13, No. 6 (1984), 1.

30. For detail on CIA and other federal agencies' refutations of Reagan administration charges of Soviet cheating and Soviet violations of nuclear treaties, see the stories in the *New York Times* for January 10 and 30, 1984;

March 4, May 29, and July 6, 1986, particularly the articles headed, "Soviet Arms Pact Breaches: Charges Questioned," June 6, 1986, and the article by Michael R. Gordon, "Joint Chiefs Find No Soviet Cheating," February 8, 1986, A6. See too Gloria Duffy, "[Reagan] Administration Redefines Soviet 'Violations,' " *Bulletin of the Atomic Scientists* 42 (February 1986), 13–17; and *Defense Monitor* 16, No. 1 (1987), 3.

31. Cited in *Aerospace Daily*, June 28, 1983.

32. *New York Times*, October 18, 1981, A46. See too the Op-ed articles by former U.S. defense official Herbert Scoville, Jr., and Senator Mark O. Hatfield on the provocatively destabilizing effects of the Reagan administration's plans for the MX in the *New York Times*, October 8, 1981, and September 22, 1983, and the letters to the same effect by Franklin A. Long, former assistant director of the U.S. Arms Control and Disarmament Agency and by Admiral Eugene Carroll in the *New York Times*, November 24, 1982.

33. Matthew Rothschild and Keenan Peck, "Star Wars: The Final Solution," *The Progressive* 49 (July 1985); Antonia Handler Chayes, Under Secretary of the Air Force in the Carter administration, "Reviewing the 'Star Wars' Program," *New York Times*, July 25, 1985, Op-ed page; John Kogut and Michael Weissman, "Taking the Pledge Against Star Wars," *Bulletin of the Atomic Scientists* 42 (January 1986), 27–30; Fred Reed, "The Star Wars Swindle: Hawking Nuclear Snake Oil," *Harper's*, May 1986, 39–48; Gerald E. March, "Dangers of Limited SDI," *Bulletin of the Atomic Scientists* 43 (March 1987), 13–14; Lord Zuckerman, "The Wonders of Star Wars," *New York Review of Books*, January 30, 1986, 32–40; David Lorge Parnas, "Why Star Wars Software Won't Work," *Harper's*, March 1986, 17–18; *Defense Monitor* 15, No. 2 (1986), 4, 6, 8, 22–23.

34. The study, "SDI: Defense or Retaliation?" is excerpted in *Harper's*, April 1986, 15–16; Reed, "The Star Wars Swindle," 48.

35. *Defense Monitor* 12, No. 5 (1983), 1; Kai Bird and Max Holland, "Capitol Letter," *The Nation*, February 1, 1986, 104.

36. William M. Arkin, "The New Mix of Defense and Deterrence," *Bulletin of the Atomic Scientists* 42 (June/July 1986), 4; and "The Strangelove Doctrine," *The Progressive* 49 (March 1985), 9.

37. T. K. Jones, Deputy Under Secretary of Defense for Strategic Threatre Nuclear Forces in the Reagan administration, asserted that "everybody's going to make it if there are enough shelters to go around." In his provocative book *On Thermonuclear War*, Herman Kahn, influential adviser to the Defense Department, assured readers that not only would a nuclear war not "preclude normal and happy lives for the majority of survivors," but it might have the salutary effect of producing renewed vigor among the population, with a zealous, almost religious dedication to reconstruction and work; cited in Helen Caldicott, *Public Letter*, September 28, 1983, and Caldicott, *Missile Envy: The Arms Race and Nuclear War*, rev. ed. (New York, 1986), 38, 75–76; Herken, *Winning Weapon*, 317; *New York Times*, June 8, 1984, article by Bernard Gwertzman; Hersh, *Price of Power*, 52, 129, 246; *New York Times*, July 13, 1983, A20.

38. Herken, *Winning Weapon*, 179. President Reagan's remarks were reported in the *New York Times*, May 14, 1982.

39. *New York Times*, January 17, 1984.

40. Draper, "Nuclear Temptations," 47. Sagan's comment is cited in Sidney Lens, "The Deterrence Myth," *The Progressive*, February 1984, 16. The antinuclear weapons pastoral letter, "The Challenge of Peace: God's Promise and Our Response," was approved by a vote of 238 to 9 at a special meeting in Chicago, May 2, 3, 1983; cited in *Catholic Almanac* (Huntington, Ind., 1986), 213–214. The pronuclear editorial appears in the *New York Times*, August 25, 1986.

41. Lens, "Deterrence Myth," 16.

42. Kaku and Axelrod, "Off with Their Heads: How Zbigniew Brzezinski Hawked the Doctrine of Nuclear Decapitation," *The Progressive*, January 1987, 29–31. See too Theodore Draper, "Dear Mr. Weinberger: An Open Reply to an Open Letter," *New York Review of Books*, November 4, 1982, 28.

43. LaRocque's address to the American Academy of Political and Social Science cited in *Defense Monitor* 12, No. 3 (1983).

44. Ruth Leger Sivard, *World Military and Social Expenditures: An Annual Report on World Priorities* (Washington, D.C., 1983). See too Yergin, *Shattered Peace*, 380; Walter LaFeber, *America, Russia, and the Cold War*, 175; David Horowitz, *Free World Colossus*, 395, 406; and *The Nation*, December 11, 1982.

45. See Chapters 2 and 3 above. See too Brown, *Dropshot*.

46. See interview with Kennan in *Nuclear Times*, November/December 1982, 20–22.

47. Bohlen, *Witness to History*, and David Holloway, *The Soviet Union and the Arms Race* (New Haven, 1982). For the public pledges of no first use of nuclear weapons by the USSR see the *New York Times*, August 15, 1980; June 16, 1982; April 20 and May 19, 1983.

48. Several polls in 1984 demonstrated that "depending on how the question is phrased, American public support for no first use has recently been running between 74 and 77 percent." Cited in Pious, "No First Use: Having It Both Ways."

49. For General Assembly resolutions overwhelmingly condemning the use of nuclear weapons see the *Encyclopaedia of United Nations and International Agreements* (Philadelphia, 1985), 574–575.

50. Kissinger's 1979 statement that "it is absurd to base the strategy of the West on the credibility of mutual suicide," is cited in Ronnie Dugger, "[British] Labor Woos the U.S.: Neil Kinnock on the Road," *The Nation*, December 27, 1986/January 3, 1987), 729.

51. Raymond K. Perkins, Jr., "Deterrence Is Immoral," *Bulletin of the Atomic Scientists*, 41 (February 1985), 34.

52. *New York Times*, December 26, 1985, A19.

53. Herken, *Winning Weapon*, 315.

54. *Ibid.*

55. *New York Times*, May 14, 1982, A16.

56. Thomas J. McCormick, *America's Half-Century: United States Foreign Policy in the Cold War* (Baltimore, 1989); Thomas D. Lairson, "Pursuing Post-Revisionism: Credibility and Hegemony in the Early Cold War"; Geir

Lundestad, *The American 'Empire'* (London, 1990); John Ikenberry, "Rethinking the Origins of American Hegemony," *Political Science Quarterly* 104 (1989), 375, 400; Robert Keohane, *After Hegemony* (Princeton, 1984).

VI. The Crusade Against 'Communist Subversion' at Home

1. Oakes's statement is cited in Ellen W. Schrecker, *No Ivory Tower: McCarthyism and the Universities* (New York, 1986), 339–341.
2. For a lively and reliable account see Robert K. Murray, *Red Scare: A Study in National Hysteria* (Minneapolis, 1955).
3. The standard and still valuable account of the notorious committee is Walter Goodman, *The Committee: The Extraordinary Career of the House Committee on Un-American Activities* (New York, 1968).
4. Two admirable recent studies which provide much detail on the anti-communist activites of the FBI under Hoover are Richard Gid Powers, *Secrecy and Power: The Life of J. Edgar Hoover* (New York, 1987), and Athan Theoharis and John Stuart Cox, *The Boss: J. Edgar Hoover and the Great American Inquisition* (Philadelphia, 1988). Also valuable is Kenneth O'Reilly, *Hoover and the Un-Americans: The FBI, HUAC, and the Red Menace* (Philadelphia, 1983).
5. David M. Oshinsky, *Senator Joe McCarthy and the American Labor Movement* (Columbia, Mo., 1976); and Mary Sperling McAuliffe, *Crisis on the Left: Cold War Politics and American Liberals, 1947–1954* (Amherst, Mass., 1978). See also Theoharis and Cox, *The Boss*, 280–300.
6. Victor Navasky, *Naming Names* (New York, 1981).
7. Cited in Caute, *Great Fear*, 296.
8. *Ibid.*, 215, 271; Herken, *Winning Weapon*, 284.
9. Ingrid Winther Scobie, *Helen Gahagan Douglas: A Life* (New York, 1992); McAuliffe, *Crisis on the Left*; Caute, *Great Fear*, 115, 126; O'Reilly, *Hoover and the Un-Americans*, 171–172; Herbert Mitgang, "Annals of Government: Policing America's Writers," *New Yorker*, October 5, 1987, 56, 84. Athan Theoharis and John Stuart Cox, "A Tale of Two Authors: J. Edgar Hoover, Political Censor," *Authors Guild Bulletin*, Summer 1989, 9.
10. Goodman, *Committee*, 82–83.
11. Freeland, *Truman Doctrine and the Origins of McCarthyism*, 216, *passim*; Kenneth O'Reilly, *"Racial Matters"* (New York, 1990).
12. Caute, *Great Fear*.
13. Navasky, *Naming Names*, 319.
14. The Truman and Kaufman statements are cited in Herken, *Winning Weapon*, 313–324. See too Theoharis, *Seeds of Repression*, 21, 117, 136–137; Freeland, *Truman Doctrine and the Origins of McCarthyism*, 146; Goodman, *Committee*, 229; O'Reilly, *Hoover and the Un-Americans*, 6–7.
15. Theoharis, *Seeds of Repression*; Freeland, *Truman Doctrine and the Origins of McCarthyism*. Eisenhower's statement is cited in O'Reilly, *Hoover and the Un-Americans*, 195.
16. Freeland, *Truman Doctrine and the Origins of McCarthyism*, 10, 125; Theoharis, *Seeds of Repression*, 137; Frank J. Donner, *Age of Surveillance:*

The Aims and Methods of America's Political Intelligence System (New York, 1980), 16, 106, 179.

17. O'Reilly, *Hoover and the Un-Americans*, and Theoharis and Cox, *The Boss*, describe more fully this educational campaign.

18. Goodman, *Committee*, 254; Roger Keeran, *The Communist Party and the Auto Workers' Unions* (Bloomington, Ind., 1980), 413.

19. Caute, *Great Fear*, 54; Yergin, *Shattered Peace*, 154.

20. Felix Frankfurter, *Memorandum Re: Rosenberg v. United States*, nos. 111 and 687, October Term 1952, Collections of the Manuscript Division, Library of Congress; Ronald Radosh and Joyce Milton, *The Rosenberg File: A Search for the Truth* (New York, 1983); Walter and Miriam Schneir, *Invitation to an Inquest* (New York, 1983); Edward Pessen, "The Rosenberg Case Revisited: A Critical Essay on a Recent Scholarly Examination," *New York History* (January 1984), 82–102; Zion, *Autobiography of Roy Cohn*.

21. Radosh and Milton, *Rosenberg File*, 433; Pessen, "Rosenberg Case Revisited," 92.

22. Keeran, *Communist Party and the Auto Workers' Unions*; Nell Painter, *The Narrative of Hosea Hudson: His Life as a Negro Communist in the South* (Cambridge, Mass., 1979); Lowell K. Dyson, *Red Harvest: The Communist Party and American Farmers* (Lincoln, Nebr., 1982); Mark Naison, *Communists in Harlem During the Depression* (Urbana, Ill., 1983); Vivian Gornick, *The Romance of American Communism* (New York, 1977); Peggy Dennis, *The Autobiography of an American Communist* (Westport, Conn., 1978); Schrecker, *No Ivory Tower*, 40–44, 61, 109–110; Navasky, *Naming Names*, 338. A judicious overview of American historians' changing perceptions is Maurice Isserman, "Three Generations: Historians View American Communism," *Labor History* 26 (Fall 1985), 517–525.

23. Schrecker, *No Ivory Tower*, 40; Keeran, *Communist Party and the Auto Workers' Unions*, 83; Athan Theoharis, *Spying on Americans* (Philadelphia, 1978), 135–155.

24. Cited in John Lukacs, "Berlin, Future Tense: Chilly Scenes of the *Fin de Siecle*," *Harper's*, March 1991, 70.

25. Frankfurter, *Memorandum*, 2.

26. Public opinion polls showed that between 1946 and 1949 the percentage of Americans who favored outlawing the Communist party increased from 44 to 68. By 1952, 52 percent favored imprisoning all Communists. Amazingly, 42 percent favored denying the press the right to criticize the American form of government. Caute, *Great Fear*, 215.

27. Theoharis and Cox, *The Boss*, 175–176, 258–260, 394n.

28. Caute, *Great Fear*, 22, 163, 182–184; Navasky, *Naming Names*, 92.

29. Navasky, *Naming Names*, 54; Goodman, *Committee*, 327; Caute, *Great Fear*, 53, 353–354, 447; O'Reilly, *Hoover and the Un-Americans*, 177; McAuliffe, *Crisis on the Left*, 62; Schrecker, *No Ivory Tower*, 111–112.

30. Schrecker, *No Ivory Tower*, 114, 169–171; Caute, *Great Fear*, 70–71.

31. Caute, *Great Fear*, 299–302.

32. Loch K. Johnson, *A Season of Inquiry: The Senate Intelligence Investigation* (Lexington, Ky., 1985), 91, 105, 223.

33. Caute, *Great Fear*, 49.

34. O'Reilly, *Hoover and the Un-Americans*, 7, 13.

35. Goodman, *Committee*, 173–179, 197, 270; O'Reilly, *Hoover and the Un-Americans*, 8.

36. Goodman, *Committee*, 300, 311, 329, 332, 464–475; O'Reilly, *Hoover and the Un-Americans*, 6–8.

37. See the interview of President Reagan by Armand de Borchgrave in *The Progressive*, December 1987, 4.

38. Navasky, *Naming Names*, 40–41; Caute, *Great Fear*, 136–138; O'Reilly, *Hoover and the Un-Americans*, 238–239; Athan Theoharis, ed., *From the Secret Files of J. Edgar Hoover* (Chicago, 1991), 118–121, 292–294, 303–309.

39. Powers, *Secrecy and Power*, *passim*; Theoharis and Cox, *The Boss*, *passim*; Athan Theoharis, ed., *Beyond the Hiss Case: The FBI, Congress, and the Cold War* (Philadelphia, 1982), 20–77; O'Reilly, *Hoover and the Un-Americans*, 47–48, 80–81, 110–111.

40. Mitgang, "Annals of Government," 42–48.

41. Cited in Edwin Bayley, *Joe McCarthy and the Press* (Madison, Wisc., 1987), 217. See too Theoharis, *Seeds of Repression*, 17–18; Freeland, *Truman Doctrine and the Origins of McCarthyism*; Schrecker, *No Ivory Tower*, 218, 263–264, 337; Oshinsky, *Senator Joseph McCarthy and the American Labor Movement*; Kutler, *The American Inquisition*.

42. Freeland, *Truman Doctrine and the Origins of McCarthyism*, 225–226, 338–339, 359–360.

43. Alan Barth, *The Loyalty of Free Men*, cited in Bayley, *Joe McCarthy and the Press*, 7.

44. *Ibid.*, 299; William Hillman, *Mr. President* (New York, 1952), 128; Caute, *Great Fear*, 35; Yergin, *Shattered Peace*, 355; Theoharis, *Seeds of Repression*, 119.

45. Freeland, *Truman Doctrine and the Origins of McCarthyism*, 217–219; Caute, *Great Fear*, 25–27; Kutler, *American Inquisition*, 157.

46. Freeland, *Truman Doctrine and the Origins of McCarthyism*, 113–117, 204–210; Theoharis, *Seeds of Repression*, 100; Caute, *Great Fear*, 276–280; Goodman, *Committee*, 195; Horowitz, *Free World Colossus*, 100.

47. Freeland, *Truman Doctrine and the Origins of McCarthyism*, 208–216.

48. Cited in Horowitz, *Free World Colossus*, 100.

49. Goodman, *Committee*, 229.

50. Caute, *Great Fear*, 50, 232–239; Freeland, *Truman Doctrine and the Origins of McCarthyism*, 218–219.

51. Belknap, *Cold War Justice*; Kutler, *American Inquistion*; Caute, *Great Fear*, 277, 154, 168, 215; Goodman, *Committee*, 285.

52. *Dennis v. U.S.; 341 U.S.* 499, 1951.

53. *Ibid.*

VII. Covert Operations Against International
'Communist Subversion'

1. Publications on which I have relied include the Senate Select Committee to Study Governmental Operations with Respect to Intelligence Activities, *Final Report* (Washington, D.C., April 26, 1976), and "Staff Report," *Covert Action in Chile, 1963–1973* (Washington, D.C., 1976); Rockefeller Commission, *Report to the President on CIA Activities Within the United States* (Washington, D.C., June 6, 1975); William C. Colby and Peter Forbath, *Honorable Men: My Life in the CIA* (New York, 1978); Thomas Powers, *The Man Who Kept the Secrets: Richard Helms and the CIA* (New York, 1979); Stansfield Turner, *Secrecy and Democracy: The CIA in Transition* (Boston, 1985); Kermit Roosevelt, *Countercoup: The Struggle for Control of Iran* (New York, 1979); Victor Marchetti and John D. Marks, *The CIA and the Cult of Intelligence* (New York, 1974); Frank Snepp, *Decent Interval* (New York, 1977); John Stockwell, *In Search of Enemies: A CIA Story* (New York, 1978); Morton H. Halperin, et al, *The Lawless State: The Crimes of the U.S. Intelligence Agencies* (New York, 1976); Young Hum Kim, ed., *The Central Intelligence Agency: Problems of Secrecy in a Democracy* (Lexington, Mass., 1968); John Loftus, *The Belarus Secret* (New York, 1982); John Prados, *Presidents' Secret Wars: CIA and Pentagon Covert Operations Since World War II* (New York, 1986); Paul E. Sigmund, *The Overthrow of Allende* (Pittsburgh, 1977); Robin W. Winks, *Cloak and Gown: Scholars in the Secret War* (New York, 1987); Frank Donner, *The Age of Surveillance: The Aims and Methods of America's Political and Intelligence Service* (New York, 1980); Martin A. Lee and Bruce Shlain, *Acid Dreams: The CIA, L.S.D. and the Sixties Rebellion* (New York, 1986); Alfred McCoy, *The Politics of Heroin in Southeast Asia* (New York, 1972); Stephen Schlesinger and Stephen Kinzer, *Bitter Fruit: The Untold Story of the American Coup in Guatemala* (New York, 1981); Richard H. Immerman, *The CIA in Guatemala: The Foreign Policy of Intervention* (Austin, Tex., 1982); Jonathan Kwitny, *Endless Enemies: The Making of an Unfriendly World* (New York, 1984); Seymour Hersh, "Huge CIA Operation Reported in United States Against Anti-War Forces and Other Dissidents in Nixon Years," *New York Times*, December 22, 1974; A. J. Langguth, *Hidden Terrors* (New York, 1978); Johnson, *A Season of Inquiry*; Philip Agee, *Inside the Company: A CIA Diary* (New York, 1975); Wise and Ross, *Invisible Government*; Philip Taubman, "Casey and His CIA on the Rebound," *New York Times Magazine*, January 16, 1983; and McGehee, *Deadly Deceits*.

2. Public Law 253, 80th Congress.

3. Dulles's and Simpson's comments are reported in Kim, *Central Intelligence Agency*, 29–35, 17.

4. Colby and Forbath, *Honorable Men*, 72–73.

5. Powers, *Man Who Kept the Secrets*, 29, 31; Johnson, *Season of Inquiry*, 101; Turner, *Secrecy and Democracy*, 75–76.

6. Truman's comments in Kim, *Central Intelligence Agency*, 20, 84. See too Marchetti and Marks, *CIA and the Cult of Intelligence*, 22–23.

7. According to onetime CIA operative Philip Agee, "Covert action is the real reason for the CIA's existence"; *Inside the Company*, 37. According to Ralph McGehee the agency's name was only "a cover for its covert operations"; "The Agency is not, nor was it ever meant to have been, an intelligence agency." *Deadly Deceits*, 190. And the Church Committee agreed.

8. This passage from Moynihan's address to the Senate on October 18, 1989, is cited in his Op-ed essay, "Assassinations: Can't We Learn?" *New York Times*, October 20, 1989, A35.

9. Powers, *Man Who Kept the Secrets*, 31.

10. *Ibid.*, 78.

11. The Church Committee reported that the "Forty Committee," appointed by President Nixon, like similar committees named by Nixon's predecessors, was authorized to exercise "political control over covert actions abroad" and was responsible for framing these operations in "such a way that they could later be 'disavowed' or 'plausibly denied' by the United States Government" and the president. *Final Report*, 4. For evidence on the haphazard way in which such presidential committees exercised their responsibility, see Halperin, *Lawless State*, 56.

12. Powers, *Man Who Kept the Secrets*, 274, 159, 119.

13. Wise and Ross, *Invisible Government*, 47; Marchetti and Marks, *CIA and the Cult of Intelligence*, 248.

14. Johnson, *Season of Inquiry*, 6.

15. Rockefeller Commission, *Report*, 14.

16. Johnson, *Season of Inquiry*, 6.

17. Turner, *Secrecy and Democracy*, 83–84.

18. Powers, *Man Who Kept the Secrets*, 277; Johnson, *Season of Inquiry*, 8.

19. The Stennis comment is cited in Marchetti and Marks, *CIA and the Cult of Intelligence*, 107. Colby's comment is in Colby and Forbath, *Honorable Men*, 401.

20. Halperin, *Lawless State*, 35; Powers, *Man Who Kept the Secrets*, 276–277.

21. Colby and Forbath, *Honorable Men*, 382.

22. Halperin, *Lawless State*, 35–36, 443; Johnson, *Season of Inquiry*, 143–155, 221.

23. Colby and Forbath, *Honrable Men*, 404; Johnson, *Season of Inquiry*, 263.

24. Johnson, *Season of Inquiry*, 263.

25. Cited in the article by Leslie H. Gelb, *New York Times*, July 7, 1986, A1.

26. Johnson, *Season of Inquiry*, 258–259; Turner, *Secrecy and Democracy*, 170.

27. This finding is cited in McGehee, *Deadly Deceits*, 29.

28. *New York Times*, January 10 and 30, 1984; March 4, May 29, 1986. A *Times* headline on July 16, 1986, said, "CIA Evaluating Soviet Threat, Is Often Less Grim than the Administration." Colby and Forbath, *Honorable*

Men, 375; Johnson, *Season of Inquiry*, 224. For the amazing intelligence capabilities of the NSA see James Bamford, *The Puzzle Palace: Inside the National Security Agency, America's Most Secret Intelligence Organization* (Boston, 1982).

29. McGehee, *Deadly Deceits*, 194, 89–90.

30. Powers, *Man Who Kept the Secrets*, 159, 307, 119. See too Marchetti and Marks, *CIA and the Cult of Intelligence*, xii, 104; McGehee, *Deadly Deceits*, 190; Johnson, *Season of Inquiry*, 224.

31. Wise and Ross, *Invisible Government*, 244, 355.

32. Marchetti and Marks, *CIA and the Cult of Intelligence*, 59–60, 175, 234, 255, 280; Powers, *Man Who Kept the Secrets*, 325; Wise and Ross, *Invisible Government*, 243; Turner, *Secrecy and Democracy*, 103, 105; Kwitny, *Endless Enemies*, 244–245, 348; Loftus, *The Belarus Secret*, 117–118; Snepp, *Decent Interval*, 78; McGehee, *Deadly Deceits*, 182.

33. Hans J. Morgenthau, "'A Heavy Price Paid' for the CIA," *Christian Science Monitor*, March 1, 1967, cited in Kim, *Central Intelligence Agency*, 59–63.

34. Turner, *Secrecy and Democracy*, 2; Marchetti and Marks, *CIA and the Cult of Intelligence*, 179, 49; Powers, *Man Who Kept the Secrets*, 364; Colby and Forbath, *Honorable Men*, 220, 354; Kwitny, *Endless Enemies*, 224–225; Carl Bernstein, "The CIA and the Media," *Rolling Stone*, October 20, 1977, cited in McGehee, *Deadly Deceits*, 31.

35. Halperin, *Lawless State*, 45–50; Colby and Forbath, *Honorable Men*, 106; Kwitny, *Endless Enemies*, 335–336.

36. Wise and Ross, *Invisible Government*, 246–247.

37. The National Security Act of 1947 explicitly barred the CIA from "police, subpoena or law enforcement powers and internal security functions." The Rockefeller Commission and the Church Committee reported numerous CIA violations of the law.

38. Powers, *Man Who Kept the Secrets*, 287.

39. Rockefeller Commission, *Report*, 9, 24, 28, 34–35, 149.

40. *Ibid.*, 33.

41. Powers, *Man Who Kept the Secrets*, 157; Johnson, *Season of Inquiry*, 223; Rockefeller Commission, *Report*, 20, 30–31, 106.

42. Powers, *Man Who Kept the Secrets*, 56, 249; Colby and Forbath, *Honorable Men*, 313.

43. Rockefeller Commission, *Report*, 37.

44. Stockwell, *In Search of Enemies*, 172–173; Turner, *Secrecy and Democracy*, 41ff. Dr. Carl C. Pfeffer, a pharmacologist, was one of several researchers who after 1964 performed experiments on behavior control for the CIA on unsuspecting "prison inmates in a program financed indirectly by the CIA." *New York Times*, November 23, 1988.

45. Rockefeller Commission, *Report*, 10.

46. McGehee, *Deadly Deceits*, 193–194.

47. Taubman, "Casey and the CIA on the Rebound."

48. Colby and Forbath, *Honorable Men*, 400.

49. Loftus, *Belarus Secret*, 9, 11, 28, 54, 66, 104, 110, 123–124, 131–132, 138.

50. McCoy, *Politics of Heroin in Southeast Asia*; Kwitny, *Endless Enemies*, 332.

51. Snepp, *Decent Interval*, 11; Wise and Ross, *Invisible Government*, 24; Colby and Forbath, *Honorable Men*, 125; Miles Copeland, *The Game of Nations* (New York, 1969), 175ff., cited on the bribe offer to Nasser in Powers, *Man Who Kept the Secrets*, 318; Kwitny, *Endless Enemies*, 91–93.

52. Agee, *Inside the Company*, 81.

53. *Ibid.*, 146, 364; Kwitny, *Endless Enemies*, 359–369; Stockwell, *In Search of Enemies*, 194–195; Colby and Forbath, *Honorable Men*, 370.

54. McGehee, *Deadly Deceits*, 57–58.

55. Agee, *Inside the Company*, 8, 84–86, 229.

56. McGehee, *Deadly Deceits*, 27–28; Kwitny, *Endless Enemies*, 171; Agee, *Inside the Company*, 56; Marchetti and Marks, *CIA and the Cult of Intelligence*, 245–246. Roettinger's comments were made during a television interview on Channel 31 in New York City on the evening of February 22, 1989.

57. Johnson, *Season of Inquiry*, 98; Powers, *Man Who Kept the Secrets*, 157.

58. Stockwell, *In Search of Enemies*, 160, 172; Kwitny, *Endless Enemies*, 57, 68.

59. Powers, *Man Who Kept the Secrets*, 125–126.

60. Cited in article by James LeMoyne in the *New York Times*, December 2, 1987, A12.

61. Church Committee, *Final Report*, cited in Halperin, *Lawless State*, 34.

62. Marchetti and Marks, *CIA and the Cult of Intelligence*, 251, 4.

63. Agee, *Inside the Company*, 558, 562; Stockwell, *In Search of Enemies*, 49.

64. Their objections appeared in the 1961 report of President Eisenhower's Board of Consultants on Foreign Intelligence Activities that they headed. Cited in James Reston, "File and Forget," *New York Times*, January 28, 1987, A22.

65. Theoharis, *Spying on Americans*, xii–xiii.

VIII. The Consequences of America's Cold War Policy

1. Draper, "Nuclear Temptations," 32–48.

2. "Between 1977 and 1984 . . . the early warning system [of the United States] generated over 20,000 false indications of a Soviet missile attack." *Defense Monitor* 16, No. 6 (1987), 4.

3. Howard Ball, *Justice Downwind: America's Testing Program in the 1950s* (New York, 1986); Richard A. Falk and Robert Jay Lifton, *Indefensible Weapons: The Political and Psychological Case Against Nuclear Weapons* (New York, 1982): Philip L. Fradkin, *Fallout: An American Nuclear Tragedy* (Tulsa, 1982).

4. Sherwin, *A World Destroyed*; Herken, *Winning Weapon*.

5. Johnson, *Season of Inquiry*, 102.

6. Cumings, *Origins of the Korean War*, vol I: *Liberation and the Emergence of Separate Regimes, 1945–1947*, and vol. II: *The Roaring of the*

Cataract, 1947–1950 (Princeton, 1990); Cumings, ed., *Child of Conflict: The Korean-American Relationship* (Seattle, 1983); Allen Whiting, *China Crosses the Yalu* (Stanford, 1974); Halliday and Cumings, *Korea: The Unknown War*; George C. Herring, *America's Longest War: The United States and Vietnam, 1950–1975* (New York, 1986); Frances Fitzgerald, *Fire in the Lake: The Vietnamese and the Americans in Vietnam* (New York, 1972); New York Times, *Pentagon Papers* (New York, 1971); J. William Fulbright, *The Arrogance of Power* (New York, 1966); George McT. Kahin, *Intervention: How America Became Involved in Vietnam* (New York, 1986).

7. See Chapter 7 above.

8. Arnold Toynbee, *America and the World Revolution* (New York and London, 1962). 92–93.

9. United Nations Development Program, *Human Development Report, 1992* (New York, 1992); LaFeber, *Inevitable Revolutions* (New York, 1984); Kwitny, *Endless Enemies*; Barnet, *Intervention and Revolution*.

10. Hogan, *Marshall Plan*; Imanuel Wexler, *The Marshall Plan Revisited* (Westport, Conn., 1983): Charles L. Mee, Jr., *The Marshall Plan: The Launching of the Pax Americana* (New York, 1985).

11. LaFeber, *America, Russia, and the Cold War, passim*.

12. Maurice G. Baxter, *One and Inseparable: Daniel Webster and the Union* (Cambridge, Mass., 1984), 319–320.

13. *Public Papers of the Presidents: Dwight D. Eisenhower, 1961*; No. 421 (Washington, D.C., 1961).

14. John Kenneth Galbraith, *The Affluent Society*, 4th ed. (New York, 1984); Michael Harrington, *The Other America* (New York, 1969); Paul Kennedy, "The American Prospect," *New York Review of Books* (March 4, 1993), 43–44.

15. Seymour Melman, *The Permanent War Economy* (New York, 1985): David Calleo, *The Imperious Economy* (Cambridge, Mass., 1982): Ruth Leger Sivard, *World Military and Social Expenditures, 1983* (Washington, D.C., 1983).

16. See Chapter 5 above.

17. Kutler, *American Inquisition*; Goodman, *Committee*; Schneir, *Invitation to an Inquest*; Navasky, *Naming Names*; Caute, *Great Fear*; Theoharis and Cox, *Boss*.

18. Mrs. Roosevelt's statement is cited in Horowitz, *Free World Colossus*, 293.

19. Bagdikian, *The Media Monopoly*; William A. Dorman, "Media," 118–124; J. Fred McDonald, *Television and the Red Menace: The Media's Road to Vietnam* (New York, 1985); Bayley, *Joe McCarthy and the Press*; Herman and Chomsky, *Manufacturing Consent*; Mark Hertsgaard, *On Bended Knee: The Press and the Reagan Presidency* (New York, 1988).

20. Pious, "No First Use," 11; Bundy, Kennan, McNamara, and Smith, "Nuclear Weapons and the Atlantic Alliance."

21. Bonner, *Waltzing with a Dictator*; Edward S. Herman, *The Real Terror Network: Terrorism in Fact and Propaganda* (Boston, 1982).

22. Pessen, "George Washington's Farewell Address, the Cold War, and the Timeless National Interest."

23. Walter Karp, "Liberty Under Siege: The Reagan Administration's Taste for Autocracy," *Harper's*, November 1985, 53–67.

24. LaFeber, *America, Russia, and the Cold War*, 275.

25. Wise and Ross, *Invisible Government*.

26. Oakes is cited in Schrecker, *No Ivory Tower*, 339–341.

INDEX

A Note on the Author

Edward Pessen was for many years Distinguished Professor of History at Baruch College and the Graduate School and University Center of the City University of New York. He was born in Brooklyn in 1920 and grew up there, attending the public schools and studying at Columbia University, where he received B.A., M.A., and Ph.D. degrees. After teaching history at Fisk University, he came to the City University of New York in 1956 and spent the remainder of his teaching career there. He published widely in articles and books, his best-known books being *Most Uncommon Jacksonians* (1967), *Jacksonian America* (1969), *Riches, Class, and Power Before the Civil War* (1973), and *The Log Cabin Myth* (1984). At the time of his death, in December 1992, he was occupying the Edna Gene and Jordan Davidson Chair in the Humanities at Florida International University in Miami.